Computer Visualization for the Theatre

Computer Visualization for the Theatre

3D modelling for designers

Gavin Carver and Christine White

ELSEVIER

AMSTERDAM • BOSTON • HEIDELBERG • LONDON • NEW YORK • OXFORD
PARIS • SAN DIEGO • SAN FRANCISCO • SINGAPORE • SYDNEY • TOKYO

Focal Press is an imprint of Elsevier

Focal Press
An imprint of Elsevier
Linacre House, Jordan Hill, Oxford OX2 8DP
200 Wheeler Road, Burlington MA 01803

First published 2003

British Library Cataloguing in Publication Data
Carver, Gavin
   Computer visualization for the theatre: 3D modelling for designers
   1. Stage lighting – Computer-aided design   2. Theaters –
Stage-setting and scenery – Computer-aided design
   3. Computer-aided design
   I. Title   II. White, Christine A.
   792'.025'0285

Library of Congress Cataloguing in Publication Data
Carver, Gavin.
   Computer visualization for the theatre: 3D modelling for designers/Gavin Carver
   and Christine White.
   p. cm.
   Includes bibliographical references and index.
   ISBN 0 240 51617 6 (alk. paper)
   1. Theaters – Stage-setting and scenery – Computer-aided design.
   I. White, Christine.   II. Title

   PN2091.S8C325 2003
   792'025'0285–dc21   2003052765

ISBN 0 240 51617 6

For information on all Focal Press publications visit our website at:
www.focalpress.com

Composition by Genesis Typesetting Limited, Rochester, Kent
Printed and bound in Great Britain

Contents

Introduction   **ix**
   How to use this book   ix

1   Setting the scene: contexts and approaches   **1**
   Setting some context, histories and traditions   1
   A case for computer modelling in set design. Why bother?   3
   The process of designing   4
   Computers and theatre design   9

2   Outlining the software and its development   **13**
   The evolution of computer graphics and CAD programs   13
   CAD   13
   Photo/Paint programs   16
   Modelling programs   19
   Specialist programs   23

3   Thinking about the hardware: an overview of relevant technologies **26**
   The platform   26
   What to look for when buying a system – what's inside the box   29
   Viewing the work – display systems and printers   33
   Input devices   38

4   Navigating the computer space   **41**
   Representing three dimensions on two   41
   Understanding co-ordinates   43
   Understanding viewports   44
   Placing the origin   47
   Making models   48
   Drawing aids: grids, snaps and selections   50
   Materials   51
   Lighting   52
   Rendering   53

5   The basics of modelling   **56**
     Using primitives   57
     Transforms   61
     Some uses of simple primitive designs   64
     More modifications and deformations   66
     Boolean   68
     AEC elements: doors, windows and AEC extended   70
     Exercises in exploratory modelling   71
     Abstract Bauprobe   71
     A word about flats and box sets   76
     A Shaker table – modelling in detail   78
     Sub-object modification   84

6   The basics of materials   **87**
     Simple colour   88
     Materials   89
     Effective material libraries   107

7   The basics of lighting   **113**
     The role of lighting on stage   114
     Lighting in the digital model   118
     Lighting the table scene – some design considerations   127
     Three-point general cover   132
     Digital light sources and their theatre equivalents   136

8   The rule of change – scenographic improvisation   **139**

9   Peopling the stage   **143**
     Why use human figures?   143
     Practical application   144
     Summary   150

10 Composition, cameras, rendering and resolution   **151**
     Focal lengths and framing   152
     Rendering environment and effects   155
     Resolution   156
     The problem of credence – reading the digital model   157

11 Advanced modelling   **160**
     Using lines and shapes   160
     More complex extrusions   166
     Lathing objects   170
     A little more about NURBS   172

12	**The design over time: storyboards and animations**	**173**
	An introduction to animation	173
	Animation (in both senses) for the theatre designer	173
	Digital animation	176
	Summary	184

13	**Project management**	**186**
	To digitally model, or not to digitally model . . .	186
	Filing and storage structures	187
	Scheduling and budgeting	190
	Organizing the design for technical purposes	193
	Sharing your work	198
	Some practicalities for conferring	202

14	**Conclusion**	**210**

Bibliography	**213**
Glossary	**219**
Index	**223**

Introduction

How to use this book

This book considers the use of three-dimensional (3D) modelling software in developing designs for performance; it considers the processes and contexts of making 3D models in the computer, rather than the more traditional methods of card, balsa, paint and glue. Tangentially we will touch on the use of paint programs (such as the fairly ubiquitous photo editing packages) or drafting programs (for technical drawing) but the central focus is the process of making digital models to explore and illustrate the possibilities of theatrical space.

It is important to say right from the start that some parts of the text are software specific, that is to say they are written with a particular program in mind, Autodesk Viz (formerly 3D Studio Viz), thus many specifics also relate to Discreet's 3dsmax (formerly 3D Studio Max, henceforward Max), a sibling product. Many (perhaps most) of the techniques will also be reasonably transferable to other software, at least in ideas and approaches. The details of the software will be explained in a later chapter. Our aim is for the book to have as wide a use as possible without becoming too anodyne; much of the book is written to be transferable; it can be read and used by a designer (or student of design) with other software, indeed we hope much of it may be of use, or at least of interest, even to those who do not (yet) work on a computer.

A fully working demonstration copy of Autodesk Viz is available as a free download from Autodesk's Web site. This will operate for 15 days free of charge before requiring a licence, and thus a fee to be paid. It may be a rather obvious observation, but plan your 15 days carefully if you choose to use it. Don't download it before a busy production week or a holiday. This book, its illustrations and provocations, can easily be followed in a fortnight.

The book takes three approaches to its subject. One of these is discursive and theoretical; these sections, found throughout the book, reflect on the process of design and the role of the computer within it. Here we consider historical precedents, semiotics, scenography. These parts, of course, relate to any software, and may be as much of interest to those that loathe the idea of using a computer as to those that are already well advanced down the path.

A second approach, sometimes woven in, sometimes separated, explores elements of practice in a fairly circumspect way; provocations for experiments and systems are offered, working practices suggested, examples sketched out. These tend to take a general approach using terms and techniques that can be found on most mid-level software. Some terms vary of course, some functions are present on one system but not another, but we believe that readers of this book will understand the thrust of the approach and find their own way around any difficulties. Problem solving is perhaps the greatest way to learn.

Finally there are a few parts of the book that say 'push this button now'. These sets of instructions relate to Autodesk Viz; the book was started using release 3 and finished using release 4, so in places both versions are referred to since some readers may well be using the, still absolutely fine, earlier iteration (most commands are very similar from one version to the next). This specific approach is largely confined to the chapters on the basics of modelling, material and lighting. Even in those we have explained what we are doing and why, rather than simply instructing the reader on sequential button pushing. These are not tutorials they are examples, which may or may not be followed by the reader. Viz, like many programs, has many features that will not be used, regularly at least, by a designer, and these are largely ignored in this book. Equally there are a number of different ways to carry out most of the functions; by and large we have kept to one or two methods rather than explore all options. (Important note: as this book goes to press Autodesk are about to release the next Viz iteration; this will be a fusion of the Viz program with its sibling 3dsmax program (produced by a subsidiary company Discreet). This will result in a more sophisticated program that will combine the architectural features of Viz with the advanced effects of Max. The exercises and illustrations in this book will remain valid, as the interfaces and operational procedures used in Viz and Max are quite similar, in many cases identical, and the authors understand that there will not be radical changes to the interface in the new version. The reader may, on occasion, have to make some minor adaptations if they are using the new product, but the core of the exercise remains. Thus, while this book refers to Viz, it may be that at the time of reading, the product will go by a different name.)

You will come across the term 'opposite clicking' in this book. This refers to the act of clicking the mouse button furthest from your thumb; for right handed readers that will be the right mouse button, hence this is normally called right clicking in computer books, however for left handed readers (who have set up a left handed mouse) it will be the left mouse button, hence we have used the term 'opposite click'.

Our experience as people who learned the software ourselves and as teachers of it, is that for the most part people stray very quickly from prescriptive tutorials. While these certainly have a very useful function, and will teach many formal processes, little known tools and facilities, most learners want to explore around the tutorials and pick things up for themselves, learning by trial and error. This book is a guide for when you divert from the path of the official tutorial. You may not always learn the 'proper way' when you divert from the path, but having to solve problems for yourself tends to be a better way of really understanding something than following a set of instructions.

Our hope is that the book will serve both as a useful introduction to the practicalities of using 3D modelling software for the purposes of designing for the theatre as much as a provocation of ideas and a discussion of contexts. This book therefore aims to introduce processes and to stimulate interest and discussion. Thus this book is not a how-to-do-it manual with precise instructions for each activity – there are plenty of those available. There are exercises in the book that may be followed by a reader sitting in front of a computer, however our intention is to have written the book in such a way that an interested reader who does not yet have the software can read the chapter and gain an understanding of principles. To this end these exercises are generally written as part of a narrative and discussion rather than as a set of instructions.

There are a number of examples and illustrations in this book, and by and large we have tried to steer clear of designing for a specific text in a specific place (there are one or two exceptions) and where an example was taken from a real project we have made it anonymous. Any creative theatre project will take on its own life because of the visions of director, designer, cast, crew, venue and so on. Our interpretation of Strindberg's 'Miss Julie' may be very different from yours. Furthermore people reading this book may not be familiar with a reference, rendering it meaningless or, worse still, may so totally disagree with our design choice that they miss the point of the exercise. The illustrations are designed to introduce certain techniques, and it is better to design a generic project that illustrates them clearly rather than crowbarring a pretend 'real' project around them.

Finally, we cannot possibly engage with all the design choices of any project that we illustrate; all designers know that ideas come from a huge range of often impossible-to-pin-down sources: the observation of everyday life, a work of art, painstaking library research, a whimsy. A book cannot capture that, and these projects were designed to introduce modelling, thus some design decisions are unexplained or may seem arbitrary. Unless they are part of your real project they always will.

Some assumptions

We assume that the reader is familiar with basic theatre practices and terminology and that they have some understanding of the process of design for the stage. A high level of knowledge or experience is not required, but a complete novice would do well to familiarize themselves with some basic approaches and questions. The following list contains some suggestions if you want to brush up on theatre design and related practices.

Designing for the Theatre, Francis Reid
Drafting for the Theatre, Dennis Dorn and Mark Shanda
Scene Design and Stage Lighting, W. Oren Parker and R. Craig Wolf
Scenographic Imagination, Darwin Reid Payne
Stage Lighting for Theatre Designers, Nigel Morgan
Technical Theatre, Christine White
What is Scenography?, Pamela Howard.

Details of these texts are in the bibliography.

The book also assumes that the reader is reasonably comfortable using a computer and has a general familiarity with Windows (or other graphical operating system), that they can navigate through file structures, manage their desktop, install software and set-up peripherals (printers, etc.). There is a section on equipment in this book but we certainly do not intend to offer a comprehensive guide to running a PC. For their part the authors have on their desks *Windows for Dummies* and *Peter Norton's Inside the PC*.

Both authors work in degree-level drama education and both work, or have worked, in theatre in design and technical capacities; as such we feel that we have come across people with a wide range of experiences and expectations. This book is based upon our teaching and practice, it is aimed solidly at designers or students of design who have developed an interest in the possibilities that the computer offers to their practice. They are likely to have seen the results of some work, or at least read about it, and feel that they should find out more. Some may have reacted strongly against the possibility, only to find themselves feeling that perhaps they need to know more. The reader probably uses a computer reasonably frequently, perhaps for word-processing, email, Web browsing and even some graphics work; perhaps using a paint program or a CAD package.

This book does not replace a software manual. Although some basic approaches are explained in fairly simple step-by-step terms (particularly some exercises in Chapter 5), the assumption is that you have access to a manual or set of tutorials. If you are developing practice (rather than reading for interest) then this book is a foil to tutorials: as you learn your software this book should offer suggestions about how you might apply your developing knowledge in contexts that are suited to theatre rather than animated space battles. This book alone will not teach you all you need about any program, and only scratches the surface of one as sophisticated as Viz.

This book may be useful for designers who are already familiar with modelling in the computer, but are interested in seeing how others (us) use it, and in engaging in some of the theoretical debate about its use. However, it is unlikely that an already competent user will learn new skills; they may however encounter new methods of deploying those skills (useful or otherwise).

This book will not be useful for people who are high-level users (or even mid-level) who are simply looking for more skills, tricks, shortcuts and tech specs. There are plenty of books that cater to that market, but this is not one of them.

We aim to set out a context for using 3D computer software for visualizations in the theatre. During the course of the book we explore particular techniques that might be used within any performance or production process. However, this is by no means a comprehensive view of the world presented by such technologies but rather a snapshot of possibilities. The best way to use this book is as an introduction to ideas and concepts for working in 3D space for theatre. There are exercises and further study recommendations along with descriptions of particular techniques that are used in the development of performance projects.

However, the computer and a variety of software do not replace the designer, nor do they obviate the need for creative discipline, rather they aid the designer to visualize the designed space. A project may be far better undertaken using conventional processes, or perhaps a mixture of the two. The precept that stage space is three-dimensional space with three-dimensional objects contained within it, some of which may be animated, and peopled by live performers, is key to our understanding of what theatre is. Thus, the research that is undertaken for any design of that stage space has to contain imagination and inspiration that can be shared between colleagues and audience. The authors are not computer people, they are theatre people who came to think that the computer might offer some useful possibilities in the processes of design; one of the authors really rather dislikes computers in general, but very much likes what they can help achieve.

1

Setting the scene: contexts and approaches

Setting some context, histories and traditions

The ability to picture knowledge is a fundamental skill involved in the creation of work for theatre and performance. Such knowledge might revolve around the outcome of research, conceptual ideas for a production and technical know-how, or it may simply be feelings and intuitions about what might work on stage and the process towards performance. How to visualize this knowledge and these ideas has resulted in practitioners determining ways of presenting their work in particular forms and at specific production meetings. This practice has established the sharing and development of work in forms such as sketches, storyboards and models to simulate the actual movement of scenic features and actors in the performance space. Furthermore, if a designer cannot create a tangible visualization of their ideas it will be harder to critique their own work, to see its strengths and weaknesses.

From the development of computer imaging in the 1970s practitioners have used computers to create work, to explore that work and sometimes to be the work. The computer has therefore become a tool for exploration but also an exciting platform for performance in its own right.

Early efforts in the world of graphic design to create images using computers produced 3D objects that were mainly confined to geometric shapes. This was in part due to the mathematical structure of wire frame grids, which have become key to working in three dimensions. Whilst we might consider such mathematical precision to be alien to aspects of art and creativity it was, in fact, Renaissance artists who used grids and lenses to view objects and then draw them. This experimentation has led to the development of our perception of depth. Grids, and what has been called ray tracing, were actually developed by Albrecht Dürer (1471–1528), a painter, draftsman and engraver. He applied mathematical systems to art in much the same way as Leonardo Da Vinci. Dürer experimented with plotting a grid over the work that he was to reproduce. He found that by doing this the artist could clearly map the area of any drawing and this method offered a guide to the length and curve of lines within the space of the canvas. This method is also used in scenic art when painters are attempting to enlarge a designer's painting onto a larger canvas or flat. Three-dimensional computer software uses these concepts of drawing to enable the artist to work in 3D space. What makes 3D software different is the ability to take the same design once it is developed in the computer and generate a number of images by moving the camera view, by changing the lighting and by texturing the objects.

This book is about modelling sets in the computer, but it is worth briefly considering how digital technologies have impacted in the wider field of performance, to understand that our practice is not isolated. In the arts of the late twentieth and early twenty-first century there appears to be increasing confluence between fine art and performed art, resulting in work known variously as live art, installation, performance art and so on; digital and media technologies have played a role in this process. Communications technology and digital visualization have developed a context in which time-based media, displaying all the elements of immediacy, ephemerality and contingency common to live performance, have created a crossover form: art/performance/film/media/ installation. This work can engage with issues of representation, authenticity and 'liveness'. The Internet is seen by many as a site of performance, and certainly it is a vehicle by which performance may be transmitted to distant audiences. Increasingly, contemporary directors and performance companies are drawing upon the facilities offered by the inclusion of the projected, often digital, image: Robert LePage, Robert Wilson, The Wooster Group, Blast Theory.

It is axiomatic that art has always been affected by the contributions of technology; the camera obscura contributed to the development of perspective just as samplers have affected music making. These contributions not only affect the form of the art but the discourses that surround it and such cultural debate has further fuelled the medium. It is a truism to say that theatre is a form at the intersection of so many creative discourses, drawing upon literature, music, painting, architecture, dance and spectacle. It has been affected by technological changes which have occurred within any of these art forms. New digital technologies have become enmeshed in many aspects of theatrical production, in acoustic modelling for auditorium design; in computer lighting desks and 'intelligent' lighting systems; for flying and hydraulic control; in sampling, sequencing and synthesis for sound; in desktop publishing and computer generated graphics for publicity; in word processing for script writing. Each of these technological incursions has an attendant theoretical dimension, which has undoubtedly had an impact on the nature of the performance event. At times, of course, this confluence of art and science has been particularly visible in the performance itself such as 'Nine evenings: theatre and engineering' (1966), a celebration of the possibilities of technology in performance; see *New Media in Late 20th Century Art* by Michael Rush for further details. Mark Reaney's 'The Adding Machine' and subsequent projects use the real-time interactive possibilities provided by computer technology, such as used in video games, to address some key issues of scenography and its relationship to time and space (see http:/ /www.ukans.edu/~mreaney/reaney/ for information). However, in the majority of cases the technological contributions are implicit and apparently subservient to the task of making theatre. Computer modelling of designs is just such an activity: as far as the audience are concerned it matters little how the design was developed provided that it works to make the production whole. Rarely will a design wear on its sleeve the manner of its creation, digital or otherwise. Or will it . . .? If a designer uses a computer, rather than paper, paint and card, in the process of making their design, in what way is the result different? There are two conceits behind this tentative theoretical exploration. The first is that the computer is not simply a tool but a working method that contributes to the process of discovery. The second is that if a designer develops their work in a digital space then this process must affect the nature of the end result.

A case for computer modelling in set design. Why bother?

The act of creating a theatrical design is almost always undertaken in a context and with media other than those that will be used in its final realization. A mark on the paper will become a piece of card that, once scaled and drafted, will be made from a piece of hardboard and painted to look like something else. Throughout the process an idea is being translated into different media. A sheet of paper is unable to cope with space other than by the trickery of perspective, and this we may only code or decode if we understand the rules. Even with these rules, as Ernst Gombrich observes, 'the paper may record what is seen, but one cannot reconstruct the scene from the paper; there are multiple arrangements of objects in space that may throw the same flattened perspective image' (1982: 192). Similarly, a card model may go some way toward offering an image of space but it has a hard job to contend with time, motion and light. There is nothing particularly natural or sacred about the use of card modelling to develop and show set designs, indeed the model has only become common currency in the latter half of the twentieth century, prior to that rendered perspective drawings were the dominant form. An engraving rather than a photocopy may have made multiple copies of the image available.

The application of computers to creative tasks has been both simplified and muddied by the suggestion that the user is simply dealing with a tool. While the metaphor of tool is commonly applied to the use of a computer, it does not seem to fully represent the complexity of the relationship that the designer has with the machine (Laurel, 1991). The computer allows one to carry out a wide variety of tasks, some of which are achieved by using a function that might be termed a tool, and might apparently simulate the function of its real equivalent, for example a paint brush. However, the range of activities facilitated by a computer, and the dialogue that the designer has with it, seem to suggest a more complex relationship. We would suggest that a more appropriate metaphor than tool is design space or studio. This is not as pedantic a distinction as it might seem for while the metaphor of the tool is applied, the implication exists that an operator uses it with a single intention and skill to achieve a known end. However, a space has an altogether more holistic effect on how a design and designer evolve and interact. In using a computer you are entering a space in which you can play and experiment. You might use tools within it to achieve specific ends but the space itself offers a creative freedom and range of approaches that cannot be equated to the use of a single tool.

Design in any discipline is a process of making choices to solve problems. Tools may be employed to assist in the process of choice making/problem solving. Wind tunnels (real or computer simulated) give a designer information about the aerodynamics of a mode of transport for example, or a white card model may explore sightlines and movement dynamics of a proposed theatre set. Once the choices have been made further tools are employed to realize the vision – first in prototype or some other form of simulation and communication of the final product, and finally tools that are used to produce the final product(ion).

A designer might use a variety of strategies or approaches to solve these problems and develop the design. Put simply these fall into two groups: systematic or technical strategies and creative, radical or non-systematic strategies (Beardon, 2000). The problems offered to a theatre designer may range from the practical: the scene has to move quickly from bedroom to town square, a helicopter has to land; to the more symbolic: the space must feel oppressive, the chair needs to be emblematic, the design needs to evoke 'Spanishness'. Nonetheless, the process will have to involve research, experiment, proposals, tests, modification, as any design project does. Some of these processes will be systematic, drafting elevations to identify masking for example; others will be creative, experimenting (playing) with objects and a torch.

An important issue is that the computer can all too easily be seen to aid the systematic but not the creative. The idea of a computer being an 'efficient tool' or a 'manipulator of data' suggests that in order to be of use the computer requires the input of known quantities, that you need to know the outcome before you set about using it. As discussed in Chapter 2 this is generally true of Computer Aided Design (CAD) programs, though even here experimentation is possible, but by and large modelling programs facilitate playful and quick creative experimentation. It is certainly true that there are propensities and suggested methods built into any system, but a careful designer need not be pulled into these. A computer can certainly be a great aid to the systematic CAD-based stages of design, usually towards the end of the project, but modelling programs offer a speed and flexibility in the manipulation of objects and textures in apparent 3D space that facilitates creative experiment. A fuller introduction to the different types of graphics program is given in Chapter 2.

The process of designing

2D exploration

The first stage is a period of exploration. The designers immerse themselves in the appropriate visual material. They consider the text and its possibilities and turn their minds to the logistics of the project. Using a variety of media a designer has traditionally used forms quite separate from theatre, such as sketching and collage, to explore possible strategies and to communicate something of their vision to the director. This period allows the designer to cogitate on the huge variety of options open to them. They need to emulate something of the multi-textual and ephemeral nature of theatre, without immediately committing themselves to the more entrenched and slower process of developing a concrete physical proposal. It is a stage of visual research and dreaming. While some design teachers may argue that it is unnecessary to separate this process, preferring instead to begin in 3D space, it is nonetheless a common, and we think necessary, preparatory period. This period of 2D exploration is most closely supported by the use of paint and photo manipulation programs; we shall refer to them as photo/paint programs. These programs are undoubtedly the most familiar type of visual/creative software to the casual user and have certainly become common currency in many design disciplines. They are the programs that facilitate the generation of 2D 'paintings' and allow for the import and modification of photographs and other scanned or downloaded images. An argument may be made that whatever your view of computer visualization, photo/paint programs (plus scanning) provide a useful aid to visual exploration. Indeed costume design has particularly benefited from the ability to import human forms and paint or paste costume proposals over them. Even the most basic package allows a user to import images, paint, manipulate and overlay them, resulting in pieces that might range from clearly abstract explorations of colour, texture or architectural forms to simulated photographs or paintings, from the retouching of a scratched photo to a piece of libellous deceit. Given the speed with which collages,

Return this card today and enter £100 book draw

Select the subjects you'd like to receive information about, enter your email and mail address and freepost it back to us.

TECHNOLOGY

☐ **Architecture and Design:**
History of architecture
Urban design
○ Sustainable architecture
Planning and design
Landscape

☐ **Building and Construction**

☐ **Computing: Professional:**
Communications
Data Management
IT Management
Enterprise Computing
○ Operating Systems

☐ **Computing: Beginner:**
○ Computing
Programming

☐ **Conservation and Museology**

☐ **Engineering:**
Aeronautical Engineering
Automotive Engineering
Chemical Engineering

○ Health & Safety
Environmental
Engineering
Plant / Maintenance /
Manufacturing
Marine Engineering
Materials Science &
Engineering
○ Mechanical Engineering
Petroleum Engineering
○ Quality

☐ **Electronics and Electrical Engineering:**
○ Electrical Engineering
Electronic Engineering
Radio, Audio and TV
Technology
Computer Technology

☐ **Security**

○ TV
Film/TV/Video
Production
Journalism
Multimedia
Computer Graphics/
Animation
Broadcast Management &
Theory
Broadcast & Communications
Technology

MANAGEMENT

☐ Finance and Accounting
Hospitality, Leisure and
Tourism
HR and Training
Pergamon Flexible
Learning
☐ Knowledge Management
Management
☐ Marketing
☐ IT Management

☐ **Film, Television, Video & Audio:**
Computer Technology
Post Production
Lighting
Audio/Radio
Theatre Performance
Photography/Imaging
○ Radio

Name:

Email address:

Mail address:

Postcode .... Date

Please keep me up to date by ☐ email ☐ post ☐ both

Jo Blackford
Data Co-ordinator
Elsevier
FREEPOST - SCE5435
Oxford
Oxon
OX2 8BR

Science & Technology Books, Elsevier Ltd. Registered Office: The Boulevard, Langford Lane, Kidlington, Oxon OX5 1GB. Registered number: 1982084 pastiches and adaptations may be generated it has been argued that the computer artist engaged in processes of this nature is no longer the creator of work but the synthesizer of it. If design for the theatre has always been about selective use of appropriate source material then the designer has always been a synthesizer. The capability of image processing simply facilitates more efficient synthesis and supports an accommodating theory. The scenographer Darwin Reid Payne, notes that it is 'increasingly apparent that the art of the twentieth century is mainly one of assemblage' (Payne, 1985: 85). He celebrates the role of the artist as explorer and expert assembler rather than creator. While the use of image processing and graphics programs is becoming increasingly common in the exploratory stage, their use alone does not constitute a significant change to the process of design. Rather, computers make the collection of material in one space very easy and they sharpen the discussion of authenticity and bricollage, but if used alone their role is largely confined to explorations using graphical and non-theatrical means.

Working in 3D – modelling

The second stage requires the designer to make a more obviously theatrical proposition, usually in the form of a series of increasingly developed and detailed models. This is perhaps the central part of the design process, the place where the work is done, and the activities that this book considers most fully. Modelling is regarded as a process with which to explore theatrical space and to illustrate your thinking to others on the team, sometimes actively 'selling' an idea. It tests the creative and practical implications of design decisions prior to their arrival on stage and it pre-empts problems. Less specifically, however, it serves as a nucleus around which theatrical ideas orbit. It is then a catalyst to the development of theatrical thinking by members of the team and a topic to energize discussion. It is in fact the only artefact that represents the intention of the production around which the team may gather and focus. In this sense it is not only an approximate rendering of the set but it is a symbol of the final product. The process of making a model is mechanical. It may come more fluidly to some designers than others but it depends upon a connected series of actions that progress forward from raw materials to simulation and from sketchy proposal to finished model.

There are two strategies for approaching a model, to which a later chapter will return in detail, but which are important to understand from the start. A model may be exploratory, a playful manipulation of objects and texture in an attempt to understand something of the practicality and metaphysics of the space. This model may be 'toyed' with, with no real sense of what the likely outcome will be. At the other end of the spectrum a model may be commenced for which the designer has a very specific idea of the outcome, its dimensions, its form, textures and materials. This latter model may be constructed straight from the interaction of research and imagination, but more usually from a series of experimental attempts. The majority of models, of course, occupy something of a middle ground. Finally, however, a model is made that appears as the final design on stage will look. A photographic or sketched storyboard will often be developed alongside this process indicating key moments in the development of the performance. An early sketched storyboard may be used by the designer to organize thoughts about time and space in the production, focusing on important details and moments. A storyboard constructed later in the process might be more specific in illustrating setting and lighting changes, and may often be a photographic illustration of the model, taken in a miniature lighting studio. The storyboard tends to deal with time and light better than the model itself can.

The modelling stage is naturally the creative period that will make greatest use of 3D modelling programs, though these programs and the processes overlap with graphics and CAD applications. Put simply (it will be explained in more detail later) a modelling program allows the user to create an apparently 3D design – apparently because of course it is only seen on a flat screen – that can be viewed from any number of angles, 'moved' about in space, given surface textures and lighting. At their most naturalistic these programs can produce deceptively real-looking images; they can of course also produce intentionally abstract, artificial images. The great advantage of the digital space is the facility it offers to combine visual research and exploration with 3D sketches, light and movement. Visualization modelling programs encourage such flexibility. They are designed to aid a designer to develop and represent creative thinking in a highly effective simulation of 3D space and, while by no means simple to use, they aim to allow the swift generation of objects. The entirely digital nature of these constructions makes them extremely adaptable. The form or the covering may be swiftly modified, replaced or rearranged. Since these programs have been designed to assist the visual designer, such as product designers, film, video makers and games designers, the philosophy of their interface is based upon the need of a user to have control over the look of the image on the screen. While these programs most closely equate with the conventional modelling process they also offer the flexibility of more exploratory sketching.

The technological drive behind visualization packages has been towards ever-increasing realism and a more interactive use of the programs. It is of course possible to produce images that do not convince. One might intentionally use very flat monochrome surface textures to specifically point to the artificiality of the generated image but one has to wonder whether this slightly atavistic desire is driven by the need to replicate rather than divert from a conventional process of theatre design. Similarly, the view that computer images look false is often derived from memories of the technology, or the use of less sophisticated programs. While certain aspects of computer visualization may still look artificial, and this is most true of modelled people, the latest generation of software produces highly credible images.

Technical schematics

The third stage is the production of symbolic representations of the design such as ground plans and construction details, which communicate specific intentions to members of the production team. This process certainly overlaps with the modelling stage. Its concern is much more pragmatic, essentially providing a means by which the creative intentions may be translated into technical instructions, and the latter depends upon a clear use of known symbols and technical precision. This stage of the process is the domain of CAD programs, which were principally developed to aid the drafting process for engineers and architects. Completely different from paint programs and sharing some elements with modelling programs, CAD provides very precise tools for data input and output and mirror the conventions of technical drawing. Perpendicular lines, parallel lines, curves, chamfers, fillets, ellipses, angles – all may be created with minute accuracy. Some of these programs work only on a 2D plane while others allow for a 3D object. The approach fostered by the interface induces a tendency towards producing construction plans of known artefacts rather than exploring the possibilities of shapes, space, texture and colour. The presumed product of working with a CAD package is a diagram of some description, while the likely outcome of a visualization program is a convincing image or animation. The functionality of the two does overlap. There is overlap between CAD and modelling; many CAD packages support the production of some kind of realistic model construction while many visualization programs do allow for technical accuracy and the limited printing of plans. However, the nature of the interface requires the user of each to think very differently.

All CAD programs, even the cheapest, allow the designer to quickly copy repeated elements and to ensure precise dimensions, angles and curves. Since a number of CAD programs also allow the generation of 3D models it is quite possible that a design may have a number of outcomes for different purposes, allowing for the production of ground plans, detailed construction drawings and a 3D model, all of which have developed from the same initial starting point. This is an important time-saving consideration given that different departments in the theatre require different sorts of information, frequently demanding time-consuming redrawing to meet their specifications.

This has certainly been seen to be the most useful application of computer graphics in the commercial environment and agencies such as Model Box Bureau (part of White Light, a theatre equipment hire and supply agency in London) have specialized in digitizing plans of theatres and sets. Their most successful commercial activity is a process of fitting the plans for touring designs into the plans of the receiving theatres and advising production companies on alterations needed for the fit-up. A natural by-product of this activity is a growing library of theatre plans stored as portable computer files that are available, at a price, to designers and tour managers, etc. It is now increasingly common for theatres to make their plans available in this way through their own Web sites. This process is only of great benefit to large productions, which demand complex plans with a significant number of elements, repeats and variations. A small design is unlikely to warrant the financial time and outlay; having said that, a number of cheap simple programs do now exist. It is worth noting here, and repeating throughout the book, that for simple activities hand drawing or white card modelling may well be more efficient than the use of computer graphics, and certainly the authors advocate the use of both digital and real modelling methods.

The practice of using CAD in the schematic stage of theatre design has become sufficiently widespread to encourage the development of common standards, ensuring that plan symbols, lay-outs and protocols can be read and understood by all users across the industry so that information is easily exchanged. This is particularly crucial in computer programs where the application itself depends upon common references including dimensions, organizational layers, etc.

An overview

While the terms and processes described above are largely universal to all design practices their application to theatre has been referred to as Computer Scenographics (Payne, 1994) or Computer Aided Scenography (Carver, 1996). The history of the development of the three types of programs has, to a large extent, determined much of the thinking on their uses in theatre. Effective photo/paint and CAD programs reached home and small industrial markets before sophisticated visualization software. The repercussions of this evolution were that computers have been utilized at the two ends of the design process more effectively than during the, perhaps more central, period of 3D exploration. In this respect, it is understandable that the computer has been perceived as an aid to the efficiency with which a designer may execute certain tasks, rather than as an effective part of a creative process. Motivated by the perception of efficiency, it was CAD programs that became the focus of early digital experimentation in theatre and, to a certain extent, this choice determined the ambivalence that still surrounds computer aided scenography. The ambivalence in the context of this process was understandable. The programs demanded that the user should think like an engineer and have a good knowledge of engineering symbols and conventions. These CAD programs did not easily allow room for visual experimentation and flexibility in the way encouraged by sketch models, and they were tremendously hard to learn. Furthermore, most theatrical production does not require plans of the complexity that warrant the use of these, originally unfriendly, programs. Paint programs, on the other hand, which by the early 1990s were quite cheap, were sophisticated and reasonably straightforward to use but did not allow the spatial or 3D experimentation required of design development. The flexibility and sophistication of modern 3D modelling programs makes them an extremely valuable tool for the designer, and the fact that there is a digital tool that can aid the creative strategies in the centre of the design process is an important development. Only from the mid 1990s have the visualization, or modelling programs, become available at a price that theatres and theatre designers could afford. It is these programs that could potentially make a significant impact on the job of theatre designers, and with which this book is principally concerned.

There are perhaps ten reasons to use a computer to assist the modelling stage of design:

1 making, editing and remaking objects is quick – an object can often be resized or reshaped in seconds;
2 nothing is wasted – every scene or object made can be saved even if rejected, you can easily use it again later;
3 the inclusion of scanned images and other visual research is easy – images can be selected, edited and fitted to an object with ease and changed as quickly;
4 a designer can see the effect of light on their design, thus integrating a consideration of atmosphere into the design of the space;
5 animations and kinetic elements can be included;
6 a design can be quickly viewed from any direction;
7 a model or animation can be sent to a team member via email or Web; communication is easy;
8 the 'unreal' possibilities of work in digital space may provide creative inspiration;
9 workflow can be made more efficient, moving easily between graphics programs, digital models and schematic output;
10 the final rendered model or storyboard can be made to look very real or convincing.

There is an eleventh, slightly tangential but very important advantage, which is that the computer can offer creative opportunities to people who have felt excluded from conventional creative processes. Some young people are made to feel that they are not creative because they cannot paint or draw. This confuses a particular set of skills in the representation of a creative idea (drawing, modelling) with the quality of the idea. It may even be for reasons of physical disability that somebody who was not able to communicate in paint and card can be freed to do so using the computer. There is no doubt from our experience as teachers that students feel empowered and en-skilled once they master a modelling program, and thus have more confidence to explore and exhibit creative ideas. Of course this does have a negative mirror; some creative students who are imaginative and communicate well with conventional techniques can become frustrated in the digital domain.

To balance the list above there are some disadvantages:

1 the software can be expensive and difficult to learn;
2 a computer model is not tactile, it can't be picked up and moved around or otherwise physically interacted with;
3 the final results can look so convincing that the viewer does not realize that they are simply an illusion, a fake, the stage will never look like that;
4 it is relatively hard to achieve an effective model of organic, chaotic or decayed forms, therefore designs made this way tend to foreground the architectural and ordered;
5 one may become more interested in the aesthetic of the computer model than the appropriateness of the design for performance;
6 the ability to make constant revisions (easier in a computer than in card) may leave a project constantly unfinished;
7 computer crashes can be extremely damaging;
8 there is a cultural antipathy towards work created on the computer, it may be perceived as 'too easy'.

Computers and theatre design

The entertainment industry as a whole has been extremely active in developing the applications of graphics and visualization technology; the film industry, particularly under the initial direction of George Lucas but continued through many specialist workshops, has made many advances in the development of creative software after seeing its potential as early as the 1970s. Most recently of course, Weta in New Zealand has claimed the development of the most advanced modelling and animation software to assist in the production of 'The Lord of the Rings'. The theatre, however, has been less quick to take up the opportunities, principally one assumes because of the prohibitive costs involved. The individual designer is likely to have a very limited budget and it is only very recently that affordable personal computers have been available that could run the complex operations required by these programs. Furthermore the sophistication of the software requires that a significant amount of time is spent learning the application before it can be used effectively; very few designers have been able to take that time. Even theatre institutions, other than the largest, would have been hard-pressed to set up the infrastructure needed to support complex CAD and visualization initiatives.

Before considering the current situation we will review the significant experiments and developments in 3D modelling in theatre design. It should be noted that many of these experiments were conducted in universities by teams that were both interested in the research element and the professional application, since for the most part the researchers were also practising theatre designers. It is only in a university context that the early experiments using expensive equipment could have been afforded.

In 1990 the American magazine *Theatre Design and Technology* published an issue in which five of the eight main articles were dedicated to computers used in various aspects of theatre, a signal of the significance of this emerging technology. One of these articles, by Mark Reaney (1990), focused on the use of 3D modelling software in set design. The article briefly outlines how a computer may be used to create apparently 3D images. He reaches a conclusion that while the computer model may not (in 1990) replace the card model it offers opportunities for animation and simulated walk-through that real-world model boxes do not. Reaney notes the limitations of the computer particularly with regard to their ability to produce atmospheric images, a limitation that is now largely behind us. The interest of this article is that while the speed and sophistication of the software has moved on considerably, the basic operational and creative concerns have remained much the same; with this in mind the authors of this book hope that while some of its technological references may quickly become obsolete the basic design concerns will not. Mark Reaney was one of the pioneers in using visualization in set design and has since gone on to create more fully integrated computer imagery in performance.

In 1993 Bob Braddy and his team from Colorado State University proposed that the computer could offer a flexible and interactive forum in which a design team, along with the director and technical staff, could collaborate on a unified, holistic visualization of the production throughout the development process, thereby enabling a highly collaborative approach to design and one in which many design and technical problems could be foreseen before the costly moment of taking to the stage. They proposed that the early development models could be seamlessly evolved into construction plans, ground plans and other schematics, thus streamlining the translation from concept, to model, to stage. Since their explorations were largely based on CAD programs, Braddy eventually found that the contemporary technology was not flexible enough to truly realize his vision for an interactive digital design studio. The technical specifications were fairly easily extracted from the computer models but, as with Reaney, these early experiments somewhat lacked the creative and atmospheric elements; cross-over between conceptualization and schematic was difficult. His basic premise has nonetheless proved to be the cornerstone of much exploration carried out since. In his book *Computer Scenographics* Darwin Reid Payne concludes that, 'The real value of computers lies not in their ability to save hypothetical quantities of time, but in the possible ways they allow design information to be effectively incorporated into scenographic design projects' (Payne, 1994: 226). Interactive flexibility has been the kernel of the argument for most advocates of computer aided design in theatre. At any stage of the production process, from initial visual sketching or collaging in a paint program, through 3D modelling to final construction schematics, radical changes may be swiftly made and the results viewed almost instantaneously. Thus a production team may quickly make decisions about space, light and music. They may input those changes and develop new models and plans without a laborious process of redrawing or remodelling.

More recently Chris Dyer has taken an interest in the collaborative possibilities offered by the technology with the development of the virtual_Stages project (now called OpenStages), where an interface has been written that is designed specifically for theatre makers. The program is built using OpenGL and uses VRML file formats, the upshot of which is that a user can view a 3D model while manupulating properties of the model. The screen presents a digital model of the set around which is located virtual equivalents of theatre control systems. The viewer and/or operator may activate fly cues, for example, or change lighting states. Although the technology is not in itself new, Dyer's contention is that in order for it to be useful and flexible it must be simple and friendly, putting the minimum computer 'noise' between the creative team and their product. The next stage of Dyer's project, and indeed a development already being undertaken by commercial software manufacturers, is to give the user the ability to transport the information determined in these virtual technical rehearsals directly to the stage. For example, you might set lighting states or hydraulic cues in the computer simulation and then have these transferred to the relevant control systems in the theatre. While this approach has drawn upon visualization technologies as well as new developments in interface design, the process is largely targeted at the later stages of the production process, aiding creativity by facilitating clear communication and technical efficiency. However, Dyer certainly sees the possibility of this work engaging with all stages of the design process. In his hypothetical account of a design for a production of 'The Merchant of Venice' at the Phoenix Theatre in 1989 he describes how a scene builder faxed through a section of the stage of the Phoenix Theatre, from which a VRML model of the theatre was created. Using OpenStages Dyer describes the possibility of now going into the Phoenix Theatre, lighting the stage with a basic cover of light, opening the scene store tool and selecting a floor with a couple of figures. He used scanned images of a cloister and painted them onto the stock scenery. He added some columns and with a few basic lighting changes he was able to show the dynamics of the proposed idea for the meeting. This example illustrates the creative and exploratory possibilities with dedicated theatre software.

Colin Beardon developed another example of similarly dedicated software. This has largely been employed in the use of computer visualization at the exploratory stages of the design process, particularly allowing non-specialists to experiment with spatial and design elements. His software, called Visual Assistant, is designed to encourage a creative exploration of theatrical image and space at an early stage of design, most significantly among student actors who are otherwise engaged in the process of improvising performance (Beardon and Enright, 1999b). In this project a straightforward interface is provided through which the user may access a 'store' of objects and images, the shape and colour of which are partly determined by the user. Through this project he hoped to introduce students to the skills and thought-processes of a designer without requiring them to engage in the full process of design development and it is a very effective simple tool for exploring theatrical space and developing sketch storyboards. However, this program does not seek to provide a digital space in which these early visions may be developed in more detail.

The work of the Kent Interactive Digital Design Studio (KIDDS) at the University of Kent perhaps fills in the middle ground between conception and production. This studio seeks, through a variety of projects, to use the possibilities of computer visualization in the development of designs throughout the modelling process. KIDDS has tended to put the emphasis on the production of atmospheric and lifelike finished models with the view that they provide a convincing theatrical environment in which to work. However, KIDDS has not sought to provide a means of integrating their final model with stage mechanisms. Unlike the projects noted above, KIDDS has not developed their own interface, deciding instead to use commercially available visualization software, which does not facilitate ease of use and requires significant training. The emphasis here

11

is not on providing a theatre-friendly interface but on using the full facilities of the more complex visualization and animation software. While projects such as OpenStages, Visual Assistant and KIDDS have been developed independently and with somewhat different intentions, there is no doubt that together they provide a most valuable illustration of the use of the digital design space throughout the process.

The projects detailed above have taken place around academic institutions, although this image may be skewed by the fact that academics publish their work whereas theatre designers tend to get on and do it. Additionally there is no denying the rather steep learning curve on the more sophisticated programs, often requiring a number of months of fairly constant use to become familiar with their functions. Universities are more able to support this learning process than the commercial theatre. More theatre or design degree courses now teach some form of computer graphics so more people are entering the industry already familiar with the field's possibilities and trained on the equipment. Taken together with the lower cost of more powerful computers and the availability of cheap and sometimes free software, it is increasingly likely that more designers will use computer visualizations as part of their tool kit for design in theatre and performance contexts.

There are more and more designers using these tools; William Dudley particularly enthuses about the potential afforded by computers used as an integral part of the process. Of the process of digital design he says 'this gave you immense freedom because you could take any risk you liked. you could even print the thing out [. . .] and then you could distress the paper and then you could put the airbrush over that. It's also sensationally good for creating the effect of light' (William Dudley, interviewed in Davis, 2001 p. 78).

The designer Roma Patel works extensively with 3D modelling tools and has a Web site dedicated to their use, with some examples of her work and exercises for the interested visitor. On the site (www.digitalsetdesign.com) she says that:

> I believe passionately that Scenography is falling behind other design professions in use of the digital technology. Digital modeling – as opposed to card modeling – allows much more experimentation at the design stage. This is because of the ease of manipulation, the portability, and the reusability that computer modeling offers. The result is an increase in creative possibilities and savings of time and money.

2

Outlining the software and its development

The evolution of computer graphics and CAD programs

Computers have been used to represent graphical data, particularly in the defence industry, from the mid-1950s; the first projects that led to the development of what we would recognize as Computer Aided Design were carried out in the late 1950s and early 1960s. In 1959 General Motors developed DAC-1 (Design Augmented by Computers) and in 1962 Ivan Sutherland, an MIT PhD student, created the Sketchpad program. This pioneering piece of software used a light pen to draw images directly onto the screen. Only five years later Sutherland, working with David Evans, created the Scene Generator, which could represent 3D scenes as a series of dots in space connected by lines. These wire frame images could then be viewed from any angle.

From these early projects the use of computers in design has been developed through a number of frequently intersecting strands. These are most simply divided into three areas (although this is a little arbitrary): CAD, paint or photo-editing programs, and 3D modelling programs, often including animation. They are not so much separated by the technology employed but by the intended context of their use. The descriptions below distil the nature of the applications in order to illustrate the points more clearly. In commercial distribution many programs of one type have features of another, so in this sense computer graphics have become ubiquitous. Our dialogue or interaction with a computer is, for most of us, negotiated by the use of graphical icons and at the other end of the spectrum most television or advertising imagery that we encounter is generated using computers for at least part of the process; computer graphics and graphics on computers are all around us. From this point of view it is rather hard to outline or identify the development of the field in a short introductory chapter as its presence is threaded through much of modern communication.

CAD

CAD is most commonly used as an acronym for Computer Aided Design, though sometimes Computer Assisted Design or Computer Assisted Drafting. This group of programs is most generally associated with the use of computer technology to assist in the development of architectural and engineering plans. The earliest CAD programs were used in industrial applications such as car design, and were available at a high price and ran on physically large computers that had

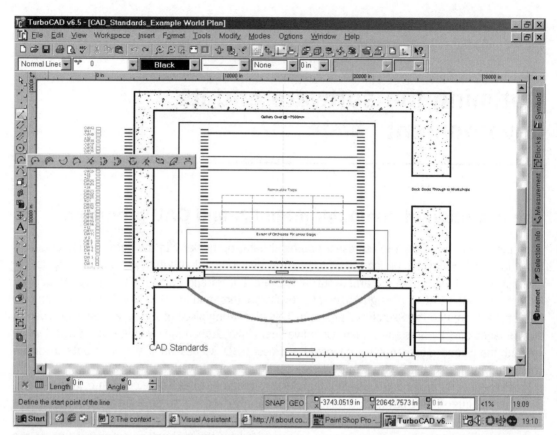

Figure 2.1 A typical interface of a simple CAD program – Imsi TurboCAD in this case. The plan on screen shows the example for CAD Standards in the theatre, developed by the Association of British Theatre Technicians. Plan drawn by David Ripley, cad4theatre

(compared with those of today) limited memory and power. They allowed the user to specify the parameters of lines on a plan and, later, in three dimensions and to adjust and modify those parameters, as points in space. These programs were initially based on calculating vectors. In this process the computer can represent a line, or a connected series of lines, which are derived from the parameters that the user has specified; the line is described by its mathematical properties rather than by its 'look'. In essence, rather than having to draw an exact square the designer could tell the computer to draw four lines of equal length, connecting with each other at the end of each line at precisely 90 degrees. If the designer then wanted to change this shape to a rectangle then, rather than erasing it and starting again, the parameters of two parallel sides can be changed to make them longer. These facilities allowed for extreme precision and quick redrawing if errors occurred. The facility for a computer to repeat operations with consistent accuracy also meant that large projects were carried out on the computer much more efficiently. More advanced programs could also represent a simple view of the designed object apparently in three dimensions. The prohibitive cost of the systems meant that they were really only of use to major industrial or government users and they were certainly out of the reach of the theatre.

During the 1980s the development of lower-cost higher-powered personal computers allowed for the development of CAD software that was aimed at the small user market (small industry and home) and, with technological advances; the features available on these products became increasingly sophisticated. In the early 1980s the Autodesk Company was established and their products have been one of the field leaders in desktop CAD applications. In the wake of the Autodesk products a number of developers have launched CAD programs of varying costs from freeware to very expensive, all of which offer varying levels of sophistication. From the early 1990s most CAD programs available to the desktop user could not only deal with points and lines on one plane but also on three axes, thus the programs were able to represent 3D shapes, displayed as wire frames, which are a series of points in space connected by lines. This development coupled with increasingly fast graphics cards allowed the user to rotate objects or buildings and to view them from any conceivable angle. Many CAD programs now offer sophisticated engineering tools that not only allow for the symbolic representation of plans but also provide structural and quantity information derived from the plans.

The CAD programs described above have largely been developed to deal with architectural and engineering problems. They demand an input of accurate geometrical data and at least some knowledge of the drafting conventions of technical drawings. They are of enormous value in representing the schematics of a design clearly and accurately but their design philosophy is less suited to the more exploratory development of design concepts. The presumed product of a CAD program is a diagram of some description, which is likely to be a step on the way to building or manufacturing the represented artefact. This philosophy determines the way in which the program is operated: it is driven by precision and real-world relevance. The technical schematic emphasis of these programs has played a major part in directing the history of the use of computers in stage design and, until recently, the computer seemed to be seen largely as an aid to efficiency in the production of construction drawings and ground plans for theatre workshop and construction departments. This process alone has been of benefit in the later stages of the production, particularly to production managers, set builders and, to a certain extent, lighting designers but it has not been of enormous value in the earlier stages of a project for the theatre designer. A CAD program is a useful aid for editing technical information developed in a 3D modelling program (or vice versa) and there are a number of fairly common protocols for exchanging graphical information between a modeller and a CAD program; there are still pitfalls, though, and some information may get lost. If you are intending to use a CAD program to develop plans for printing do remember that the size of printer necessary is prohibitively expensive, and it may be necessary to get designs printed by an agency.

In general most theatre needs little high-end drafting and many of the simple programs available will meet the needs of the independent set designer. A useful CAD program will have a number of functions for precision drawing. It will allow the input of points and lines by keyboard, mouse or digitizer. It will have functions that snap lines and points to specified relationships with other lines, centre point, right angle, etc. It will allow for the creation of exact curves and chamfers (a rounded corner). Most CAD programs also have a number of pre-defined architectural units, allowing the user to insert doors, windows, stairs, etc., to user-defined sizes and designs without having to create them from scratch. CAD programs should allow for the inclusion of dimension lines, annotation, scales and rulers, as well as fill textures such as cross-hatching, line types such as dashed, broken, etc. Drawings will be organized in layers. Not all of these features of course will have 3D representations but one must remember that these programs are more suited to preparing paper plans rather than virtual models and most will have sophisticated tools for the preparation of scale printing.

The authors use IMSI TurboCAD (this is not a recommendation but rather an observation). For less than £50 this offers the range of generic tools required for standard plans and schematics, and it is capable of operating in 3D. Material can be moved fairly easily from Viz to TurboCAD. It should be noted, though, that Viz (the modelling software generally cited in this book) is specifically intended to work as part of the Autodesk suite, and it is probably worth investigating some of the Autodesk CAD products. Autodesk have dominated the small business and desktop CAD market with the program AutoCAD and its simpler iterations such as AutoSketch and AutoCADLT. All but the most complex theatre design will simply not need the features of the full package and, if the program is only to be used for the preparation of paper based plans, any one of the simpler programs available will be quite sufficient. Autodesk products have an advantage that because of their ubiquity it is easy to move files created in them to other programs, including modelling applications, particularly Max and Viz. However, there are file transfer protocols that the majority of programs can import and export.

Some programs aimed specifically at theatre lighting design make extensive use of CAD technology and interface feel. These programs tend to foreground the production of lighting plans including symbolic representations of lanterns, rigging positions and electrical installations. They may also produce databases of units, their hire costs, weights, hook-up information; gel cutting lists and cable inventories may also be derived from the information. In general these programs are more applicable to the engineering side of lighting design than the aesthetic, though more programs do offer some form of modelling as part of the package. The latest and most expensive may offer very high quality simulations of the effect of the lighting design on stage.

Photo/Paint programs

Alongside this history of CAD applications and emerging from the same Sutherland experiment, a parallel and often overlapping strand of development in computer graphics took place more oriented to the artist than the engineer. While the vector-driven CAD packages were ideal for dealing with the mathematical properties of line and form geometry, they could not so easily handle the less formal sides of graphics. In particular they were limited in the way that they reproduced surfaces of objects with colour and texture. Furthermore they were designed to deal with the image as a symbolic representation of an object (to be built) rather than, first and foremost, as a picture. Paint programs were developed that dealt with the appearance of the image on the screen represented by pixels, rather than being driven by the mathematical properties of the line. This, in effect, meant using the screen as a canvas rather than as a drawing board. When using a paint program you are giving the computer instructions about how to represent every small element of the picture on the screen (a bitmap) rather than specifying the properties of a line (which is the vector process of CAD

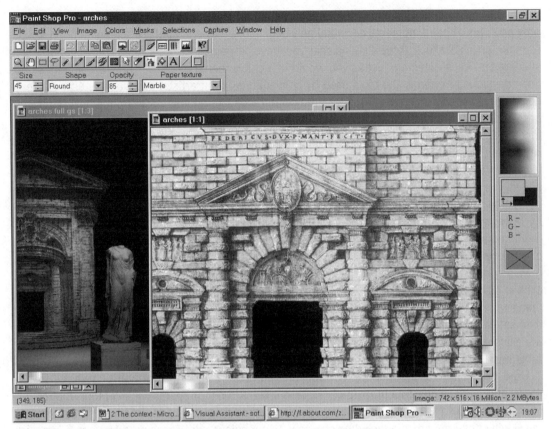

Figure 2.2 A typical interface of a simple paint program, Paintshop Pro 4

programs). These programs became increasingly significant and popular with the development of raster display technology, which scans the screen much like a television allowing for the presentation of a complex and easily redrawn image, not possible with earlier computer display equipment. This in tandem with the development of the colour monitor allowed artists to see their work more accurately. The key player in the development of graphics programs has been the entertainment industry, particularly film and television makers and game designers who, together, have been responsible for the majority of significant developments in the field. In the mid-1980s Thomas and John Knoll set about designing a program aimed at graphic designers for the developing desktop computer market. The end result of their work, released by Adobe in 1990, was Photoshop, which is still one of the mainstays in the growing paint, photo and graphics program market.

While emerging from the same root as CAD, these graphics programs have developed a significantly different place in the market. Their strength over vector-based programs is their emphasis on creating a finished image rather than a schematic for a project to be finished in another media; their final product is the graphic, not the built environment. Significantly, most paint programs are not designed to represent apparently three-dimensional worlds. Unlike CAD programs, photo/paint programs generally only deal in one plane, that of the screen. In other words, to make an object look three dimensional you have to paint it to look three dimensional, using shading and foreshortening, just as you would in a conventional painting. These applications have been developed to mimic the tools used by conventional paint artists, allowing the user to create computer generated images (CGI). These may either look like photographs or paintings, or have an aesthetic integrity of their own. The other significant attribute of paint programs is their ability to incorporate or import images from elsewhere, and image manipulation programs, designed for retouching photographs, share many features with paint programs. Once it is digitized by a scanner, video capture, digital camera, or taken from elsewhere in the digital domain, an image may be edited, manipulated and incorporated into other works (a film or 3D model, for example). Some paint programs, if they have an animation tool, can deal with the moving image as well as the still, by breaking it down into frames. Video titling, effects and editing is a reasonably recent line of multimedia software and is only of use to the theatre designer who works in multimedia, and plenty of other texts deal with this area.

Paint programs alone (without the use of CAD or 3D modelling) are generally the tool of 2D artists, graphic designers and multimedia authors. The latter is a burgeoning area of computer graphics sales and as such their application in theatre is more frequently in the domain of publicity than set design but there are certainly other uses that these programs may have and some of these are explored later in this book. The popular use of scanners and digital cameras has made these programs increasingly popular for image manipulation and photo-retouching.

Used principally for assembling research images, assisting in the creation of textures for the model and perhaps final touching-up of rendered images, most programs will offer tools that equate to those used by a 2D artist using conventional methods, such as pen, brush or spray can, and many will offer virtual media including charcoal, water-colour, oils. These programs are particularly good for assembling several images together, one fading into another, for cutting and pasting parts of one image into others. Importing figure silhouettes and painting costume over the top is a common and useful process for costume design. One particularly useful feature is the ability to select areas of a certain colour range to be excluded or deleted from the image, allowing one to separate an object from its background.

The final image file can be used as a texture map in a modelling program, that is to say it can provide the surface for a 3D object. It may also be printed, emailed or included in an on-screen presentation. It is likely to be the case that an image created in a modelling program will be imported into a paint program for preparation before printing. The paint programs are certainly useful for adjusting the size and colour balance to match the printer.

Depending upon the approach taken by the designer they may or may not use top end features. In June 2000 we purchased Serif Photostudio for £9.99 and this offers many of the features that most designers are likely to use to support digital model making and simple texture design. It includes basic painting tools, effects, selection and copying facilities. The shareware program Paintshop Pro is also effective for basic use, and old releases are available free.

However, if you tend to rely heavily on 2D work you may be advised to purchase a program with more advanced creative features. Adobe Photoshop (now on its sixth release) is perhaps the best known and is generally highly regarded. It can be bought for about £500. As with CAD programs certain features of paint programs turn up in modelling programs, particularly with regard to applying textures to surfaces. Indeed the final output of a modelling program tends to be an image of the kind dealt with in a paint program.

Modelling programs

Rather than being a strand on its own, modelling, which is sometimes called visualization or 3D graphics, is more properly the hybrid between CAD and graphics programs. Ever since the first Sutherland experiments the computer has been used to create virtual images of the world, representing space in three dimensions. The first major applications were for flight simulators, which were designed for the US Navy in 1972 by the General Electric Company. Such images rely on the ability of a computer to generate co-ordinates and lines to represent 3D forms and, to varying degrees, to give surface properties to those forms in order that they might look real. This is a combination of vector-based geometry and pixel-based painting. As with all the applications discussed so far these extremely expensive programs were only really available to academic, government or high-end industrial users until personal computers of sufficient power were available to small business users. The programs produce apparently 3D worlds and objects, often involving animation, and are exemplified in a number of uses: video/computer games design; architectural walk-throughs; film special effects; simulator landscapes; flying logos; pre-production product models. In the 1980s 3D modelling, carried out on extremely expensive systems far beyond the domestic sphere, were being used in film and TV production; the ability to animate 3D scenes is a major feature of these programs, and the film industry has been responsible for significant developments in the sector, and thus many programs have sophisticated animation and associated effects tools. At first this commercial application consisted of the ubiquitous 'flying-logos' and the augmentation of title sequences, often already undertaken with 2D graphics programs. However, by the late 1980s and particularly the 1990s animation was used for more sophisticated narrative purposes, creating characters and worlds with their own aesthetic. The production company Pixar have contributed greatly to this with a number of animated short films as well as the full-length 'Toy Story' (1995) and 'A Bug's Life' (1998) for Disney. In the process they created a new piece of rendering software, Renderman, now used widely in the industry. Every year it seems more software is developed, more artistry and techniques employed.

In the more mainstream market, in 1989 Autodesk (the creators of AutoCAD, a very popular and sophisticated desktop CAD program) launched 3D Studio, a visualization program for the desktop market. While this and similar programs depend heavily on the vector mathematics of CAD programs, they have been created with the designer in mind. The later generations of these programs depend not so much on the input of precise co-ordinates but rather on the more intuitive or free creation of objects that can be simply modified to meet the designer's needs and vision (that being said, complex geometry sometimes needs very precise inputting). Once the form of an object or scene is constructed, frequently using a mesh framework linking points in 3D space, the program then utilizes digital 'paint' technology to give it surface textures. Once the objects have been assembled and surface textures provided the scene can be rendered from conceivably any viewing position; that is to say the computer calculates the effect of light on each surface and how it is perceived from the viewer's position, and then creates a bitmapped image of the scene, perhaps modified by specified effects including fog, lens flare, blur, etc. Recent advances in the way that the computer calculates the final image have meant that the end result can be very realistic and certain programs and protocols have been established simply to carry out the rendering for models constructed in CAD programs that do not have this facility.

Many of the advances in visualization applications over the past decade have been in the rendering of the final image based upon the properties assigned to an object's surface, and how accurately those properties, and the effect of light upon them, are represented. Rendering engines have the ability to calculate not only lighting on a surface but also the effect of bounced light, transparency, refraction, reflection, fog and mist. These calculations of the behaviour and effect of light not only make for convincing images but are naturally of great benefit to architects and theatre designers. Other advances have made the modelling and animation of organic objects more effective. This has meant the philosophy of these programs has resulted in a fairly constant move towards increased realism in the final image. This is a processor-hungry means of rendering but results in high quality, photorealistic images.

Since many visualization programs have been developed for the games and film industries, a major feature of many programs is animation and associated effects. In the higher-end software this is extremely sophisticated, allowing the animation of one object to be influenced by another, connecting objects in the manner of a skeleton or other mechanical device. Motion capture facilitates the recording of live action movement that is mapped onto a digital 3D model; the result may be a very fluid animation.

Visualization programs have found their way into many fields of design, their output appearing regularly in interior design, archaeological reconstruction (for example, Channel 4's 'Time Team'), accident reconstruction, product advertising, as well as the more ubiquitous computer games and film effects. Visualization programs are designed in different ways depending upon the anticipated user group: some are more geared to animation and effects while others share features with CAD programs and are largely designed to be used by architects and product designers. However, visualization is not of course solely concerned with making computer models of an apparently real artefact. Visualization is a tool used in any field to create a readable, communicable and often interactive image of data. These data may be purely mathematical, demographic, topographic, medical and so on using numerical data which may be given visual, often apparently 3D form in order to aid understanding. From the point of view of the theatre artist the data are, of course, a combination of the creative response that the designer has to the text coupled with the engineering and architecture that are imposed on its structure.

Theatre falls somewhere between the fantasy creations of the film and games industries and the needs of architects to visualize the built environment. Theatre designers need the freedom to create complex and imaginative worlds, modelling to a high degree of realism. They are likely to welcome sophisticated calculation of the effect of lighting and smoke. Most designers would probably be keen to be able to import and export CAD plans, and use certain drafting conventions. The easy generation of architectural forms, doors, windows, etc., would also be a bonus. However, a scenographer is less likely to need to create convincing biological entities (representatives of figures certainly, but not substitutes), nor are they likely to need certain camera and animation effects that replicate the effect of explosions and the like. We outline this to explain our choice of Autodesk Viz to illustrate this book.

Autodesk is the parent company both of one of the best selling desktop 3D modellers, 3D Studio Max (produced by a sub-company Discreet), and for AutoCAD, the field-leading CAD package. 3D Studio Max is highly regarded as one of the best of the mid-range programs; it is certainly one of the most popular. At slightly over £3000 it offers high-level modelling, animation and realistic rendering, however it is expensive. Autodesk have since capitalized on working in both domains (the imaginary and the built) and have developed the Viz product, specifically targeted at design visualization and architectural renderings, very much the kind of work undertaken by set designers. Viz offers extremely powerful 3D modelling tools but lacks advanced animation and effects features. On the other hand Viz does include a number of extremely useful drafting aids not available to Max (some more useful for large architectural practices than individual designers). Viz is half the price of Max which makes it particularly attractive to the individual user. At about £1500 it offers almost all the features that we can imagine a designer needing, and is far cheaper than programs of comparable sophistication. An educational price is available to students, and this should make Viz reasonably affordable at about £350. Since the interfaces are quite similar a user can migrate from Max to Viz (or vice versa) reasonably easily, and files can be exchanged between the two programs.

For the purposes of the approach taken in this book, the modelling program is the heart of the theatre designer's system and should be selected with care. They range in price from over £15 000 to free, and sometimes the cheaper software will do what the designer needs as effectively and often more easily than the expensive versions. However, it is worth being prepared to pay for software that really does provide the features necessary. Building a model is a reasonably time-consuming project compared with the quick sketch or an exploratory plan but it is the most closely related to the intended end-product, that is a 3D representation of the world of the text. Though it is unlikely to be the only means of exploration it does yield the most useful information about the arrangement of space, the play of colours, textures and forms, and the practical details needed about sight-lines. The initial sketches lead into the model and the final plans are derived from it. In traditional approaches a designer may be moving backwards and forwards between the means of graphic representation quite frequently and the same is possible in a computer. However, the proper use of a sensibly chosen modelling program will minimize the need to change between modes. Many programs can carry out a range of the activities needed in much of the design process for theatre.

Since the high-end software is really designed for the commercial production of games, television and film effects, they offer features that are unnecessary, complex and expensive. It is worth considering for whom the software was designed. The needs of an interior designer or architectural model designer are rather different from a film effects specialist or the creator of flying logos. Bear in mind that frequently the more expensive programs take far longer to learn, at least to learn fully, and often need far bigger computers to run them.

At the top of the range Alias Wavefront's Maya, and SoftImage are powerful programs that were intended, originally, to run on Silicon Graphics Unix systems rather than the more domestic PC. These systems are far more complex than will ever be needed by a theatre designer, and basically are not designed for the job. In the mid range fall Viz and Max by Autodesk and their subsidiary Discreet, respectively, as well as Lightwave by New Tek, which has just released a 'lite' version. Lightwave was originally designed for the Amiga type of computer, a platform that was initially strong in the field of home graphics, but more or less disappeared from the scene a decade ago. It is really designed for the film and games market and despite its impressive features it is slightly less suited for theatre design than 3D Studio Max or Viz. Of the three, Viz probably has the best range of features for a theatre designer at the price, particularly if you can purchase it at the educational discount. The latest version of Viz and Max contains photorealistic lighting facilities, which means that it replicates the behaviour of real light – this feature, often called radiosity rendering, is available in many high-end programs now. This may be seen as a bonus to theatre design, but it should be taken with some caution. Max and Lightwave will of course serve very well (they support many of the animation and effects requirements better), but the lack of architectural features may sometimes frustrate, though Max, of course, integrates with other Autodesk products. As noted in the introduction the successor to both Max and Viz will be a combined product, incorporating the main features of both. Although this is likely to cost more than Viz currently costs, it should be an extremely effective package.

In the budget range, Strata 3D is a useful program with two versions: the entry level 3Dplus and the advanced 3Dpro. (An old version of Pro was recently attached, free of charge, to the cover of a computer magazine.) A great advantage of this system is that they share a common interface and logic, so that one may use the base version in the first instance and then choose whether to upgrade. The main differences between 3Dplus and 3Dpro are that the latter offers more complex animation facilities and a greater range of effects, though many are available as plug-ins for 3Dplus (i.e. may be added-on later). The Strata package is available for the Mac or PC, and at 2003 prices 3Dpro is available at a litle over £500.

Two other effective packages in the cheaper end of the market are Eovia's Carrera Studio and Calgori's TrueSpace. For free one can use the idiosyncratic Blender (which is not really suited to theatre work but is interesting to try) and of course use one of the many demonstration releases that are now available. There are other programs, and products come, go, change hands and get upgraded with such regularity that any purchaser must undertake full research before they buy, rather than relying on an out-of-date book.

Since Viz and Max and indeed pretty much all software products are constantly being upgraded, it is sometimes possible to buy discontinued versions at a competitive price. The user will rarely be negatively affected by the obsolescence of their software. Although later versions of the software have made some processes more easy and improved the 'realistic look' of the design many of the founding principles have remained much the same and an old version of a program may win out over newer versions simply through ease of use brought about by familiarity.

Chapter 4, on working in a modelling program, explains the principles of 3D modelling in more depth, and you should read this before buying a program since it will help you to understand basic terms and reference points. It goes without saying that by the time this book is published features will be advertised that we have not even thought of, so you should always consult specialist magazines such as *Computer Arts*, *Digit* and *3D World,* as well as reputable dealers (those that specialize in 3D) and experienced users.

Briefly the features that a set designer is likely to need include:

- a good range of approaches to making models, using pre-made primitive forms, extruding, lofting and lathing 2D shapes;
- tools to edit objects by moving, scaling, rotating them and ideally bending, twisting, tapering and squeezing them;

- facilities to modify an object by moving its component parts of vertices and edges;
- light sources that emulate spotlights, take projections and cast shadows;
- if light is a major concern you will require the ability to render accurate photometric lighting simulations using a radiosity rendering engine – in brief you will want to produce photorealistic picture;
- the use of complex materials including bump mapping, transparency, opacity mapping, ideally reflection;
- the ability to change the scale of materials;
- the facilities to animate the location of objects and the level and colour of lights.

Also useful for the theatre designer are:

- facilities for sharing files with CAD programs;
- a good set of drawing aids that help locate precise points in space;
- use of a range of measuring units;
- the use of layers to organize the model;
- architectural features such as the creation of doors, windows, stairs, etc.;
- the ability to represent the effect of smoke, or haze, in a light beam.

Do remember that if a feature that you require is not available on the software that you would otherwise purchase it may be available as a plug-in program. Otherwise there is probably a way around the project to avoid the feature.

There are some additional programs that work with modelling programs, but are not complete solutions in their own right. Curious Labs' Poser is an excellent, easy-to-use figure-generating program that allows you to select character types and arrange them in a number of poses. These figures may be imported into many modelling programs to provide humanity for the scene. A Poser demo may be downloaded from the Curious Labs' Web site for free.

Where most modellers apply pre-made textures to surfaces some programs allow you to paint directly onto the surface of the model, and carry out a range of graphic effects in 3D. These can be particularly effective both for highly detailed material application and for applying effects to avoid the predictable look of computer realism. MeshPaint 3D from Texturetools, or Deep Paint 3D from Right Hemisphere are two such products, allowing the user to 'paint' directly onto a computer model, providing highly individual and detailed surfaces.

Specialist programs

Digital modelling for theatre has developed significantly over the last five years and a number of programs now exist to support the design process, developed specifically for theatre professionals. Lighting has particularly benefited from this attention, with a number of products offering digital support for the lighting designer. Lighting has always depended heavily on symbolic plans to represent the lighting designer's intention; unlike set design there is no easy way of producing a scaled-down replica of the intended end-product. Furthermore, lighting design, particularly for large events such as concerts and trade shows, produces a large amount of data: patch plots, loading charts, hire costs, cable lengths. Unlike set design this is reasonably formulaic, with calculations based around known units. This makes it the perfect activity for digital support. Principally using a CAD-type logic and interface, the lighting designer may draw or import the theatre plans and the set plans and then may place barrels or truss at specified points in 3D space, often selecting symbols with 3D representation from existing libraries. Luminaires, generic or manufacturer specific, may be hung, sourced, focused and patched, with all the necessary information existing on printable spreadsheets.

Some programs, such as WYSIWYG, offer real-time interactivity with lighting desks. A real desk can be used to set levels in the program and thus stored on the desk or, in the absence of a real control, a virtual desk may be created. These high-end programs can render the lit perspective or isometric image for design consideration. At their simplest these are specialized CAD programs with symbol libraries and associated data files, the schematic- and information-based part of the design. They can offer modelling and rendering tools for 3D visualization of the design and interaction with theatre lighting systems. The drawbacks have tended to be a limited set of modelling features and rendering of lower quality than dedicated 3D model programs and renderers. A render from one of

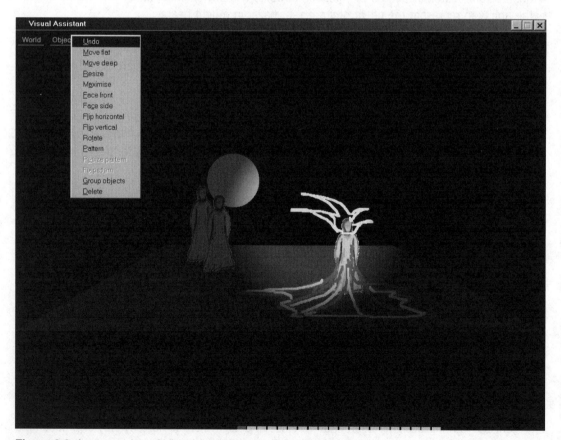

Figure 2.3 A screen shot of Visual Assistant showing a sketch design

these programs is unlikely to use algorithms that provide totally realistic lighting simulation; this is changing, however, and at the top end these features are appearing.

From the set designer's point of view these are of limited value and files are not portable between model program and lighting program to a satisfactory level. The more likely process is for a designer and lighting designer to work together in a good modelling program and then for the lighting designer to translate the vision into practical information in lighting software. However, it will not be long before this slight schism is overcome. The argument against experimentation with lighting in a modelling program is that it does not offer theatre-specific lighting information. Gel numbers or lantern types are not represented or translated into rendering information. The response to this is that the programs allow the designer to find the ideal representation of their vision. The task is then to transform it into theatre-specific reality. One looks at the way a particular light plays on a surface on the screen, the task is then to find the real-world equivalent. A good designer, working with a lighting designer, will know what is possible but a sophisticated rendering engine assists the process.

Finally, Visual Assistant is a free, straightforward program that allows the user to arrange simple, apparently 3D scenes (in fact it is not a 3D program, it simply scales 2D bitmaps as you move them away from the plane of the screen). The user calls upon simple geometry and graphic tools to arrange objects and people in a stage space. It provides an extremely useful facility for creating multi-image storyboards and is an ideal exploratory theatre sketchpad, though it is not intended for detailed design development. It is a useful foil to the overbearing tendency towards visual naturalism in computer modelling; an example of an interface and a scene are shown in Figure 2.3. Visual Assistant can be downloaded from http://www.adr.plym.ac.uk/va/index.html

3

Thinking about the hardware: an overview of relevant technologies

It goes without saying that between writing this chapter and you reading it much of the software will have gone on to a new release, faster computers will be cheaper and someone will have marketed a tool that we have not even thought of. Therefore this chapter focuses on generic issues with only occasional mention of specifics. Its purpose is to provide a broad grounding so that the designer entering this field, perhaps for the first time, has some idea about the technological context and the meaning behind some of the numbers. If nothing else, it is hoped that this will enable you to become an informed purchaser, however there is no substitute when buying a system for consulting dealers, reference manuals, other users, the main Web sites and regularly published magazines. A list of some of these appears at the end of this book. Your hardware needs will vary depending upon your aims, the type of work that you'll be undertaking and the software that you'll be running. Simple 3D packages from the budget end of the range, used to produce simple, still images, will run on the sort of computer that most people have at home (if it isn't too old). These are often what are called 'entry level' computers, but are still sufficient for simple graphics work; one can be bought for less than £1000. However, if you intend to run Max, Viz or an equivalent program with a variety of add-ons for the production of high resolution animations you should expect to buy the very fastest equipment available, and spend, at 2002 prices, about £1500–£2000 for the computer and monitor and at least £500 for peripherals. It is in general true, however, that 3D graphics demands a lot from a computer; it is one of the few occupations that genuinely warrants the high specifications that we are sold.

This chapter is likely to cover territory known to those who have already spent some time researching what computer to buy. Equally it will be out of date very soon so, in general, specifics have been avoided. Where prices are mentioned it is for comparative purposes only.

The platform

This book is written from the perspective of a user running Microsoft Windows (hereafter referred to as Windows) on an IBM-compatible PC. This section will briefly explain the meaning behind this, and the reason for that choice. References are made to alternative systems, but the main focus is the PC/Windows platform.

'Platform' is a term that refers to the combination of electronic architecture and operating software that provides the basic operational parameters of the system. In order to provide a usable base (or platform) from which to run programs such as word processing applications, spreadsheets, modelling programs and so on a computer needs to provide an environment in which these were designed to work, and which will provide the interface for the user. This environment tends to be made of, or at least defined by, the design of the processing core of the computer, and the programmed operating system. Thus, a platform might be referenced in terms such as 'Windows 2000 on an (IBM-compatible) PC'. This phrase indicates the combination of the software operating environment, i.e., Windows 2000, and basic configuration of the electronic hardware, i.e., IBM-compatible PC, that make up the platform.

In the modern market place, and for the purposes of the individual user wishing to undertake design work, there are two main platforms to consider: PC or Macintosh. These are the only two serious contenders for the desktop market, although there are a few variations worth considering. At the higher-end of use, for film production for example, the Silicon Graphics iteration of the Unix platform is generally favoured above the domestic choice of PC/Windows or Macintosh, but the cost of the Silicon Graphics platform puts it beyond the reach of a theatre designer.

The distinction between the two, and their rather different status in the market place is, at least in part, down to the commercial philosophy behind their release. As small, or personal, computers were developed for the home and small business market in the 1970s and 1980s a number of individuals and companies developed different systems for handling information and interacting with the user. As IBM developed their personal computer (PC) they made public much of the technical information behind its design; they used an operating system designed by a third party, Microsoft; and a processor designed and manufactured by Intel. This openness about the system, coupled with the contracted-out provision of key elements meant that other manufacturers could enter the market and hence a number of companies make very similar machines, frequently using Windows as the operating system. Naturally this competition gave rise to competitive pricing and developments that attempted to elevate one manufacturer's machine above another's. The term PC, though really standing for any personal computer, has tended to be used to specifically refer to computers designed to the original IBM specifications. PCs do not have to run Windows – other operating systems such as Linux can also work to provide the user's environment – but for the purposes of this book Windows is the most obvious choice.

Technically a Macintosh is also a PC. Macintosh, produced by Apple, used a different internal structure, meaning that their programs were not compatible with those for IBM-type machines. It is common now to refer to the IBM-derived computers made by many companies as PCs, as distinct from a Macintosh computer.

The Apple computer company, makers of the Macintosh family of computers, took a rather different approach from IBM, keeping their system much more in-house, providing their own hardware and operating systems. The Macintosh computers made significant headway in computer graphics in the early years of home computing, notably with paint programs such as Adobe Photoshop, which was specifically designed for this platform. CAD and 3D modelling for the desktop market however, were initially more commonly employed on the PC. Autodesk, a particularly influential field leader, originally designed software for the PC only. There is probably more option in terms of software for the PC, particularly in the 3D modelling area, though inevitably there are some Mac-only applications.

The advantage of the PC is that, unlike Macintosh, the system is manufactured by a large number of companies, each with slightly different details in the manufacture. (Indeed IBM now has only a very small share of the market that they created.) Each manufacturer may slightly rework the architecture to suit different needs and budgets. As such there is a larger range of PC variants available and the high-volume market has resulted in extremely cheap prices. The disadvantage, of course, is that this multiplicity leads to an irregularity between systems and you cannot be entirely certain that particular add-ons will work with your system. The Macintosh system is more predictable and stable and accepts extras far more readily. A Macintosh, however, is generally more expensive, though frequently prettier!

The authors are PC-based and this book is written from the perspective of a PC running Windows but much of the general material remains relevant to both. Since Darwin Reid Payne's excellent book *Computer Scenographics* focuses on using a Macintosh system, this book might, perhaps, redress the balance.

A word about the Windows operating system

The operating system (OS) is your way into the computer, and not only is it your first contact but, to a certain extent, it is the first contact of any other software that you load onto your PC. A modelling program that does not understand your OS, and vice versa, will not work properly. The OS is the layer that communicates between the users and the deeper levels of programming that make the PC work. For the PC the ubiquitous OS is almost certainly an iteration of Microsoft's Windows. Historically IBM produced the first PC using the internal architecture that has now become synonymous with the term PC and they chose to use the emergent company Microsoft's operating system called DOS. This was simply a text-based system at first but, as graphics and display technology improved, Microsoft developed a Graphical User Interface (GUI) to work on top of DOS, making the system more user-friendly. This system has developed into the many incarnations of Windows which now does not work on top of an OS but contains its own OS. Ironically, although IBM contracted the OS for their systems to Microsoft, it is now Microsoft that dominates the small home computing markets.

The Windows family falls roughly into two genealogies: the Windows 9x strand including Windows 95, 98 and ME was targeted more at the individual users wanting flexibility, while the Windows NT and Windows 2000 family was targeted more towards corporate users or those who needed stability and security. Though they all look fairly similar to the user they operate in rather different ways so there is no guarantee that a piece of software designed for Windows 2000 will operate effectively on Windows 98. The latest version is Windows XP, which is derived from the NT/2000 line but is also attempting to appeal to the needs of the individual user. Check with dealers which operating system your chosen modelling software will work with, and then check with a user community. New releases of operating systems and modelling applications may be fraught with bugs, and this can be particularly problematic if both new releases are being used with each other for the first time.

Windows prides itself on its intuitive interface, an interface that is emulated in all applications that run on Windows. It relies on a heavy use of graphics to represent commands through buttons, icons and 'fly-out' or 'roll-down' menus. Needless to say it is only intuitive if you are used to rolling a mouse in one hand while looking at a screen, before moving a cursor (going at a different speed from your hand) over a tiny button that looks very little like the intended action – and then trying to decide whether one or two clicks will do the job.

What to look for when buying a system – what's inside the box

Most 'multimedia' computer systems currently available (usually advertised as such) will run all but the most complex computer graphics programs, indeed most 'entry-level' systems will run basic programs. Only a few years ago in order to undertake 3D modelling with any degree of efficiency one had to purchase a bespoke system costing as much as four times the price of a standard computer, however a basic machine is now so powerful that its use by many people simply as a word processor is a little absurd. Of course, it is in the interests of manufacturers to persuade a user that they need a more powerful computer and, to support this carousel, software manufacturers frequently produce new releases that need a higher specification machine than the last. While many advances will be to the advantage of a high-end graphics user one must also be aware of when it is time to stop the carousel and accept that the current system (software and hardware) is sufficient.

Today you might see a computer advertised as an AMD Athlon XP2000, 1.68 GHz, 256 MB DDR, 80 GB Hard Disk, 32 MB Graphics. In this section we will explain what this jargon means. The order in which this is expressed is usually, but not always: Central Processor Unit, usually described as a name (Intel or AMD), a model type (e.g., Pentium 4 or Athlon XP2000) and sometimes its clock speed in MegaHertz or GigaHertz; amount of Random Access Memory (RAM) measured in Megabytes and often qualified by RAM type; size of internal storage; specifications of the graphics card; other details on CDs, DVDs, monitors and sound cards will follow.

The CPU

The first in this list is usually the Central Processor Unit (CPU), which is located on the main piece of engineering, the motherboard. Frequently, though perhaps erroneously, termed the brains of the system, it is the CPU that is the computational centre of any computer and its capacity will define what the rest of the system is capable of. Intel set the standard for PC CPUs when they designed the x86 series (of which the Pentium 4 is the latest iteration) for IBM, though other manufacturers make compatible processors with only minor functional differences. Intel still have a large market share for processors but competitors such as AMD offer equivalent products (or even ones that AMD will claim are superior), with the new high-end AMD Athlon processor generally being regarded as better value for money than the equivalent Pentium 4, though the latter is perhaps the better option for video and animation. Naturally, both Intel and AMD are working on a new design for the next generation of processor. The imperative behind the design of new processors is towards ever-increasing speeds for the handling of data. It does this by being able to receive instructions, measured in bytes, more quickly and to deal with them more efficiently when they are received, finding ways to deploy parts of the processor efficiently that might otherwise be waiting for new instructions.

The frequency figure related to the CPU refers to its clock speed, or speed of operation. A clock speed is necessary in a computer to ensure that all parts function synchronously. It is like a conductor's beat. The faster the clock speed, the faster the computer will deal with data. In fact this is only the speed of the CPU; most other components of the computer run substantially slower. The CPU operates at a multiple of the basic computer clock speed. This occasionally causes problems when the CPU is waiting for information that is slower in arriving. Increasingly however, the memory is capable of keeping up with the CPU, despite the overall increase in clock speed of the ISA input and output bus. This is a part of the computer that allows you to plug extra bits in and it still runs slowly in order to ensure backwards compatibility. Therefore any older card that is plugged into a fast computer will not benefit from the new speeds. PCs offered for sale in summer 2002 were advertised with PCU clock speeds in the order of 2 GigaHertz, which is quite sufficient for modelling software.

Overall 3D modelling and computer graphics in general require the computer to carry out such a large number of calculations that a fast processor is necessary but this must be matched to an appropriate memory. By the time you read this book no doubt Intel and their competitors will have launched new versions, and 1.5 GHz will be considered too slow.

If you are buying second-hand but with the intention of running the latest version of software the authors would recommend no less than a Pentium III or AMD K6 III running at a minimum of 350 MHz with 256 MB RAM. This will, however, be slow and frustrating.

Random Access Memory (RAM)

RAM is the short-term operational memory of the computer, the place where data is stored prior to being accessed by the CPU. RAM is readable and writable; it is where data is rewritten during the operation of a program, later to be saved in a long-term storage location once the task is complete. The more complex the program the more RAM it needs, and 3D graphics programs handle a lot of complex data.

CPUs can work with far more RAM than a user is ever likely to put in, but software may be limited to how much RAM it can make use of. Windows, for example, can currently only address 2 GB of RAM, though this is still far more than most PCs will ever be equipped with. The configuration of the computer may limit the way that memory is installed and, while that may not limit the maximum amount, it may make upgrading from the present configuration quite complex. It is worth checking about how easy it is to upgrade the RAM before you buy a computer.

Most RAM is supplied as Synchronous Dynamic RAM (SDRAM) that is designed to carry large amounts of short-term data and to deal with it in step with the computer's internal clock. These are not the fastest memory chips but they can store more data than the faster Static RAM (SRAM), which is also more expensive. If you need high speed but low volume SRAM would be preferable but, since insufficient volume of RAM also slows down processing, the more usual and cost-effective method is the provision of larger quantities of Dynamic RAM (DRAM). DRAM is also available in specifications other than Synchronous. Each of these has particular advantages, notably WRAM or VRAM, which enhance the use of Windows and Graphics, respectively.

In the drive to increase processor speeds a bottle-neck has been created, since RAM is not capable of being accessed fast enough to keep up. The latest SRAM design, known as Double Data Rate (DDR), is designed to address that problem, maximizing the efficiency of new CPUs running at an excess of 1 GHz.

If you do not have enough RAM for the complexity of the operation, or the RAM is not accessed fast enough, your computer will run more slowly than it should as it tries to move information from limited storage to the processor. How much is enough? Windows alone uses a fair amount of memory simply to function and when you then run a 3D modelling program on top of that, perhaps rendering images with a lot of data for example, high colours, complex shapes, even shadows and reflections, you will rapidly use memory. In reality, to use a moderate-level graphics or 3D modelling program you should have at least 256 MB of RAM but doubling that would be more sensible. Basic software will be able to run well enough on 128 MB. Paint programs are also quite memory-hungry, but not generally to the same extent as 3D modelling. However, whatever we write here and now will be obsolete in a year or two, and new releases of software, including Windows, have a tendency to require more RAM and faster processors. RAM is cheap compared to the rest of the system – get as much of it as you can.

What are bits and bytes?

Information is generally measured in bytes, which is a grouping of 8 bits, a bit being a single 1 or 0 binary. Since a binary basically represents a yes or no answer, or on or off, you can use it to represent any piece of information for which there are a set number of options. By logically asking yes or no questions eight times you can identify one item from a list of 256 possibilities. Each time you add a bit to the binary number needed to record information, you double the number of options in the set to which the binary string refers. For example, to identify all symbols and control strokes on a keyboard, of which there are usually 128, requires 7 bits, that is 7 zeros and ones. The 8 bit byte allows for large character sets.

For work in graphics environments the position above is extended. Imagine a screen showing an image made of 1024 dots, or pixels, by 768 dots, that is a total of 786 432 dots. If each dot can display over 16 million colours, which is common in graphics now, it will need 24 bits, which equals 3 bytes per pixel to identify the right colour. This is called the colour depth. This means that this display would require 2 359 296 bytes to store the screen graphic information. Although this is not of direct use to most designers, knowing that computers store information this way will explain why so many functions are based around certain numbers: 16, 32, 256, 1024, etc. Remember, for these purposes 0 is also a number, so options 0–255, often used in colour choice, offer 256 options.

Storage

'Storage' is where completed operations, recorded as files, are sent for long-term keeping. Operations are committed to this long-term memory when the save function is activated, or when the computer is instructed to remember settings. The form of storage generally integrated into a computer is the hard disk drive. Although they are commonly confused this long-term storage is quite different from the short-term memory (RAM) that is rewritten during the operation of the computer. RAM is where data is stored temporarily while being worked on, storage is where it is sent to once complete, albeit able to be recalled for later reworking. The storage medium can be the hard disk inside the computer; a floppy disk, which has limited storage but is cheap; a writable CD; a ZIP drive; or a hard disk remote from the computer, such as a network server. The files that make a program work will generally be stored on the computer's internal hard disk so as to be accessible to the user and, similarly, files created by programs (i.e., the project that you're working on) will generally be stored in the first instance on the hard disk for quick retrieval. Other forms of storage are generally used for the transportation of files or the provision of back-up storage. As with RAM the capacity of the storage is measured in bytes and, as with other specifications, graphics work requires large-capacity storage. The programs alone may take a thousand million bytes, a Gigabyte, to store; Viz Release 3 typically requires 350 MB (0.35 GB). Computer image files generally require a large amount of storage space, although this will depend upon the size and quality of the image.

There are differences between hard disks, most notably the method by which information is transmitted between the disk and the operational components. The faster of these systems uses a Small Computer Systems Interface (SCSI) connection, however this is substantially more expensive and often harder to set-up than the standard Enhanced Integrated Drive Electronics (EIDE) system. Since hard disks are used to provide temporary operating memory you do need fast access to them to speed-up the memory-hungry process of rendering. Thus, buy a fast-access hard disk. Look for a high data transfer rate.

The smallest hard disks available today are in the order of 40 GB, which is quite sufficient if you are working with still images. However, if you intend to create animations or work with video you may well need to double or quadruple that hard disk specification; indeed under these circumstances you are likely to make use of large external hard disks for storage purposes.

Hard disks can fail so it is extremely sensible to invest in some form of stable external storage. This can also provide a very useful archiving resource, allowing you to keep previous projects away from your hard drive; this both frees space and protects archive work from accidental damage or erasure. Similarly remote storage is useful for holding large image libraries and other visual resources. External storage media are also generally more transportable than a whole desktop computer, thus useful for taking your work to meetings away from your studio. While floppy disks are very portable and sufficient for storing small files they will not accommodate large images and animations very easily. At present the most sensible and portable system is probably a writable CD, and since most other computers have a CD reader if not a writer or DVD (Digital Versatile Disk) it is a fairly straightforward procedure to view your work on a different machine. Other storage options are an external hard disk or a ZIP drive. Each storage device attached to your computer, whether it is inside or out, is mapped with a letter code (conventionally followed by a colon). Conventionally a floppy drive is mapped as A:, hard disk as C:, and then any additional or removable devices from D: onwards. It is increasingly common for manufacturers to provide a hard disk that has been internally partitioned, effectively making two hard disks of smaller size. This allows you to separate program files from your own work. In this case the hard disk may have multiple drive letters. A compression program will allow you to minimize your file size for ease of storage, bearing in mind that a decompression utility is needed to expand them on retrieval.

As with all specifications listed here, 3D modelling takes a lot of space to store, and requires a lot of time to move. The faster and larger your system the more efficient you will be.

Viewing the work – display systems and printers

The accurate representation of a designer's work is of course vital to the quality and efficacy of their work, and rendering, particularly complex animation, will only fulfil its function to describe your vision if the display system is up to the task. The display system is generally made up of two elements: the screen itself and the video card, sometimes called a graphics card or a graphics adapter. Both the speed with which the display redraws itself and the quality (resolution) of the image are naturally most important to designers working in 3D.

The importance of resolution

Any discussion of a computer-based image, its construction and display (through whatever media: monitor, projector, print), is dependent upon an understanding of resolution. All images produced on the computer are ultimately constructed from a number of dots, generally called pixels, an abbreviation of picture elements. Each stage of the creation, manipulation and output process describes the image around the number of dots it contains and how many dots over what area, are used to show it. Three factors warrant consideration when specifying resolution: how complex is the image (how many shapes and colours); how large will its final output be (either monitor display, print copy or even projection); and how high quality does the output need to be (public performance where critical clarity is vital, or production meeting)?

Naturally the more dots in an image the more detail that image will be able to show: a picture of a landscape made up of 100×100 (thus 10 000 pixels) will be able to show only 1 per cent of the detail of the same view composed of 1000×1000 (1 000 000 pixels). To think of it another way, the view of 100×100 pixels could be a small detail of a larger view (1000×1000) but shown with the same clarity. Not only will this ratio specify the complexity of the image, but also describes its aspect ratio. Since in most circumstances a pixel has an aspect ratio (proportion of the measurement of its sides) of $1:1$ the images above will all be square, an image constructed with a resolution of 100×200 will have portrait-type layout with an aspect ratio of $1:2$. This, however, is not the end of the story since the final image will also depend upon the resolution of its display media. Generally speaking the display medium will have a preset resolution: a monitor for example has only a limited number of resolutions that it can display comfortably, or a printer will usually print a particular number of dots per inch. There may be variations within these, but the options tend to be limited and prescribed.

Taking the monitor first, the number of dots a monitor can show will depend upon its size (there are other factors, but not for discussion here). There are standard resolution ratios that a monitor can be set to show, the most common being: 800×600, 1024×768, 1280×1024 and 1600×1200, note the recurring proportions of $1:1.333$. A standard 17" CRT monitor (see below) will comfortably display resolutions of 1024×768, although it can be set to show smaller or larger resolutions (800×600 or 1280×1024). The reason for this limit is that the monitor will display the image in dots (known as pels in a monitor) that are approximately 0.27 mm apart, known as the dot pitch. This means that each square inch (reverting to inches here since that is still the common unit for such specifications in the UK) of screen contains roughly 5184 (72 × 72) dots. At a very high magnification the bitmap would look like an abstract pattern of squares. Viewed at a normal magnification the areas coalesce as a picture. The physical size of the monitor is therefore a clear determinant for the resolution that it can display. Flat screen monitors can display a slightly higher resolution for their size.

A monitor with its resolution set to 1024 × 768 will therefore display any image of that size or smaller in the equivalent proportion of the screen, displaying each pixel of the image by one dot or pel on the screen; this is the ideal display configuration. An image 800 × 600 pixels will be displayed in about 66 per cent of the screen area. Most software allows you to zoom in on the image so that it occupies the entire screen, but your image information is here being spread over a wider area than intended, and thus will lose clarity. Similarly it is possibly to zoom out, compressing the image to a smaller screen area, but since there will not be enough pels to show each pixel you again lose resolution. The ideal situation is to have one pixel shown in each monitor pel, and whatever the actual image size this relationship will show a consistent quality of image. This logic will suggest that if you opt for too large a monitor for the type of image that you normally produce the images will look less convincing than they would on a smaller monitor with a lower resolution. It is not the case therefore that the bigger image is always better.

It is of course also possible, and sometimes necessary, to create an image with a higher resolution than your monitor is capable of displaying. In these cases you will either only see part of the image on the screen at any one time, or you will have to zoom out to see the full image, thus potentially losing its quality. An image of 2000 × 1400 will either be viewed a quarter at a time, or zoomed out to a ratio of 1:2. This situation is only likely if you are producing images for print output (see below), or photographing as transparencies, where generally the resolution is expected to be far higher than those shown on a screen.

Monitor types

The common choice and the cheaper monitor for a PC is a Cathode Ray Tube (CRT), though the liquid crystal display (LCD) monitor is becoming more common and more affordable. The former works by shooting an electron beam at a coated screen – in fact there are three sub-beams, one for each of the primary colours (RGB). As the beam hits the screen a small circle of light is created (the pel described above) and it is the balance of the three primary colours that dictates the final colour. This beam sweeps across the screen punching a number of these small circles of colour at regular intervals and then going back and starting again. A modern CRT monitor will redraw the entire screen this way between 60 and 120 times a second. Given that many displays and images use 1024 horizontal dots for each of the 768 lines, this means that the monitor is drawing about 50 million dots per second (its bandwidth). These dots quickly fade, remaining visible for only a small fraction of a second. The quick redraw rate and the fact that the light persists in our vision between the fading and redrawing of a dot accounts for the apparently constant image on a screen.

The size of the monitor you have will affect the work you create. There are two ways that we might measure the size of a monitor. There is the physical diagonal distance across the screen (the visible screen size) or one may consider the resolution, which is the number of dots that the screen is capable of showing horizontally and vertically. The designer should be able to have access to a number of resolution settings on the monitor: the most common are likely to be 800 pixels wide by 600 lines high (800 × 600) and 1024 × 786 and possibly 1280 × 1024. Only a designer working on printed graphics is likely to need higher. For a CRT monitor a screen dimension of 17" (with 16" viewable) should yield sufficient resolution, although 19" may aid detailed modelling work. A much larger monitor will be extremely bulky and hard to house and, ironically, it may show a less good image than the smaller monitor since the same resolution image may be spread over a larger area, hence the image may look a little less crisp. CRT monitors are now available with flatter screens than previous models, and this is worth spending the little extra money on since the image is generally a little larger for the size of the unit, and of better quality.

You should aim to choose a monitor with as low a dot pitch as possible, nearer 0.26 than 0.28, and a vertical scan rate of at least 72 kHz to avoid eyestrain. You should be able to adjust the image quality on the monitor easily (colour, brightness, contrast).

LCD monitors (sometimes known as TFT – Thin Film Transistor) are much slimmer than CRT since, rather than shooting an electron beam at the screen therefore needing distance from the gun to the target, they have each pixel set electronically. LCD monitors display images by raster scanning but, unlike a CRT screen, the dots on the LCD screen remain lit almost indefinitely, until reset. The drawback with these monitors is that they cannot be redrawn at the speed of CRT displays. The upshot of this is that they are very good for static images but less good for animation and video. They do take up less space than a CRT and are coming down in price. Generally a LCD monitor will show more pels in a given area than a CRT monitor, thus a resolution of 1024 × 768 may be shown on a monitor with a smaller diagonal dimension. These monitors currently start at about £300.

Graphics cards

The second element of the display chain is the graphics or video card, sometimes called an accelerator. This is a piece of hardware with associated software (called drivers) that may either be built into the computer motherboard, or sit separately in an expansion slot. The function of this piece of equipment is to store the image data in such a way that it can be quickly accessed by the CPU and the image output circuit. The more advanced graphics cards also have a processor to handle the computation of colour and the brightness of the pixels, saving the central processor from the task, and hence accelerating it. Simple characters displayed on a blank screen require very little graphics information but an image made up of complex colours and hundreds of thousands of pixels, perhaps changing 30 times a second, requires a large amount of memory and very fast processing and retrieval rate of the complex information. A highly specified card is needed if you are intending to produce detailed, high quality animations that utilize a large number of colours. In this scenario you would require the graphics card to compute and provide the information for perhaps 800 000 pixels, each with a possible 16 million colours, though this is rarely used, 30 times a second for smooth animation. This is particularly complicated when the computer is calculating the effect of hidden objects from a moving point of view in a 3D world. Still images need far less highly specified graphics cards. Colour depth is a term that frequently arises when describing graphics equipment; the term refers to the amount of memory needed to store data for the colour of one pixel. To store information about 256 colours takes 8 bits (one byte), whereas to store information for about 16.7 million colours takes 24 bits, 3 bytes – this is a full colour display. Some systems claim 32-bit colour depth – the extra byte holds other information about the image but does not increase the colours.

A large image, say 1024 × 768 with full colour, known as true colour will need nearly 2.5 MB of memory on the graphics card to store the image information, and if the image is to include sophisticated elements such as transparency it will require over 3 MB of memory. If this is to be animated one needs to increase the video RAM in order to have information on the next frame available to the display quickly. If the image is to have more pixels the required memory will increase, as it will if the card is to carry out the calculations needed for fast 3D display. The increased card memory allows for the fast handling of image data, taking the load off the RAM. Most current cards for these sorts of applications will have at least 32 MB, and many advertised as part of a system have 64 MB of RAM, so base level specifications are high enough for most users. The graphics card RAM only limits what can be displayed on screen, it does not actually limit other than by practicality the size of the images that you can make. The majority of graphics cards are now accessed by the CPU through an Advanced Graphics Port (AGP) bus, designed specifically to move image information such as video very quickly through the system, where necessary bypassing the CPU. This AGP bus can either connect to a card housed on the motherboard or, more commonly, to a card located in a slot inside the computer. This allows the user to decide on their preferred card, or to upgrade.

Graphics cards normally output to a computer monitor, but many have the capability to output to analogue S-Video.

In summary, since most graphics cards, other than the very bottom end of the market, are designed around the needs of the gaming community, which is demanding of high quality fast graphics and interactive 3D, most cards are suitable for the 3D designer.

Printers

The other common method for viewing and presenting your work is by printing it. The type of printer used will depend on the function of the output. Large technical drawings and ground plans will require the use of a plotter or other printer capable of taking paper up to A0 or at least A1 size. These are expensive bulky items that are of limited use since they will not print photographic quality full-colour images. The designer is better served taking their file to an agency that will plot it for them at very little cost. Companies such as these tend to be listed under Printers or Draughtsmen and Tracers in the phone directory. The cost varies depending on how much work needs to be done to set the file up for printing and obviously on the size of the plan or design.

Of more everyday use to the designer is a printer that can reproduce full-colour images of seemingly photographic quality. The most common form of printer available is the inkjet, which operates by painting ink, usually three colours and black, onto the paper. The three colours when used together and properly aligned can create the full range of colours used in the image. These printers vary in cost enormously but the technology behind the application of ink to paper is much the same. Many printers are now capable of producing such images at 1440 dots per inch (dpi), quite sufficient for all but the most demanding viewer of the image. Images that the Kent Interactive Digital Design Studio (KIDDS) have framed and mounted for exhibitions have been printed on a cheap Epson Colourjet 700 (now superseded). As important as the printer is the type of paper that is used and, for a colour image, one needs to print onto either photographic paper or specially designed gloss or satin inkjet paper. Most of these printers are restricted to A4 paper, but some are available that print onto A3, naturally at a higher price.

Printers create the image by controlling the colour applied to single tiny dots in the same way that a monitor fires electrons at the screen one dot at a time. A printed dot can simply recreate one pixel from your image but a pixel may be represented over a number of printed dots without sacrificing much of the quality of the image. For the purposes of printing the resolution tends to be referred to as dots per inch (dpi). Since many low-budget inkjet printers can produce images with in excess of 1400 dpi, some up to 2800, one can see that they are quite capable of producing high quality renderings of digital models, quite sufficient for production meetings. If an image is intended for printing and photographing as a transparency one can aim for a much higher resolution than a monitor is capable of showing. This results in a sharper image that is capable of showing more detail. A very high quality image for 35 mm slide projection may well be 5760×4320 pixels which, if printed one pixel per dot at 1440 dpi, would result in a paper copy of $4" \times 3"$. Should images be required for publicity purposes you are likely to be asked to supply a high resolution file (rather than print-out) directly to the graphics or publicity office for them to insert into the document directly.

Dye Sublimation printers offer an expensive alternative to inkjets, creating the colour on the paper by briefly vaporizing dye in close proximity to the surface, upon which it then solidifies. These produce very high quality graphic images but are slow in operation and are best suited for small formats; these are of little relevance to the individual theatre designer.

Laserjet printers, properly named Xerographic printers, are prohibitively expensive for most individual users requiring colour printing and they are currently of more use in office environments where their near silence is of benefit. Unlike the printers above, the image is first described using electro-static information onto a mediating surface such as a drum or belt which, when covered with charged toner, is transferred to the paper rolled over the drum. Colour laser printers are falling in price, so it is possible that these will soon be a viable alternative to the inkjet.

In conclusion a good quality inkjet printer is the most sensible choice for the independent designer, and those from Epson have been particularly highly regarded for the quality of their graphics output. The designer is not likely to need the fast printing speeds or silent operation that are important features for office printers, instead the quality of its graphic output is paramount.

To summarize what we have discussed so far in this chapter, most computers are over-specified for what their users need. However, the manufacturers of hardware and software must, in order to sell more items, constantly upgrade the specifications needed by the program and therefore offered by their machines. This is bad news for the home users who only want to word process but good news for the designer since many machines on sale are capable of running graphics software. Graphics, particularly 3D and animation, do need a lot of memory, a fast processor and a sophisticated graphics card feeding a high quality monitor. Unlike word processing you really do need the highest specifications offered. The PC you buy for visualizations for theatre should have a fast processor at least equivalent (even if bought second hand) to a Pentium III 350 MHz; a new computer will be faster. At least 256 MB RAM and ideally double that. A hard disk of at least 20 GB, though ideally 40+. It should have other storage systems such as a zip drive, or a writable CD. A large monitor, 17" or 19", capable of displaying at least 1024×768 but ideally 1280×1024 pixels and supporting a refresh rate of around $100\,Hz$, or at the very least $60\,Hz$. A graphics card connected by an AGP bus, with at least $16\,MB$ memory and drivers that support OpenGL. A box that will allow you easy access to upgrade and a number of expansion slots.

Input devices

Other than a keyboard and mouse, common input devices are a scanner, pressure sensitive pad, digitizing tool, digital camera, Video Cassette Recorder (VCR) and, for some applications, a joystick.

A scanner is probably the most useful input device for the designer. It allows pre-existing images to be captured and imported into a variety of graphics programs. A flat-bed scanner is the most sensible option, rather than one that automatically feeds pages through, since original images of various sizes and thickness can be placed on it. It is even possible to scan the surface of 3D objects. A3 scanners are available, which may be useful since art reference volumes (often used by designers to provide initial inspiration material) may be larger than A4. However, an A3 scanner is of course more expensive, and takes up a significant amount of desk space, particularly if one also has a 19" monitor and an A3 printer. The software that drives the scanner is often accessed through a paint program and can control a number of settings related to the image quality. It will allow for zooming and re-sizing of the original image. The final outcome of scanning an image is a bitmap. This is a pixel-based image but some software can read the bitmap to find letters and characters, hence being able to convert a paper document into a word-processing file. However, scanning is a slow process and a scanner that is to be used frequently if possible should be connected to a computer via a SCSI or USB connection, rather than the older and slower Standard Serial Port. The best choice is a SCSI connection as this is the fastest method of communication. Many scanners are sold bundled with software; from a designer's perspective look for high quality graphic or paint software in the bundle rather than the Optical Character Recognition software that is of more use to those working with text.

Pressure sensitive pads and digitizers are both sophisticated variations on the common pointing device, the mouse. They are effectively similar devices used for different purposes. A mouse uses a relative set of co-ordinates, that is as you move the mouse across the table the cursor will move but if you pick the mouse up and put it down 30 cm away, then move on the table again the cursor will continue from where it last was. This is not a useful way to enter certain types of graphical information, particularly precise measurements. The digitizer, however, allows a designer or engineer to input precise relationships between co-ordinates in the real world via a pointing device, the digitizer stylus, by moving across a sensitive tablet to input absolute co-ordinates Thus the top left corner of the tablet relates to the top left corner of the digital plan, the bottom right to the bottom right, etc., the distances between each point being precisely set. A digitizer may therefore accurately translate co-ordinate points off a plan and into a computer aided design or drafting program. CAD work requires large digitizer tablets, which allow the user to input existing graphical data and to work in absolute units. Again, it's worth remembering that CAD agencies can digitize existing plans for a fee.

A pressure sensitive tablet may allow some of the above but it is principally used for the creation of graphic images and may therefore be no larger than a mouse mat. Such a tablet will normally operate in either relative modes (as does a mouse) or absolute mode (as does a digitizer). The advantage of the tablet is that the user holds the pointing device like a pen or brush. It is therefore much more accessible to the conventional artist and the pressure with which the stylus is applied to the tablet may instruct the computer to make a mark that is heavier or lighter, thus emulating a conventional medium such as charcoal or ink. Certain graphics programs specifically support the use of pressure sensitive tablets.

Scanners

A scanner is an important piece of equipment for the designer: it is vital to be able to import found images. A designer needs a scanner with good graphics capabilities and a reasonable data flow, but does not need to worry unduly about the quality of its text read (optical character recognition). It is important to get a flat-bed scanner rather than the feed-through document type for handling books and scanning the surface of 3D objects. Also, if space permits, buy one larger than A4. Given the graphic nature of the work the scanner must be able to scan full colours (i.e., 24 bit, representing 16.7 million colours) but since they will be capturing images to apply as textures in a scene, resolution does not need to be overly high. A native resolution of 300 dpi should be sufficient if you are only scanning model textures, although most machines will be higher. If you are scanning to build up a library resource you will need good resolution, but do remember that higher resolution images take more storage space.

Make sure that the scanner is supported by TWAIN protocols since this will allow direct input into paint programs. Finally, scanning can be slow, so a fast connection is a bonus. However, a designer is not likely to have to deal with a huge volume of material so this may not be a key issue.

Slide scanners take an image straight off negative or transparency, thus giving very high quality; some work at incredible resolutions such as 2820 dpi.

It is possible to buy a number of different devices that scan or digitize a 3D object, producing a mesh that is of use in a modelling program. At present these are very expensive or, at the cheaper end, very slow and limited to the size of the scanning surface. Undoubtedly these will be of great benefit to 3D modelling in the future, but are currently not really practical or affordable. However, a number of pieces of software can make a 3D image (of sorts) from a photograph (or photographs) as the user inputs data about key points and vanishing points.

Digital cameras

A digital camera is an increasingly useful tool for capturing samples from the outside world and bringing them into your digital model. As with scanners you will find that resolution is not as important for modelling work as it is for normal photography (for print or nostalgia) since the final image is likely to end up as a small part of a large scene, seen only on a computer monitor. Thus price and ease of use are more important than the often touted resolution. A camera that can take a close-up photograph of a texture will be more useful than one with high resolution.

Finally . . .

A drawing board, scale ruler, fine-tipped drafting pens, compass, set-square, flexible curve, craft knives, hot glue gun, mounting board, foam-core, mixed bag of balsa, fimo, acrylic paints, a range of pencils and brushes of different sizes and shapes, scenic artist charcoal, gesso, a pair of scissors and a good eye. Not everything in set design is done on computer.

4

Navigating the computer space

This book is about digital three-dimensional (3D) modelling for the theatre; the irony of course is that none of the programs discussed actually produce a genuinely three-dimensional object, but rather they present an illusion of a 3D object, seen from a prescribed point in space. This chapter will briefly outline some of the principles behind 3D modelling, explaining how the computer constructs and shows a model, and how the user may interact with this environment. Many of these aspects will be covered in greater detail in later chapters – this provides an overview.

Each object in a digital scene is constructed by telling the computer where all its key points are in a notional three-dimensional space (we say notional because it is a function of maths) and these points are joined up with lines that, together, make surfaces; it's a lot like 3D join-the-dots. Once this framework has been established we tell the computer what the surface is like (this is usually called mapping), we then identify where lights would be in our mathematical void, we assign them colour and intensity, and finally we identify where we are seeing the whole thing from, and how distorting we want the perspective to be (maths again). We then render this image, which gives an illusion of seeing the object (or objects), lit, textured and apparently three dimensional. The end result, on our monitor, will look like a painting or a photograph, but the difference with a computer model is that we can (almost) instantaneously view the scene from a different location, or rearrange objects in it, these things are only possible in 2D graphics if the whole image is re-drawn or re-photographed.

Representing three dimensions on two

The art of illusion is of predominant importance in the 3D space and the means by which illusion is created has its heritage in the language of the human visual system and how that system has been presented over centuries in Western art. Creating three dimensions out of two has been a painterly practice and has involved techniques of perspective. It is worth noting that perspective is a technique of presentation and representation and not a truth. The viewer is given clues as to what the artist intends us to see. These clues include terms such as occlusion, size differences, linear perspective, texture gradients and shading, and atmospheric perspective. It is by these devices that we are enabled as viewers, to perceive objects and illusions. Occlusion is a depth cue and it is indicated to the viewer by placing objects behind one another. Size differences again give the viewer a sense of distance with those objects, those that are larger appearing nearer. Linear perspective offers a greater sense of distance and is illustrated where parallel lines appear to converge in the distance. Textured gradients such as a chess-board will appear more dense in texture when they are further away and so, in order to replicate this look, we must increase the density of the squares on the board. Shading results from light shining on objects and thereby making other objects look darker in some areas. The parts of an object that look further away from the light also thus look darker. Atmospheric perspective refers to the distance and therefore fuzzy nature of objects that are at a distance from us. It is usually caused by particles of dust in the atmosphere that refract light and so cause this effect to be perceived by the viewer. As Hubert Damisch has argued, it 'does not imitate vision, any more than painting imitates space. It was devised as a system of visual presentation and has meaning only insofar as it participates in the order of the visible, thus appealing to the eye' (Damisch, 1994: 45).

Many Renaissance artists worked from a theory of art, which refers to a vanishing point and a horizon line with receding visual rays. The vanishing point is a point on the horizon towards which the viewer is looking and towards which all parallel lines appear to converge. There can be more than one vanishing point but there is usually a principal vanishing point. The viewpoint to any image is the point where the viewer stands and in 3D computer environments this refers to the camera view or scene view. Visual rays are another important tool from theories of art, which are related to 3D computer environments. The visual rays, which come in essence from the standpoint or view of the spectator, allow us to create distortion which can imply a distance from the object. This is called foreshortening and it is achieved by making that nearest part of an object appear larger than that which is furthest away.

In 3D modelling many of these devices of perspective and use of rays are built into the programs. The nature of distance and space is already calculated through algorithms and these mathematical points result in wire frames. These wire frame images can be confusing because they may present every edge of an object or form including those that are hidden, or occluded. This science of drawing is not new. Its heritage is based in the 1500s when Albrecht Dürer (1471–1528) experimented with methods of drawing objects that involved stretching a string from the point on an object and marking the other end on a piece of paper. In addition Dürer's woodcuts show the use of a grid set over a vertical frame placed between the artist and the image to be drawn. This use of a grid, or squaring up as it is called, of a design is often used by scenic artists for the painting of large scenic cloths for the stage. The grids, rays and plotting points of a computer then all have an artistic heritage, which allows for the precise plotting of an image in the 3D environment.

The picture plane and 3D views

Before considering 3D in the computer further, it is worth briefly exploring the idea of the picture plane, and how it is used to represent 3D space. Imagine that there is a plane of glass, an arm's length away from you, through which you view, let's say, a town. If you were to shut one eye and reach out with a pen you could sketch a view of the town on the plane of glass, and this view would show the town as it appeared to you. What the glass has done is intersected each beam of light from the town to your eye at a given point. Of two objects of the same size (say lamp-posts) the one further away looks smaller because the rays of light converge towards your eye. This presents the world as it appears to an artist, but would be of little use to a draftsperson who needed to represent real, not perceived, dimensions. They would not want the rays to converge towards a single point, but to hit the plane of glass parallel to each other, and perpendicular to the glass, thus creating an image that showed their real size. This method of representation, known as orthographic or axonometric projection (depending upon the orientation of the viewing plane – see below), sets the principle for viewing models in a computer that we shall return to later. This is impossible for a human to achieve, because we occupy a small and specific point of vision: a view will always converge on us. However, drafting conventions, such as a ground plan, assume this parallel approach (i.e., elements in the far corners of ground plans are not curved, nor do we draw sets of treads becoming larger as they rise above the stage).

The computer can therefore show two kinds of view: the parallel view for accurate construction of a scene, or the perspective view for convincing images of the end result. Many programs will allow you to view the scene from any angle in either mode, though some may provide preset viewing positions for each mode.

Understanding co-ordinates

Most objects that you will make in a computer model are constructed by placing points in space (vertices), and joining these points up (with lines) thereby creating a mesh. A vertex is located by its co-ordinates in three planes for 3D modelling or two planes for 2D drawing. The line may be curved or straight, although for most basic modelling purposes a curve is generally made up of a number of short straight lines connecting numerous vertices. Generally a shape is a 2D form made by a connected series of lines. It has no thickness and all its points exist on a flat plane. An object is a 3D form, defined by a number of vertices in space, which are located in three planes. A mesh is the term given to the representation of the basic form of an object. The mesh shows the vertices and lines for the whole of the form (literally as a mesh; a more complex or detailed form has more vertices and lines and is thus a more complex mesh).

The co-ordinates of the 3D world are based on what is known as a Cartesian co-ordinate system. René Descartes (1596–1650) was a French mathematician and philosopher. He developed the idea of a number of axes that allow objects to be described by points, lines and planes in space. On a flat plane (such as a piece of paper) there are two perpendicular axes: one running along the width of the paper (side to side) and one running along the length of the paper. Axis X in geometry normally represents width and Y represents the length. If the paper is lying on a table Y will be forwards or away from the viewer, if the 'paper' is vertical (such as a screen) Y will be the height. Therefore any point in 2D space can be represented by two numbers: the co-ordinate on the X axis and the co-ordinate on the Y axis. For 3D space we need a third axis, Z, which will define the 'depth'. In a computer, height, width and depth are relative to the point of view of the 'observation point', and it may take some time to become familiar with co-ordinate orientation. The representation of solid objects in this space is also sometimes referred to as the Euclidean system named after Euclid (c. 300 B.C.) who was a mathematician from Alexandria. Unfortunately not all 3D computer programs use the same axis conventions as Euclid. Understanding how your program names and identifies each of the three axes is extremely important to the efficient operation in digital space and you are strongly advised to spend time with your specific manual in order to be clear on this. Different programs orientate the axes in different configurations relative to the viewports, however the principles remain constant.

Once the axes are set they are each divided into a set of measurement units, like a ruler. These units may be imperial (inches, feet), metric, parsecs or just generic units, the effect is the same. In computer space it is generally not necessary to work in a reduced scale (such as 1:25), rather, one works by using units that represent the real world size. Thus any point in space is located against these three measures. The plotting of an object in space can thus be given a mathematical formula. Since there is a point in space where all three axes intersect, called the origin point, co-ordinates may be either negative or positive numbers. The origin point itself, the centre of the world, is at point zero on each of the axes, written as 0,0,0.

Most objects that you make or place in the scene will be created via a number of short-cut methods so that you don't have to enter each vertex location via the keyboard.

If there are three axes that define the three dimensions of space (X, Y, Z) one might also perceive that we can consider three planes crossing the space, each perpendicular to the other two. Each plane is therefore constructed from two of the axes: XY, YZ, XZ.

Units will be set up in a configuration or options menu. In Viz this is accessed from the Menu Bar under Customize > Units Set-up.

Understanding viewports

The computer will usually show you the 'space' from a variety of positions, known as viewports or view-points. In general your program should allow you to choose which view you wish to see, and to see multiple views at the same time. Although they have little meaning in the mathematical space of a digital 3D model, most users (and programs) will orientate the scene around a notional set of axes (see below) indicating up/down, front/back, left/right. Each of these pairings can be called a plane. Therefore it is possible to view the scene from named positions aligned with these orientations. If viewed in parallel mode (i.e., not perspective) these are called orthographic views.

These viewports can be scaled so that they can represent the entire scene (or wider) or clipped to show a small portion of the scene. They are absolutely the equivalent of plan, front and side elevation used in construction drawing – all objects are seen as if each point was extended to the viewport by a line perpendicular to it, there is no accounting for diminution over distance. For this reason it is usually a good idea to construct objects in such a way that they have one or more faces aligned to a pre-set orthographic viewport (although it should be possible to align a viewport to an object).

Many programs, Viz included, allow the user to create viewports on any plane, not just the six named planes. This is achieved by rotating or orbiting the view around the centre of the scene. Such views, if seen in parallel projection, are axonometric views, to all intents and purposes the same as orthographic.

Different programs use different axes to define the front, top, etc., planes. In Viz the top viewport (i.e., looking 'down' on the world) is designated as XY, and the front XZ, whereas, for example, in Strata Studio the front view is XY and the top is XZ. See Figure 4.1 for an illustration of this. The Viz definition is useful for theatre since the top view (or plan view) can also be thought of as looking down on a ground plan, which if generated in a drafting CAD program will also make use of the XY plane for the ground plane/plan view. Of course up, left, front, etc., are fairly meaningless in a world where there is no gravity, and where the user can re-orientate the world and their own position instantaneously – however these orientations are applicable to theatre designs.

So when an object is created (or its vertices) it is constructed with reference to a set of co-ordinates. These are often known as the world co-ordinates (such as the Viz orientation described above) and in this system 0,0,0 is the centre of the universe. However, it is not as simple as this since in addition to the world co-ordinates you may also need to reference your viewport co-ordinates, and perhaps individual object co-ordinates. The reason for this is that you will carry out certain actions relative to the viewport (which may not be parallel to a world plane) and certain actions need to be relative to an object. For example, if you move an object you will often want to move it relative to its current position as you see it, e.g., 5 cm to the

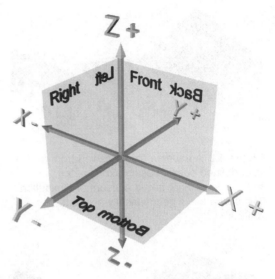

Figure 4.1 An illustration of axes, planes and viewports. The orientation is derived from Autodesk Viz; some other programs use different orientations

left of your view or, if you wish to rotate an object you will normally wish to rotate it around its own origin point, not the world origin. In general the screen co-ordinates (often used when moving an object) will always describe the plane of the screen as being the XY plane, whatever the world co-ordinates, thus Z falls away from the viewport. Additionally each object will have its own axes with its own origin point, the location and orientation of these will depend upon the method of creation.

To summarize there may be at least three sets of co-ordinates in operation:

- the world co-ordinates, set by the software to describe up/down, forward/back, left/right. These tend to be absolute, fixed references that cannot be changed;
- the co-ordinates relative to an object, that is to say an object will have a specified front, top, etc. – often related to the position that it was created in. If you rotate an object (let's say to tip it on its back) you may end up with its front aligned with the world's top. These are often called local co-ordinates;
- finally the screen itself is a flat plane (with apparent depth) and one may use co-ordinates absolute to the screen/viewport, rather than the virtual world or object. Generally the screen co-ordinates will have X running left to right, and Y top to bottom – this will be the case whatever the orientation of the scene. This is useful when moving objects in a scene, since the designer does not have to work out the orientation in the world, or with respect to the object, but rather moves it left/right, up/down as it appears in the current view.

Many programs also allow the user to create custom, or user-defined, axes, independent to those mentioned above. These can be particularly useful for viewing and manipulating objects that are not aligned to standard world co-ordinates.

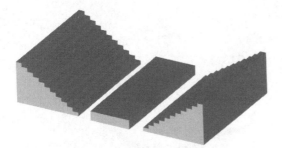

Figure 4.2 A traverse stage viewed from a user-defined position using axonometric projection, i.e., not taking account of diminution. The scene looks geometrically accurate, but artificial

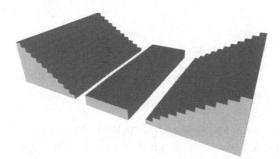

Figure 4.3 This figure shows the same traverse stage, viewed from the same position as Figure 4.2, but with a perspective view applied. This is a more natural point of view, and the effect of the perspective can be varied. In some programs this is also known as a camera view, where the effect of different lenses is applied

In addition to being able to view the scene from one of the named planes it is also possible to customize the viewing position so that the scene is viewed from a plane that is not aligned to world XYZ. In these cases one might choose whether to have the view shown with or without the effect of perspective. A user may specify a viewport that does not align to the world planes but that still uses parallel projection. This view, though showing an object in 3D form, does not try to mimic natural perspective (that is, showing how the object will look in the real world) but rather it demonstrates how the parts fit together; see Figure 4.2. These kinds of diagrams are often used to demonstrate how flat-pack furniture should be fitted together by the customer.

You may, however, wish to specify a view that recreates the effect of perspective, converging lines over distance, creating the appearance of diminution; see Figure 4.3. Usually you should be able to view the scene from any position in perspective (including from font, left, etc.). Generally the user can specify the parameters of the perspective effect, specifying the field of view and creating more or less distortion over distance. These processes are also used to create and control specified camera positions in a scene. The perspective and camera views are the only views that properly mimic the effect of a single person's point of view, showing a scene as a viewer would see it, all other views should be schematic representations to facilitate easy working. (We say 'should', since some programs do seem to include single observation points and vanishing points (i.e., perspective) in their orthographic views.)

It should be clear that the types of viewport have particular functions:

- the main orthographic views support detailed construction work, these are the views in which most scenes will be created – top, front, left, etc.;
- user-defined axonometric views allow the designer to re-orientate a viewport to align it with a part of their scene, but the image is still unaffected by an illusion of perspective. This is useful for detailed work on objects that do not line up with a main plane;
- perspective and camera views show the scene as it might appear to a single viewer in the real world. These views are useful for showing your work to others at a design meeting but can be difficult to work in.

Practical summary

The user will therefore have control over the number of views shown and the alignment of each of these views. In Viz this can be achieved in a number of ways (not all are listed here):

- to set up a complete schema of viewports, either select from the menu Customize > Viewport Configuration > Layout, or opposite click (frequently a short-cut to commands) over the viewport title in its top left corner and select Configure > Layout;
- to change one viewport to a different view, either opposite click over the viewport title in its top left corner and select Views to choose a new view, *or* use a keyboard shortcut such as F (front), T (top), P (perspective).

Most viewport navigation commands in Viz are located at the bottom right to the full program window where there are eight buttons that control zoom and alignment functions:

- to enlarge one viewport so it fills the screen use the Min/Max toggle button, by default the bottom right button of the viewport navigation buttons;
- to re-orientate a viewport (becoming a User view) use the Arc Rotate function from the viewport navigation controls.

The program will display the co-ordinate location of the cursor relative to the world axis, but when an object is selected for moving or rotating the computer will normally display the position relative to the object's axis (though it is possible to change this).

Placing the origin

We suggest that for any major project the world origin of 0,0,0 co-ordinates is taken to be the intersection of the centre-line (Y axis) with the setting line (X axis) at stage floor level (i.e., at stage floor level Z=0). For theatre in the round, place the centre of the circular stage at the centre of the 0,0,0, co-ordinates. This would normally be known as the datum point, and should be set (whether on digital or paper plan) for all productions since it is from this point that key measurements will be taken; it therefore makes sense to ensure that the same datum point, and thus the same centre line and setting line (sometimes known as the datum line) are used by all involved. All theatres vary so there is no absolute rule about locating these lines, though in a proscenium arch theatre the setting line, also known as the plaster line, is the axis that connects the upstage corners of the two proscenium arch uprights, or sometimes it is the upstage line of the safety curtain. The centre line bisects the arch opening.

An advantage with the computer is that these lines can be relocated (or more frequently the whole design moved) if the designer finds that they are in error, or if the production is touring to different venues. Ultimately a fixed reference point will be needed for any project since many measurements and co-ordinates will be taken from it when the design is constructed. In theory this reference point could be anywhere on the design, provided it is clearly identified on all plans and made known to all involved (stage managers, production managers etc.), but in practice it is most sensible to place the 0,0,0 origin in the computer at the intersection of the centre line and setting line at stage floor level.

Making models

The details of model making will follow in a later chapter, but it is important to outline just what a computer model is before proceeding much further. A model is made of objects, or groups of objects, which are generally represented in the computer as a mesh or wire frame, and are defined by identifying points in space and lines connecting these points. The computer is then told (or often 'works out') where the surfaces are (as opposed to holes) and material is applied to it. Most of the time these meshes are made using shortcut tools and rarely will the designer have to locate each point in space for each object.

An object (generally the word used for a 3D form) can be made either by defining 2D shapes that make it up (its sections and outlines) or by going straight into three dimensions and utilizing pre-made 3D objects as building blocks that are modified to create the required shape. Put simply, a pillar could be constructed from a number of 2D drawings that illustrate sectional views (either horizontal or vertical) or it could be constructed by utilizing a number of pre-made blocks, cylinders and other 3D forms, and modifying and assembling them to fit the required shape. The assembly method is more given to exploratory modelling, quickly experimenting with forms in space, but the schematic method may be more suited to design requiring precision.

In a drawing we can make a simple point on a paper plane that is a visible entity. Once we make a second point and connect the two with a line we certainly have a graphic presence. This is not how a computer model works, since points and lines do not themselves define form and generally cannot be used in a final rendered scene; it is only when lines enclose space that a form is identified. Thus lines are used as a method of defining and creating form.

An object's mesh can be as simple or as complex as the object requires. At the most simple three points in space, vertices, connected by three straight lines make a triangular surface (often called a face), and these faces are the basic elements of many objects in a digital model. This face is not itself 3D, but when joined with others it may become so. Once three or more vertices are connected we therefore develop a face and edges to those faces. A rectangular surface is made from four vertices, although it may also sometimes be considered to be two triangular faces. A cube is therefore eight vertices arranged in 3D space with 12 apparent edges and four square faces. The more complex the object the more points and edges it will have, which will usually be broken down into an arrangement of four- or three-sided polygons. Once constructed, of course, individual vertices, edges and faces can be manipulated, moved, rotated, deleted and so on. Generally such modifications are dealt with on a whole-object basis, thus moving, scaling, rotating or deforming the whole.

This process gives rise to the name of the most common form of modelling, polygonal modelling. This process constructs every object from vertices joined by edges to make faces, the whole is called a mesh. Thus, even a sphere is actually made up of a large number of straight edges and flat faces. Curves and organic shapes are not always easy to achieve and the objects may have a high number of vertices to look convincing, and this can make a scene hard to work on. Nonetheless, if you are prepared to use a very high number of these faces for curved objects most artefacts can be made this way. It is a logical and conceptually easy way to work, if sometimes frustratingly fiddly. Since a lot of set design involves architectural, manufactured and rectilinear objects (walls, platforms, chairs), polygonal modelling is quite suitable and will be the main process described in this book. It is also the form of modelling tool that is generally present in cheaper modelling programs.

Spline-based modellers work in a different way to polygonal modellers, though frequently both approaches are available in the same

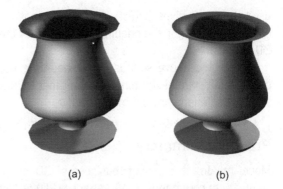

(a)   (b)

Figure 4.4 A vase made from the same outline but constructed as a polygon object (a) and a NURBS object (b). Note how the edges of (a) are visible as short straight sections, whereas the edges of (b) are far more smoothly curved

program, and it may be possible to convert an object made as a polygonal model to a spline equivalent. These objects are formed by curved lines and faces instead of a number of short lines connecting vertices. Unlike polygon modelling these lines are not modified directly but have a control line or control vertices that affect them. These control lines and vertices are 'invisible' – they are never rendered but they act on the curve of the line and, thus, because shapes are made from lines, the curve of the shape. The word spline derives from the practice of curving wooden staves by applying tension at each end, this is a useful image for visualizing how moving control points modifies the curve of a line. There are a number of methods (or calculations) for producing splines: NURBS (Non-uniform Rational B-Splines), B-Splines, Bezier. It should be clear that spline-based modelling (normally NURBS) is most suited to the creation of organic forms and any curved surface that will be seen in close-up and needs to maintain a smooth curved profile.

Both of these approaches model the surface of an object; a different approach entirely, called solid modelling, considers objects to have weight and volume, and the modeller creates form by manipulating the whole volume. This process is generally the domain of architects and engineers and is not covered in this book.

The theatre designer will need to take rather different considerations into account than other digital model makers. The designer is not making a finished, polished image, their final models are simply indicative of the built object, thus it is not always necessary to ensure that each curve is perfectly smooth in close-up for example. Neither is the designer usually making a complex scene for real-time interaction (though there are exceptions) and thus they will not have to be too worried about how complex the geometry is. A video games designer will have to ensure that their scene can be re-drawn almost instantaneously as the scene and point of view change; this requires the scene geometry to be quite simple. The theatre designer, however, is not so dependent upon these fast re-draw speeds and thus need not overly worry about what is known as the polygon count. Finally, of course, we must realize that a theatre designer can always make a conventional card model if this will serve the project better. This book introduces approaches in roughly the proportion that we have used them ourselves (which is of course not to say it's the ideal proportion), that is to say it emphasizes polygonal modelling, and generally creates objects from 3D building blocks rather than 2D shapes.

If all of the above sounds rather daunting then take heart from the fact that most software provides substantial shortcuts for a number of these processes, and generally one will find that the simplest solutions are the most effective.

Practical summary

Model making is the main business of 3D modelling programs, so it is difficult to give a brief summary of commands. In Viz, shapes (2D) and objects (3D) are generally created from the Create Panel, a function of the Command panel, but certain basic primitive shapes can be selected from preset icons located by selecting the Objects tab from the Tab panel. Using icons to create basic objects and lines is a common practice in modelling programs.

Objects may be created using a mouse (or stylus), frequently employing the 'click and drag' process. More complex objects may need several mouse actions. For purposes of precision you should be able to create an object or shape by specifying its location and dimensions via keyboard entry.

In Viz modifications are undertaken by:

- selecting the object and changing its parameters in the Modify panel;
- using a select and transform tool such as Move, Rotate, Scale;
- selecting an object or shape and then selecting an icon for a modification under the Modifiers tab.

Drawing aids: grids, snaps and selections

A number of tools are provided to aid model making (and drawing), particularly to aid precision. Grids are non-rendered objects that appear in a viewport to act like graph paper. The user may define how far apart grid lines are (using specific units), thus aiding accurate drawing. The grid spacing will depend upon the units that you're using: a model being made of an outdoor production of a grand opera is unlikely to benefit much from a grid spacing set at 5 mm.

The other major function of the grid is that it serves as the construction surface (or plane). If you are creating an object in a viewport you are only active in two axes, thus the computer sets the third and this is always set as the active grid – it acts as a 'table-top' for the object that you're creating. Thus if you are making a box in an active top viewport you can specify all the dimensions, but in practice you can only locate it relative to world X and Y (where in the screen is it). Thus the computer places its base on a preset construction plane (grid), by default Z0. When building this box a positive Z value will build the box above the construction plane, a negative Z value will build it below. Of course any object may be moved after it is built, but it is clearly more efficient to build an object in the right location first, particularly if there are multiple objects. A designer should be able to specify their own grids thus setting their own construction surfaces. These may not only be at different locations, aligned to the default grid (e.g., an XY plane at Z:2200 mm to aid the construction of an upper level), but they may also be set at angles to the world plans, thereby construction objects that are not automatically aligned to the world axes.

The default or home grid can have its parameters set in Customize > Grid and Snap Settings and then clicking the home grid tab.

In Viz a grid is created like any other object from the Create panel, selecting the helpers icon. During the creation its parameters may be set. Once created it can be activated or deactivated (thereby reverting to the home grid) via Views > Grids > Activate Grid Object. Once activated it serves as the construction plane for any objects created. Viewports can be aligned to the custom grid rather than the world axes. Opposite click over the viewport label (top left of viewport) and select Views > Grid and then the chosen view.

Snap settings are a valuable aid to accuracy. Once activated they 'snap' the cursor to the nearest specified point; this may be a grid point, the centre-point of a line and so on. They operate when the cursor comes within a boundary distance of a defined target. Although useful they should be used with discretion since leaving this function on can result in a frustrating and jerky process. The snap settings are set in Customize > Grid and Snap Settings and then clicking the Snaps tab. Once set, Snap is switched on or off from the toggle button at the bottom of the screen.

Once an object exists in a scene it will frequently need to be selected for further modification. The simplest way to achieve this is normally to place the cursor over one of the wire frame lines in the active viewport and click to select (a fly-out should appear with the name of the object). In a busy scene, however, it may be easier to filter your selection so that the cursor only picks up objects (geometry), lines, lights and so on. In Viz this selection filter is activated from the Toolbar in Viz. It is also possible to select the object by name from a drop-down list. You are not restricted to having only one object selected at a time; multiple selections are possible. These may either be chosen from the named list, or frequently selected by clicking and dragging in an active viewport. Depending upon the selection setting either all objects that are entirely within the window are selected, or any object where part of it falls within the window.

Materials

Once the skin of the object is specified using polygons or splines the designer will normally assign a material (sometimes called texture) to it. Most modelling programs will have a materials editor that will facilitate the creation and modification of these surfaces. In some cases a model needs to be exported to a texturing program, particularly if sophisticated texturing is not available in the modelling program. This is more commonly the case with CAD packages than with custom made 3D modelling programs. The material or texture is the surface applied to an object, which will appear when it is rendered (that is to say when the computer is instructed to generate an image of the scene), giving the model its finished look. By default materials are flat colours but they may have patterns, highlights or the appearance of bumps, transparency, reflections and even animations assigned to them. The manipulation of the colour that materials take on in shadow and highlight, coupled with the size and intensity of that highlight, will determine if a material and thus the object looks shiny, dull, metallic or non-metallic.

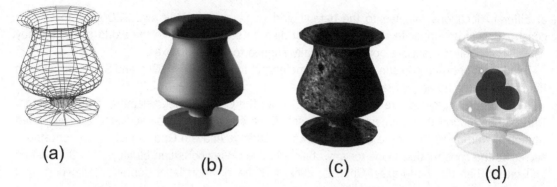

Figure 4.5 A vase with different types of material. (a) No material applied, shown as a wireframe, (b) a default material with a flat colour and slight highlight, (c) a material with an image applied to give a 'texture', (d) a transparent material applied with a reflection assigned, looking like glass and revealing three spheres inside

For anything more than a monochrome surface colour the designer will apply a map (or image) to the surface. These maps may be images such as those captured by a scanner and edited in a paint program, they may be images created from scratch in a paint program or often a hybrid of the two. These are known generally as bitmaps. Alternatively the map may be a pattern created by the computer (after parameters have been specified), this is known as a procedural map. However they are created, maps may be assigned to an object to represent surface pattern, reflection or, even, using the greyscale of a map, the bumpiness of an object's surface, or areas of opacity and transparency. Maps may be scaled and tiled over an object to generate a repeated pattern, applied as a single map, realigned in direction and even distorted in proportion. Like working out how to wallpaper a room the designer will instruct the computer how best to apply the map to an object. This is variously known as setting mapping co-ordinates, UVW mapping or texture mapping.

Lighting

Three-dimensional modelling programs generally allow the user to specify the location, type, intensity and colour of the lights illuminating the scene. Programs at the lower end of the market may have more limited facilities and when purchasing the software a theatre designer should make sure that the lighting options are sufficiently sophisticated. Lights are created as objects in the scene that do not appear when rendered (the effect of the light does of course appear).

Most modelling programs offer lighting options and where they do not users will import their models into a rendering program to complete the scene. As with all of the above it is advisable for the theatre designer to use one program for the whole project. There are now a number of programs available that are created specifically with performance lighting design in mind, but these really meet the needs of a more technical approach to lighting design. A number of modelling programs offer options that are quite adequate for exploring the contribution of lighting to the design, and this facility is one of the major advantages of the digital model over the physical. What is important is that in the digital model, adding lights to the scene is as easy as adding objects and within the computer environment form and texture are really a function of light. The set designer working in the digital environment must therefore engage with the effect of light.

Generally three types of light are offered: an omni-light or point source, which is equivalent to a bare bulb with light radiating in all directions from it; a spotlight, which has a defined directional beam; and a parallel or direct light source which replicates the effect of the sun. There will also be an ambient light setting that controls the overall, non-directional, general background light. While a designer might use an omni-light as a kind of working light early in the process it is the spotlight that will replicate theatre lights most closely. To be really useful a spotlight should have the properties of variable colour, variable intensity, a variable beam angle and an edge quality of hard and soft. Advanced features that are useful are attenuation and decay of intensity over distance and the ability to project bitmaps and even animations. The projection feature is extremely useful in replicating gobos and slides, allowing for the prediction of, and compensation for, key-stoning. The lighting facilities should allow for the calculation of shadows but most programs will defy nature and allow the designer to specify which objects in a scene will cast shadows and which will not. It is also possible to use a spotlight to create negative light, projecting a shadow into an otherwise lit area.

A number of programs contain libraries of the optical details of actual light sources (such as Lightscape). These are architectural facilities allowing for the replication of the properties of specified sources. Theatre-specific programs now do the same for theatre luminaires. While apparently a valuable facility it is not essential since at this stage the designer is creating the intended look of the scene, rather than identifying specific tools to do the job in reality. We have found that once a scene is created using generic lighting there follows useful dialogue between designer and lighting designer about how that look will be achieved on stage. One must also remember that the scene shown on the monitor will rarely be a facsimile of the actual theatre conditions, however accurate the data.

Rendering

In most programs the designer builds the model while looking at it in wire frame or simple flat surfaces; this construction version of the model will then be rendered to see the more detailed effect of light, surface texture, etc. Generally this rendered image cannot be manipulated in real time, so the designer views the result and then returns to the model to make alterations. There are two simple reasons for this. Firstly it is far easier to work on the details of a design while looking at its component meshes, and secondly most software does not have the capability to allow the user to modify a fully imaged scene in real time, showing all the effects of materials, lights, reflections, etc. This latter situation is changing but even if the software allows for real-time interaction with the fully lit and textured scene it may not always be desirable. Whatever else, there are moments when a final 'image' needs to be taken on the design; at these moments the 3D modelling file is rendered as a 'flat' image file (often a jpeg), effectively fixing the scene as a photograph. This image may then only be altered as one would a flat image in a paint program.

The rendering component, often called the rendering engine, is therefore the means by which the computer turns a scene made of meshes and other symbols into a realistic-looking image or animation, viewed from a specified position. The computational side of rendering calculates the effect of light on surfaces and produces a pixel image that represents the interaction of light, pigment and form. At best it will also simulate the different textures of surface materials, showing their apparent shininess, or transparency. It will also calculate and represent shadows. The rendering on a computer is equivalent to trompe l'oeil in painting. It paints an image to the screen based on a series of rules known as algorithms, which describe the behaviour of light in the real world. Rendering can take a long time; a scene with multiple light sources, shadows and reflections, perhaps even volumetric lighting can take many minutes to render to a high resolution and a short animation may take days. Rendering may be sped-up by either rendering a lower quality or smaller image with less detail, by reducing the complexity of the scene, by upgrading the computer (!) or by rendering across multiple machines on a network (not really an option available to an individual designer).

The simplest and cheapest programs will render using simple algorithms, perhaps only being able to show objects as flat colours with lighter and darker shades of the same colour to offer cues to the 3D nature of the form. More complex algorithms may add specular highlights, which indicate how shiny an object is. For the purposes of this introduction there are three types of rendering system that one might come across in desktop software. Radiosity is generally considered to be the system that produces the most realistic results, since not only does it calculate the effect of lights on objects but also considers indirect lighting reflected off each object. In the real world, of course, every object, even soft black drapes, reflect some light and light continues its path to illuminate other objects. The Radiosity algorithm calculates the effect of this bounced light and as such, a scene generally appears subtle, with softer shadows and complex colour ranges. Given the fact that these rendering systems will also calculate reflections, transparency, defraction, etc., they can take an extremely long time to render even a still image and animations frequently take far too long in these systems to be viable. Nonetheless, a Radiosity renderer coupled with photometric lighting data in the scene will produce very accurate images. (This of course still depends on the ability of the designer to arrange the scene appropriately, and the quality of the monitor or printer.)

Raytracing is perhaps the next best option, for while it does not calculate the effect of bounced light it nonetheless computes the passage of light back from every pixel, allowing for very accurate depiction of reflection, refraction and transparency.

Scanline rendering is a less complex process than the two above but a good system can come very close to the appearance of raytracing, without the excessive rendering time, however accuracy of calculation is sacrificed. Using algorithms that calculate horizontal lines across the image, rather than rays of light, these systems tend to be less effective at representing transparency, reflections, shadows, atmospheric effects and refraction. A good scanline rendering engine may be quite sufficient for indicative theatre design use where the emphasis is not on a photoquality final image. The algorithms used in scanline rendering are often named after their inventors, with Phong algorithms, named after Phong Biu-Tuong, being the most commonly used, and allowing for smooth surfaces, specular highlights and transparency. Many versions are able to represent shadows, transparency and reflection. Gouraud rendering is based on a simpler algorithm and is useful for images that require real-time interaction but it lacks many realistic details.

Most programs will allow the user to specify which rendering algorithms are to be used, as well as the resolution of the final rendered image, thus giving the designer control of the speed and quality of the image. Similarly, most programs will allow the user to specify whether shadows, reflections and atmospheric effects are to be rendered. Until recently the low end programs have tended to be restricted to scanline rendering, often using simple algorithms, however some freeware applications now support raytracing and it is likely that rendering of high quality will be available in most packages you consider. Of course it is quite possible to create a model in one program and export it to a rendering program for texturing, lighting and final rendering.

The art of 3D programs uses geometry and co-ordinates to produce the images you see on the screen. The pixels (derived from the words 'picture elements') produce the screen images in the same way that a television screen presents shapes and faces. For the theatre designer working in this environment it is sometimes disorientating to navigate your way around the space, world or view presented on screen. The key idea for working in this fictive world is to be patient and to learn the operating program that you are working from. This will take time. As we have implied, 3D space can be given a number of names depending on the program, although scene, universe, world and view are the most common. Much of the learning of new software involves learning the vocabulary for modelling, lighting and handling surfaces. Once you have learnt one program you will find a similarity to the terminology and to the devices used within the programs. We will talk about modelling in the generic sense. You should be able to follow the principles within any 3D computer program noting the particular features of how your own program operates.

5

The basics of modelling

In the real world of a design studio a model may be made from one, or several, of the following approaches:

- card, balsa or other medium is marked out (with a template or plan perhaps), cut to shape and then assembled with other pieces to make a 3D form;
- card or balsa is cut roughly to shape (a cut-out silhouette) but has the illusion of a 3D form pasted or drawn onto it, thus removing the need for detailed modelling. Even quite fundamental objects can be made this way;
- found objects (or parts of previous models) are taken or bought, and adapted for the specific context;
- collection of found objects may be assembled into a new object;
- a plastic material such as clay is pressed into solid form.

The computer also provides a number of methods, some of which have an equivalent in the process above:

- 2D shapes may be created that describe elements of a 3D shape (a plan or section) and are then turned into that 3D form. The equivalent in the conventional process is perhaps the making of a paper template or plan before cutting the card to shape. This forces a certain precision and pre-planning, but it is a good way of making complex or detailed forms;
- a 3D object may be made by assembling primitive 3D forms, adapting and modifying them so that when assembled they look like the desired object. In the conventional process of modelling this would be making a table out of matchsticks and a balsa top. This can be a simple way of experimenting with form, and a multitude of objects can be made this way;
- a surface can be made that has an image applied to it, perhaps even making an outline or silhouette, effectively creating a 'cut-out'. This is a wonderfully quick and playful method of experimenting with scenography, but is very much an initial experiment since it does not offer the spatial detail necessary for most contemporary designs. Colin Beardon's Visual Assistant software works on the principle and is an extremely useful tool for quick conceptualization.

Very often all three processes will be used, often on the same object. In this chapter, however, we will concentrate on what is probably the simplest to grasp, and certainly the process that will see the most immediate results – that is using primitive (simple) 3D forms with which to create models. For this section we are only going to consider polygonal models. This process is limiting, but it is an easy way to get started and thus become familiar with the program and its possibilities.

Using primitives

This is undoubtedly the most simple approach to modelling, and can produce some credible results, particularly where the aim is the initial exploration of form, space, balance. Even when your intention is for a more detailed or complex scene this basic approach may well provide a foundation for the model. Certainly, if you are unsure about finished detail, this method of creating simple suggestions of forms will allow for a quick rendition of a suggestion of the space and arrangements.

Your program will offer you a number of pre-made mesh objects, generally representing essential geometric forms: cube (box), cylinder, sphere, cone, pyramid, torus, tube; these are represented in Figure 5.1. It may also provide a number of advanced or extended objects, frequently modifications of the previous list. In Viz the Extended Primitives list also includes a capsule, a chamfered cylinder, a spindle, a prism and oil tank, and a hedra. These are slightly more complex shapes, many involving rounded corners, but nonetheless are simple adaptations of basic geometry.

Generally these forms will be created by the simplest of commands, probably clicking on the primitive of choice (either represented as an icon, or from a menu) and then clicking and dragging in a viewport (see viewports above). In Viz an object is either created from the Create panel on the Command panel, selecting Geometry (icon), or from the Objects tab (Viz 4) or Create Surfaces tab (Viz 3) on the tab panel at the top of the screen, selecting the icon of your chosen form. (It may also, in Viz 4, be created by opposite clicking in a viewport and selecting the modelling menu, but this is a shortcut, and thus should be used only when familiar with the full method.) During the creation process or immediately after the software will allow you to specify the parameters of your object.

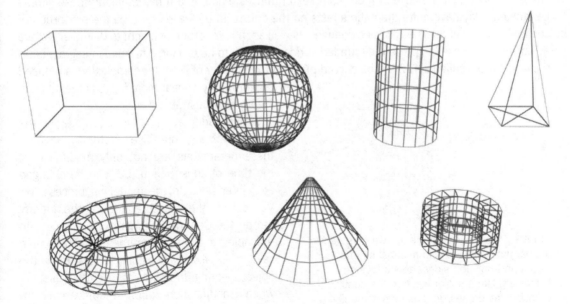

Figure 5.1 Primitive meshes. Top left to right: box, sphere, cylinder, pyramid. Bottom left to right: torus, cone, tube

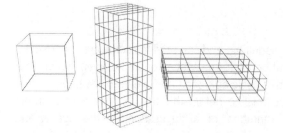

Figure 5.2 The box on the left was created with equal dimensions in each axis (X,Y,Z) and minimal complexity; the central box (rotated here for ease of viewing) was constructed with an increased height (Z) and divided into segments along its height (Z) and depth (Y before it was rotated). The box on the right clearly has less height but is deeper and wider: this has been divided once on its height and three times along its width

These parameters will naturally differ slightly depending upon the nature of the mesh, but will effectively allow you control over its size, proportion and complexity. In the case of a cube one may specify the size, in units, of each of the three dimensions, and how many segments the cube is made from, i.e., how complex the mesh is (in Viz this is referred to as the segment parameters, in Strata Studio it is the object complexity). These parameters may be specified either by keyboard entry or click and drag, often both. In Viz you may create using click and drag for dimension properties, but segment properties need to be entered through commands in the creation dialog box.

Note that in Viz, as well as many other programs, there are many alternative methods for carrying out commands; you are advised to consult your reference manual for these.

The control over the complexity of an object is very important for any future modification that you may carry out since the more segments there are the more flexible the object will be to change later. Imagine a box made out of a flexible mesh such as chicken wire with many subsections, and one made out of twelve rods, one for each edge. The chicken wire box will be able to be pulled about and transformed in a variety of ways, whereas the box made of rods on the edges will have very limited flexibility. In the case of more complex primitives, such as a tube, changing these simple parameters may have quite dramatic effects on the object. In the case of a tube the proportion of central hole to wall thickness can be changed as well as the proportion of height to diameter. Where an object is supposed to present a rounded surface it needs to have a large number of segments (in these instances called sides) on the curved plane. If the number of sides (or complexity) is reduced the form may appear more jagged or rectilinear. Figure 5.3 illustrates this.

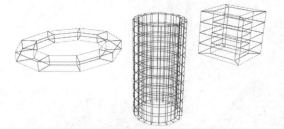

Fig 5.3 The cylinder on the left was created to appear flat and wide with minimal segments of height and only ten sides, hence looking something like a nut or washer; the central cylinder was created to look something like a pipe and the one on the right, having its sides reduced to four, is more like a hollow box

Similar adaptations may be made in the creation of any primitive. Naturally each of these parameters are not only modifiable at the time of construction, but can be changed at a later point in the modelling process. (In Viz 'select' the object and click the Modify tab on the Command panel to have access to the object's creation parameters.) This being said it is always sensible to construct the object bearing in mind its eventual use, as when modification upon modification are made to objects results may become unpredictable.

Therefore when creating primitive objects you should consider how likely you are to need to modify them (twist, taper, bend – see below) and how rounded they may need to look – both these factors will influence the complexity. Since this may tempt you to make all objects complex (i.e., with more segments) you should bear in mind that the more complex objects there are in the scene the bigger the file will be, the slower it will be to load and re-draw.

Many of the objects needed in a set design can be made from assembling primitives together. Indeed a flat or a rostrum can clearly be represented by simply providing a box primitive of the right dimensions. At its most basic this may involve creating one or two primitive objects and moving them into an appropriate relationship with each other.

The problems with primitives, certainly the basic forms, is that if used alone and in a fairly unmodified form they do look rather rectilinear and artificial; scenes created this way tend to look like computer-generated scenes, and this aesthetic envelope will undoubtedly have an effect on the way initial model explorations are viewed. This observation is of course equally true for white card exploratory models and the designer, in whichever medium, must be aware of the potentially powerful effect of the early methods that they use. An early computer-based investigation of space for a production that depends upon more organic forms may lead to some rather off-putting artificial imagery; the director/designer rapport may be compromised at an early stage.

The name and colour of primitives

It is very important to understand the complexities and conventions of naming objects. A complex scene may contain scores or hundreds of mesh objects, each with a multitude of mesh lines on show; selecting and modifying these objects may be extremely difficult. Thus each object, when created, may be given a name and a colour. The name is self-explanatory: by default this is often the geometric form and the number of its iteration, therefore 'box03' will be the third box created in that scene. This name will become confusing so a name should be assigned that clearly identifies the object, and while 'chair' might seem like a good idea for a chair, it becomes less appealing when there are perhaps eight of them. Ideally identify each piece individually, perhaps by stage location or purpose. You are also likely to be offered the opportunity to set the colour of the mesh, i.e., to specify how the object appears in the construction windows. In Viz this is set in a dialog box next to the name panel. This helps identify geometry in a complex scene, and will allow you to identify all objects created for a similar purpose (perhaps used in the same scene) with the same colour – the rationale will of course depend upon the nature of the project. A further use of this colour setting (in most programs) is that when an object is rendered (i.e., the computer generates a solid, probably lit, image of the scene) the computer will show it in this original construction colour unless a more complex material has been applied. Thus a designer can use this to quickly assign a colour to an object without having to create a material – particularly useful in a book such as this since materials do not come until a later chapter!

The location of the created object

In general the creation method will fix the object in one plane, allowing you to locate it in the other two. Commonly a user will create an object in the top or plan view (perhaps replicating the way one tends to work on a sketched ground plan). In this case the computer will generally place the object on what it takes to be the ground level, i.e., the XY plane where Z is 0. This is often called the construction or ground plane. Since it has been provided by the computer it is sensible to make best use of it and consider it to be the stage level (for more about this see the section on organizing your project, and an explanation of grids and axes in the previous chapter). Some objects (for example, a sphere in Viz) are created by default with their centre on the XY plane, thus the lower half of the object sits below ground level. This is quite easily rectified by moving the object after construction. Most other objects are created with their 'base' on the construction plane and if their height (Z dimension) is given a positive value they will extend upwards. (A negative value would also have them below the stage.) This is an effect of each object being created with a pivot, an important concept to understand.

The pivot point

When an object is created, by whatever method, it is assigned a 'centre' or focus, sometimes called the origin point, transform centre or pivot point; this is the point of origin of the three axes of the object, and thus this is the point on the object around which transformations of all kinds take place. At the moment of creation it is likely to be set on the construction plane for the viewport you are using (i.e., the ground plane or XY if you are creating from the top viewport). Thus a sphere has its geometric centre as its pivot point but a tube may have a capped end as its pivot point; this will be the end that is located on the construction plane as you create the object. Thus the creation method may define the initial location of the transform centre.

This centre becomes the locus of most transformations. If you rotate the object it will do so around its pivot point (even if this point is outside of the object), if you scale it, it will scale, on one or more axes, towards or away from this point. Similarly, but using different terms, if you increase or decrease the dimension of an object in one or more axes the zero point will be at the pivot. It can be possible to set multiple pivots for an object. Your program will allow you to move the pivot point of the object without moving the mesh itself, thus, for example, an object can be made to rotate around its physical centre, rotate from one end, or rotate around a point outside of its geometry. In Viz this is achieved by selecting Hierarchies in the Command panel, then Affect Pivot Only. In Strata Studio this is achieved by holding down the control key while moving the origin point to its new location.

Selection

Once constructed you are more than likely going to have to select an object later in the project in order to transform or deform it in some way. Selection may usually be carried out by choosing a selection icon (an arrow) or other icon that automatically selects an object (such as the move icon, rotate icon or scale icon) and clicking on the object. If you are working in a wire frame (or mesh) view you may have to ensure that you click on the line, not the space between. Holding down the Ctrl key (Viz) or Shift key (Strata) while selecting will allow you to choose multiple objects; once selected they can be operated on as one, e.g., moved together or all scaled identically. The program may also allow you to select from a list of objects in a drop-down menu, perhaps even filtering the list by type (camera, light, geometry). Finally, objects may be selected using a click and drag region selection tool: where the cursor is dragged over an area on the screen, all objects falling wholly or partially (depending upon setting) within the area are selected. In Viz this is a button on the main toolbar with a dotted rectangle icon. You should be able to change the shape of this selection device from rectangular to circular or even freeform. This process is extremely useful in complex scenes where cursor-based selection would be difficult. It is vital that your scene is well organized to allow for ease of selection, ensuring objects are clearly named and that appropriate mesh colours are chosen. See 'organizing the design' in Chapter 13 for more information.

Transforms

Once they are created there are a wide variety of modifications that you can apply to a primitive object (or indeed to many forms of object once created). Some of these may be applied by keyboard entry through a Modify dialog box on the Control panel (Viz) or other Object Properties panel; other modifications or transformation may be applied by clicking over a command icon and operating on the object mesh in the viewport.

Moving objects

Moving an object is the most simple of the transform possibilities and, quite obviously, involves moving the object around the world co-ordinates. This modification is generally carried out by clicking a move icon (crossed arrows) and then clicking and dragging the object. The only point worth noting here is that successful moving depends upon having good control over your viewports. To be precise in the location of the object one should inspect its location from viewports reflecting the three key planes: top, front and side (left or right depending upon the scene). While it may be sufficient to examine the location of the object from just one or two of these, or perhaps only from the perspective or isometric viewport, this can lead to errors of location that may be harder to rectify when the scene becomes more complex. This is particularly important when assembling one large object out of a number of sub-objects. Don't forget that you can zoom in to your viewport almost indefinitely, thereby ensuring millimetre accuracy.

Most software will give you the opportunity to constrain the axis through which an object moves, that is to say that if you want the object to move only stage left, but not up- or downstage, not off the ground) then you can restrict the movement to the X axis (the X axis of world co-ordinates, assuming you are operating in the top viewport, as if in a plan – this will also depend upon the axis orientation of the software). In Viz this is achieved by selecting the move function and selecting the object to move (in a viewport that illustrates the plan of movement) and then clicking over one of the two move arrows on the object pivot. This will constrain the object to move only in that direction. In Strata Studio the same is achieved by clicking over one of the object handles, although in this case the object can also be moved in the plan perpendicular to the viewport (e.g., it can be moved up and down even in the top viewport). To move without constraints one normally clicks anywhere on the object and drags it to the new location. Remember, if working in a wire frame view that it may be necessary to actually click on one of the lines that make up the object rather than simply inside its geometry.

Scale/dimensions

Although, like location, this is set at the time of construction, it may be modified at a later date. Indeed for the set designer this is one of the most useful functions as the relative size and proportion of scenic elements may be tested and quickly changed. Scaling and dimensioning are different functions, but may appear to have a similar result.

A very sensible way to change the size of an object is to re-enter its dimensions through the same interface or mechanism as you entered them when you created it. In Viz this process is achieved by selecting the object and then clicking on the Modify tab in the Command panel (Object Parameter in Strata); one may then access and change the original dimension parameters (and any other creation parameter). The size of the object may therefore be changed.

Scaling may be a more confusing process. If a scale modifier is applied (often by selecting an icon and clicking and dragging on the mesh) the object may be increased or decreased in size, often measured by a percentage of the original, along any or all or some of its axes; as with moving an object, axis constraints can be applied. In more complex operations scaling may also allow for squashing, i.e., maintaining the same internal volume, thus scaling down one dimension and scaling up the others. However, be warned, scaling may not change the original object dimensions (as displayed in the Object Properties dialog box) since it has been applied as a modifier on top of the original object rather than actually changing the initial specifications. Thus an object scaled up (say 133%) along its height may apparently become 2000 mm high, but the original object parameters will still indicate that it is 1500 mm. Thus care is needed not to confuse the issue, since you may eventually use these details to aid in the construction process. Furthermore, applying a non-uniform scale (i.e., scaling only in one axis) may have an unusual effect on any other transforms (such as bend) that have been previously applied. Remember that scaling increases or decreases the dimensions towards or away from the pivot. To scale an object accurately within a scene this may mean careful adjustment of the pivot location.

Ideally therefore change the size of an object by changing the dimension of the original. Scale might be most usefully applied when merging a complex mesh or group of meshes in from a library (having been created for a different project) and needing to change their size or proportion for your scene. For example, a figure merged from a scene created using one set of units (say 1 unit = 1 inch) to a scene created using 1 unit = 1 cm will need scaling up approximately 250 per cent.

Rotation

The last of the simple transforms is the rotation of an object around an axis. By now you should be familiar with the function and location of the pivot point as the locus of the axes and it is very important for this transform. If the pivot is at an extreme edge of an object (say the bottom) the object will rotate as if toppling over; if the pivot is in the centre it will appear to spin around its centre, or at the top it will appear to swing. The pivot may be set outside the object, in which case it will seem to orbit. Rotation will normally be constrained to one axis; imagine that the active axis, the one around which the object will rotate, is a pin holding the object to a surface, you are only able, therefore, to rotate the object clockwise or anti-clockwise around the pin, thus around one axis.

Naturally the rotate tool is very important: all stage designers are aware of the strength of the diagonal lines over the stage space, and the appropriate angling of furniture and setting for sightlines, movement and dynamics. However, you are advised to create your objects as fully as possible in a perpendicular and parallel relationship to the three main planes before rotation, for once rotated it becomes increasingly difficult to carry out adjustments to objects.

Clone

More a creation method than a transformation this is an extremely useful and time-saving function. At any stage of the process of making/transforming an object you can clone it. (We are all used to this 'copy' function in word processing, the idea is the same here.) In general a clone can be activated when undertaking any of the transforms described above. In Viz one simply holds down the Shift key while effecting the transform, which will create a duplicate as it operates, leaving the original intact. The simplest version of this is holding down a Shift key while you move an object. Once you release the cursor you will find that you have created and moved a copy. Technically you can create three kinds of clones in Viz, a copy, an instance and a reference. A copy is the most straightforward, and will be the term implied throughout this book: it is a unique duplicate of the original which, when created, operates as a stand-alone independent object. If you make a change to any instance all instances derived from the original (and the original) are affected by the change. A reference is somewhere between the two; the cloned object may be modified independently, but if the original is changed all references are so affected. For the most part when we clone an object we intend to copy it. Strata uses a copy command that is more like a word processor: when an object is selected one may choose the edit > copy function, thereafter pasting back into the scene.

There are some sophisticated variations on this theme including the Array function, which creates copies or instances on specified steps along a specified pattern or path (linear, circular, etc), and the Mirror function, which reverses the selected object. We will undertake an array later on.

Naturally this ability to copy objects exactly is a great advantage over conventional model making where, unless you have the facility to make moulds, each piece, however frequently repeated, must be made by hand. The copy function here can therefore allow more time to be spent detailing elements, and of course the instance function can allow for very rapid editing of a collection of copies, again not possible in conventional model making. The downside of course is that it may be tempting to make too many objects by this production-line method, perhaps losing the organic originality of elements.

The other creative advantage of this clone tool is that it encourages escalation and repetition, which may be a highly effective theatrical device.

Grouping

A final process that is very useful for even the most basic project (as we will be undertaking in a moment) is grouping. This is the process by which a collection of separate objects are organized as one unit. This aids selection and transformation. The simplest, albeit short-term, group is a multiple selection, allowing you to move, rotate or scale (and clone) a number of objects simultaneously. Thus, for example, if a table was made of four boxes for legs and a box for a top, all five objects could be selected to move or rotate the table as one. The slightly more robust method, though, if the objects are logically related to each other such as a table top and its legs, is to create a named group and assign each object as an element of the group. Groups may further be collected under an umbrella group. Hence one may have a group of primitive objects making a chair, all grouped under the title 'chair'. This group may then be copied ('chair01', 'chair02', etc.) and then grouped alongside a table object group, under an umbrella group perhaps called furniture. Elements of groups can be detached or ungrouped for further modification. This makes the organization of the scene quite straightforward and facilitates handling of complex forms.

Some uses of simple primitive designs

Render.
If you are attempting to follow this while in front of a computer you must remember that in order to see a finished model you need to render your mesh (see the previous chapter for details). While you are undertaking simple exercises it may not be necessary to render at all; simply viewing the model in a working viewport set to flat shading may be sufficient. This will also allow you to navigate around your model, changing the views while looking at it. However, to view any more detailed work you will need to render the image.

We have briefly explored some simple and fundamental modelling processes, available on even the simplest software. Used alone you may find the methods limiting (and certainly not warranting spending £1500 on the program), but nonetheless a number of activities can be carried out using only these methods.

The most basic exercise is the testing of straightforward spatial relationships, examining stage arrangements using quickly constructed 'stand-in' objects. Collections of primitives can quite easily be assembled to suggest a number of architectural forms, and the resultant model can be re-sized and adapted extremely quickly to test the effect of changes in size and layout.

The two figures 5.4 and 5.5 were modelled very quickly using only primitives. Figure 5.4 was modelled in about 20 minutes; the pillars were made with a box as the base, on top of which was placed a torus and then a cylinder. The approximation of the Ionic capital was made from a torus, a box and two cylinders 'on their sides'. The objects were grouped as 'pillar' and then copied. The roof (or cornice) is made from two boxes, rotated to match the angle of the pyramid that makes the pediment. The total dimension of each model is the same (i.e., in the real world height, depth and width would not vary) but each had components re-arranged to test the proportion and spatial relationships. Varying the depth of the tread on the flight of steps, the diameter and number of the

Figure 5.4 A simple 'temple' façade modelled quickly using only primitives

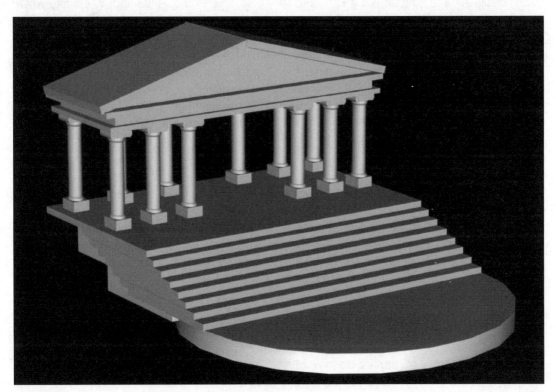

Figure 5.5 The original temple (Figure 5.4) modified using simple clone and scale transforms

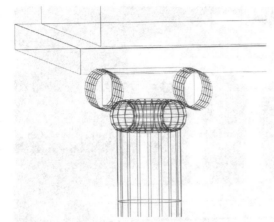

Figure 5.6 Capital, seen slightly from above and the side, a torus mounted on the main cylinder and on top of that a box flanked by two cylinders

pillars and the shape of the forestage element all affect the quality and feel of the space. The models also show the possibilities of being able to see a scene from a variety of perspectives. This exploratory modelling would be hard to achieve as quickly and neatly in card form (though of course not impossible) thus the designer may miss the ideal combination for the scenography. Naturally one has to be careful not to rely too much on this quick form, but it is a useful playground. They enable you to facilitate on computer the German Bauprobe. The Bauprobe functions as a full-scale mock-up on stage of the set. It is done to try to see the nature of spatial depth within the theatre space. Very often this is achieved (in reality) by using stock scenery and shapes, similar to our computer-generated primitives, and placing them on stage in relation to one another. Naturally, this movement in 3D space needs to be read by the designers and director but it can save taking up time in the venue and, of course, where productions are touring the computer can allow a general sense of the feel of shapes in a variety of theatre spaces. The purpose of the Bauprobe is experiment before commitment to design, and this is the freedom offered by quick primitive sketching.

Similarly, even deploying only these basic tools, spaces and objects can be created and tested that would be frustratingly difficult to produce as a maquette, potentially putting a designer off trying a complex but interesting idea. Figure 5.7 is an example of an object that would be extremely difficult to mock-up quickly using conventional approaches, but was quickly made by assembling digital primitives.

More modifications and deformations

The processes described above (primitive modelling, moving, scaling, rotating and cloning) do allow for quick scene generation, but are not enough to facilitate anything more sophisticated; one is left with clearly simplified toy-type forms. Edges tend to be clean, lines are straight and detail is lacking; this allows for only simple test forms and the designer must be careful not to permit this aesthetic to permeate their work for too long (unless of course this is the most suitable scenography).

Viz provides a number of modifiers that may be applied to a form simply by clicking an icon from the Modifiers tab panel including: bend, skew, twist, stretch, taper, wave, ripple, spherify. These modifiers may be applied to any object. You will remember how we discussed the complexity of the primitive object earlier in this chapter, here it becomes very important as the more segments there are the more successful your deformation will be. In the example below a

Figure 5.7 An arrangement that would be difficult to achieve using card and balsa, but easily achieved in the computer

tube has been bent through 90°. In Figure 5.8 one example (on the left) was constructed with only three segments while the other was constructed with eleven. The object with more segments bends more smoothly.

To illustrate all deformation possibilities would be a daunting task: each of the main deformations has a number of variables usually operating around negative and positive values of the 'amount' of deformation, the axis upon which it operates, the direction (in the case of a bend), the bias (usually changing the centre of the effect) and a number of others. Figure 5.9 illustrates a range of common deformations, all applied to a tall thin box, except the ripple modifier (on the bottom object), which was applied to a thin wide box (like a tile).

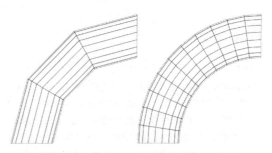

Figure 5.8 An example of the effect of increasing the number of segments in a mesh, seen here after applying a bend modifier

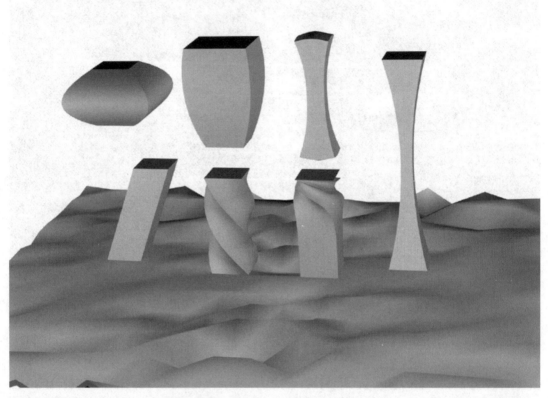

Figure 5.9 An example of modifiers applied to a box primitive. Top row from left: a negative stretch modifier (therefore a squash!); a taper modifier with curve; a squeeze applied with axial curve and radial bulge. Bottom row: a skew; a twist through 180°; the same twist (object copied) but biased towards the top; a positive stretch modifier. The ground is a box with a ripple modifier applied. All of these were effected through their default axes. A modifier applied to an inappropriate axis can have startling effects

Boolean

We have considered moving objects and grouping them to make a more complex object out of component parts. Boolean functions take this a stage further, allowing each component part (or operand) to have a logical geometric effect on the other; essentially one may create a form out of the intersection, union or subtraction of two original forms. This is a calculation worked out by the computer as an algebraic formula. The devices were named after George Boole (1815–1864). Boole developed algebra to solve logical problems. Put more simply one may create an object to act as a tool on another object – a large box-type object may be a 'wall flat', a smaller box object can be created the size and shape of a window and this latter object is used to remove the equivalent geometry from the first object. In Figure 5.10 one box has been created to resemble the proportions of a flat, and two further boxes have been created to suggest a window and a door. You should be able to see this from side and front elevation. Note that these latter two boxes extend all the way through the 'flat' box, since they will be used to remove a section of the wall; the only important aspect of their depth is that they project though the wall object front to back.

Once so constructed the Boolean operations can be performed. There are several ways of going about this in Viz. Select the 'flat' object that is to have the holes made in it, this will be known as Operand A. Then select Create > Geometry > Compound Object from the Command panel, and then select Boolean. You now have to select the operation (subtraction, intersection, union) and pick the second operator. In our example we will select Subtraction A–B where we pick the door block as Operand B. The computer will remove the original door block and remove the equivalent intersecting geometry from the wall. This can be repeated with the window block. Make sure you fully complete the first operation, leaving the function, before commencing the second. Figure 5.11 illustrates the result.

The advantage of this to the designer is clear. Simple openings in flat surfaces may be created easily, making fast work of door flats, windows, etc. More complex operations are of course possible, and geometry is not simply limited to cubes. Figure 5.12 shows, on the left, two spheres created to overlap: the centre example illustrates the subtraction of the smaller sphere from the larger, and the example on the right illustrates the Boolean result of the intersection of both spheres.

One should be aware that excessive use of the Boolean function on one form may make the geometry behave in rather unpredictable ways. Save your work frequently.

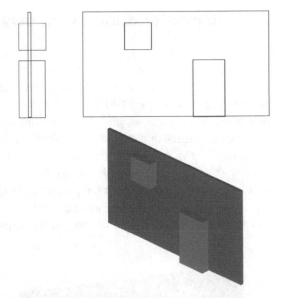

Figure 5.10 An illustration of two smaller boxes placed in a 'wall'-type box in preparation for a Boolean subtraction

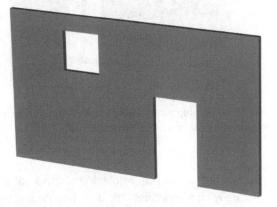

Figure 5.11 The result of the Boolean subtraction established in Figure 5.10

Figure 5.12 Two spheres overlapping (left) and the result of Boolean subtraction (centre) and intersection (right)

AEC elements: doors, windows and AEC extended

In addition to the creation of primitives (box, tube, cylinder, torus, cone, etc.) and extended primitives (capsule, hedra, chamfered forms) Viz also provides architectural forms that can be simply created and modified using the same type of instructions as one would for other primitives. Thus windows and doors (Create > Geometry > Doors/windows) may be created with the user specifying overall dimensions, hinge location and opening method, the design and proportion of the panes and the panels, etc. Viz also facilitates the construction of stairs in a number of formations, straight, turned through 90°, turned through 180°, spiral. Tread depth, riser height and construction (open, closed) are all variable. These tools are of enormous help to the designer, though of course one must be most careful not to lazily fall back on the straightforward default forms offered, at the expenses of design and research.

Figure 5.13 Door and window opening created with Boolean functions, door, window and stairs objects added from AEC features in Viz

Figure 5.13 shows the 'wall flat' that was created above (with Boolean subtractions for door and window openings) now with a standard door and window (from AEC functions in Viz) inserted in those holes. A simple L-shaped stair has been sketched in (with limited detail). This outline model could be used to examine spatial relationships within a scene and to test certain practical details. In this example there are a number of problems with the arrangement: the window opens onto the staircase (it should either be a sash type, or open outwards) and is at an unresolved height, appearing to be neither a ground-floor nor a first-floor fixture; this makes it look quite clumsy and arbitrarily placed. It also seems rather small for the proportion of the rest of the wall. The whole form looks rather flat, lacking in spatial interest and dynamic. Naturally the specifics of any text will provide the information necessary to test these arrangements; the point being simply that these tools are of great value to the designer at early stages.

The extended AEC function offers 'foliage' (of moderate use – simple default plants allow the designer to suggest greenery), 'railings', allowing for the quick generation of railings on stairs, and the very useful 'wall' function. The user specifies the height and thickness of the wall and then creates the object, in the top viewport, by clicking to locate one end, moving the cursor to the next corner, clicking again and so on. An opposite click ends the run of flats (which is effectively what has been created). The wall creation function facilitates the rapid specification of flat objects; once created the wall can be further sub-divided into sections, with each component having variable angles and dimensions. Doors, windows and other apertures may be easily constructed.

To recap

So far in this chapter we have examined the basics of constructing objects from primitives (and, in Viz, the possibility of Extended Primitives, and Architectural Objects). We have looked at the most common modifications and transformations, and the application of Boolean functions. These are still the more basic operations but provide enough flexibility to allow the designer to undertake some exploratory exercises.

Note that at this point we have not covered textures, lighting or camera creation, thus most outcomes at this stage will look a little devoid of life – texture, lighting and a properly set-up camera are often the key to a convincing and engaging image. However, the point of the exercises that follow is to deploy techniques learned so far in simple exploratory modelling exercises, investigating some preliminary aspects of design.

Exercises in exploratory modelling

There is of course no formula or rule that insists on a chronology of design development. As we have indicated earlier in this book a designer may undertake a period of research, followed by graphic storyboarding and exploratory modelling, progressing onto more detailed 3D explorations. All the while the design is being tested for spatial, theatrical and symbolic properties. Sometimes of course the design may begin by focusing on one detailed object or one scene, perhaps modelling it in quite some detail before 'pulling back' and imagining the element in context. Usually, however it has been arrived at, a designer will move towards a tentative model (often in white card) suggesting layout without becoming too obsessed by detail, atmosphere or texture. While this process has its drawbacks, and the computer, as we will see in later chapters, deals well with atmosphere and colour even early in the process, these exercises work towards the equivalent of a white card model – a spatial testing ground.

In order to carry out these exercises you will need to be familiar with the processes described above, and know how to navigate viewports and use dimensions and grids. Elements of these will be refreshed in the tutorials. We have not covered materials or lighting in this book to this point, so these exercises will all use the default lighting setting and the simple geometry colours assigned to the object when it was created, or later modified. This will certainly result in a flat slightly artificial look, but this is sufficient for these explorations.

These exercises are designed for Viz, however most of the activities can be carried out on other 3D modelling packages. It is expected that you will have your manual to hand (or have an on-line reference available) and that you have familiarized yourself with the basics of primitive creation and modification (size, location). We will detail some more complex procedures, but will gloss over creating and location.

Abstract Bauprobe

Even before a designer begins to consider the design for a specific text, theatre or location, simple object modelling can teach some useful lessons about spatial arrangements that will hold fairly universally true, and can be applied to the majority of projects worked on. What follows are a series of etudes designed simply to explore space, balance, proportion, movement. Theatre design is fundamentally about shaping space, about giving it form, meaning, life. It doesn't really matter whether the end result is scenic naturalism or abstraction; an understanding of forms in space is central.

Some practicalities:

- we made a basic stage floor – we find this helps ground a project, it is not totally necessary;
- size doesn't matter here, it's all about proportion and arrangement;
- consider how arranged forms express dynamics. Is a scene formal, chaotic, well proportioned, uneasy, playful, harmonious and so on;
- for this book all elements are greyscale; they need not be, this can be a good way to test how one colour on one shape stands against a different colour on another shape – how does colour create balance, focus, disharmony;
- since we have so far only covered simple geometry, not lighting, cameras or materials, these images are really very simple, a light has been added for impact on the page, but even that is not necessary. Obviously the same exercises can be done with greater complexity – particularly moving viewing positions to replicate different auditoria;
- the software need not be complex: simpler programs (such as Visual Assistant) are well suited to this form of sketching and exploratory imagining.

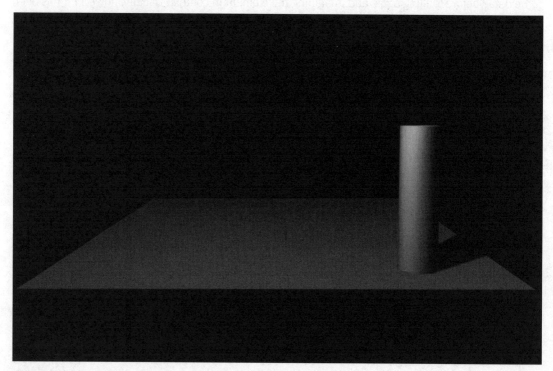

Figure 5.14 A strong position on stage, but perhaps a little lonely

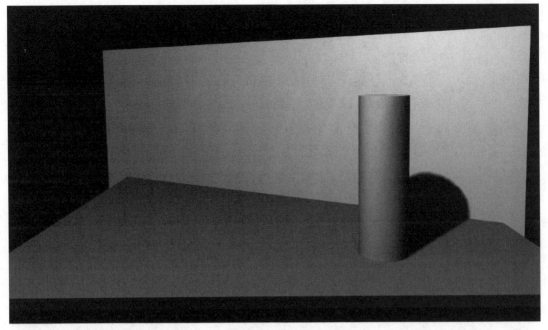

Figure 5.15 A diagonal adds a strong sense of movement, slicing through and off the space. It also takes our eye from stage left to stage right, and the powerful stage position occupied by the cylinder. Diagonals are important to create energy, particularly if the diagonal opens the space beyond the stage

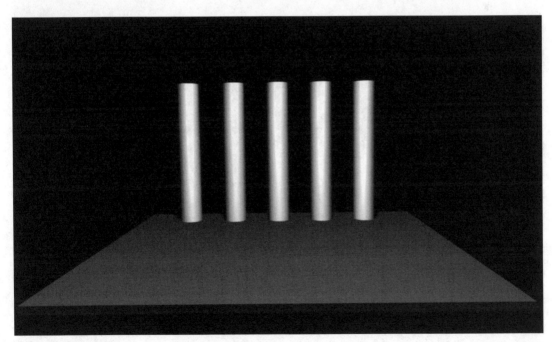

Figure 5.16 Powerful, formal static, immovable

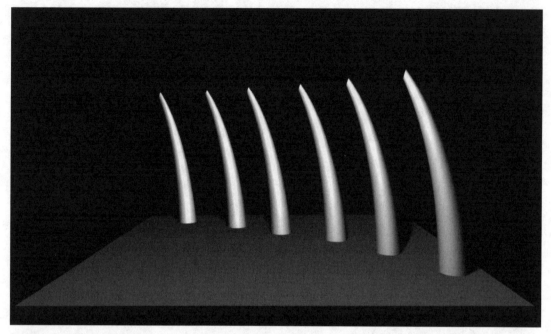

Figure 5.17 The same forms bent and moved on a diagonal – fluid, dynamic, perhaps even a little restful, but still formal

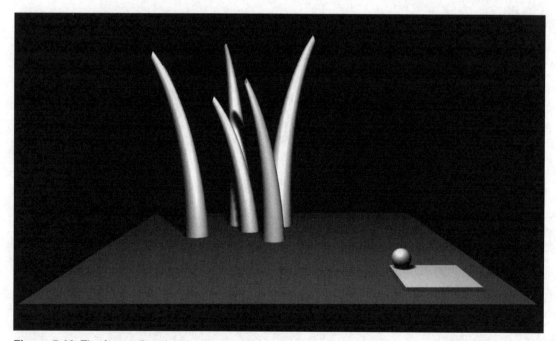

Figure 5.18 The forms disordered upstage right – chaos, nature; but down left there is order

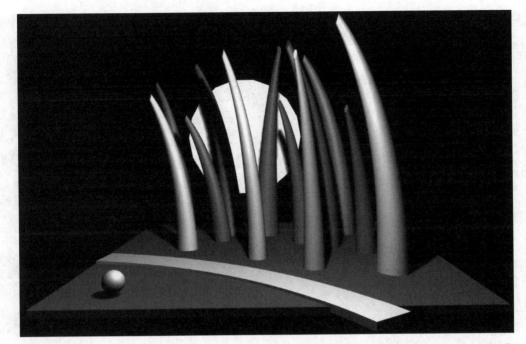

Figure 5.19 A line onstage is a powerful thing; this one also opens up the space by continuing off, the 'path' being constructed from a bent box. It allows the sphere alone to find some status against the growing chaos. A narrative perhaps

Figure 5.20 Restful, fluid, harmonious. The curved form is simply the box from the previous image bent again, the dark mirror/shadow of the circle on the floor is a cylinder

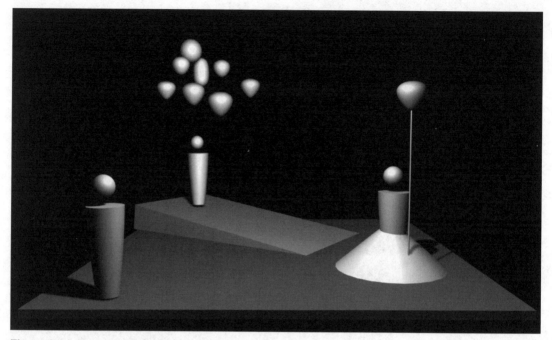

Figure 5.21 Narrative with simple forms: the spatial relationships tell a story, and simple, adapted primitives suggest characters effectively

A word about flats and box sets

Any number of tools in modelling programs facilitate the construction of 'flats'. The simplest is probably a wide, tall but thin box (these terms depend upon where you are looking from; we will assume the conventional terms). The box can be moved, scaled, rotated, bent, copied, Booleaned as you like. There are other ways; Viz provides a wall making tool under Create > Geometry > AEC Extended > Wall. Creation can be via keyboard or mouse drag and click. You specify the thickness (in the units of the scene), height and the line that you create it on; centre justification will usually serve our purposes. It is also possible to extrude a 2D line, perhaps one imported from a CAD program. Extrusion will be covered in a later chapter.

A flat, of course, can mean a multitude of things. It can simply be a framed piece of black cloth to act as masking, it can be a piece standing alone with an abstract image on it, or it can be the main component of a box set. If you feel the need to use flats to suggest walls then consider the following.

Flat surfaces, unless needed for their formal qualities, expose all the weaknesses of construction and joining. They are also too dominating and bland for most purposes. Add texture and detail. Break up height with pipes, picture rails, dados, hanging implements, shelves, tiles – whatever the scene demands. Even a bleak space may simply use a distressed texture to reduce the 'blockishness'. For most purposes aim to make a flat scenic unit darker at the top and edges.

Flats parallel to the audience/setting line tend to be lifeless, unnatural, too square; there are of course many occasions when such a formal arrangement is required, but generally speaking, diagonals give more energy to a theatre space. Instead of imagining you are removing a fourth wall from a room imagine you are cutting a diagonal line through it. In his preface to 'Miss Julie', an important treatise on scenic naturalism (and its problems), the playwright August Strindberg pleaded with designers to use asymmetry and suggestion, to do away with painted detail, and to make use of diagonals.

Sketch (pen and paper, CAD – anything) the plan of a room and play about with cutting planes, that is to say explore ways in which the space can be divided to provide an interesting and appropriate playing space. Consider the need for diagonals, for architectural interest and for including elements that indicate period or other aspects of setting. In a modelling program you can make the whole room (e.g., chimney breasts, all the windows, doors, shelves, alcoves, etc.) and then decide where to cut through it; see Figure 5.22. It also gives you, the designer, a greater feeling of the reality of the place and will tend to make details more lifelike and convincing; rooms rarely have neutral architecture – if they do, plays are rarely set in them. Too often an inexperienced designer makes assumptions about architectural spaces that are not borne out by research, and more often than not a real space is more dramatic and exciting than an imagined space. However abstract or theatricalized a design may become, most of the time one of its key functions will be to evoke in the audience a sense of place.

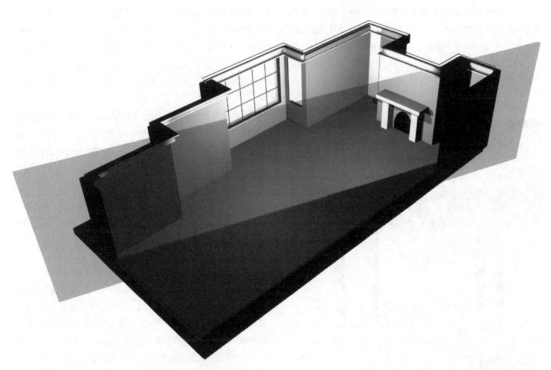

Figure 5.22 A realistic room layout, the 'glass' plane suggesting a cutting plane to create a scene design

Once the cutting line has been set and unnecessary walls removed you can edit details, widening any 90° angles to aid sightlines, making walls higher, the stage deeper, forcing perspective, enhancing or theatricalizing elements, making strong diagonals for entrances, ensuring there is suitable space for action around each area. Albeit a rather acme approach to design (and the box set, thankfully, is no longer common) this is a useful process for seeing how architecture can be translated to the stage, and aid the design process.

A Shaker table – modelling in detail

This small exercise comprises simple modelling techniques using primitive forms and modifications in order to make an item of furniture, a Shaker table. This item has been chosen as its form is sufficiently simple to construct using only techniques covered up to this point. This item will be used in a later exercise so when working on it save it as 'shaker table'.

Much of the art of making models in a digital environment is based upon an understanding of how the real-world equivalent is made. This is, of course, also true of conventional model making, and it is axiomatic that a key skill for any designer is the ability to really look at the world, to understand its form and function. Making a model of any object brings you to a closer understanding of the object, thus modelling is not simply a means of communicating a design idea, but a means of research in its own right.

The Shakers were an extremely disciplined religious order, emerging out of Manchester in the late eighteenth century but making their future in the northeast of the United States of America. Their doctrines were severe, they lived in communities separated from the outside world, the sexes were separated and worship was extreme. Their work was central to their existence and was carried out with dedication and skill. They were industrious, inventive and committed; Shaker artefacts were simple, unadorned, functional and beautifully made.

Figure 5.23 A Shaker table

The intention of this exercise is to reproduce the table shown in Figure 5.23 as accurately as possible. Naturally, as a designer, we may wish to make adaptations later on so that the piece best suits the overall concept and communicates effectively, but at this stage we are going to make an exact copy so that we understand as much as we can about the table.

Along with the initial image (Figure 5.23) we have the following dimensions: it is $25\frac{3}{4}$" high, $28\frac{1}{2}$" wide (i.e., side to side from the front) and 21" deep, front to back. To make construction easier we need to translate these to millimetres, since metric is used across Europe this will be our working unit. There are 25.42 mm in each inch, 25.4 mm will produce accurate enough dimensions, therefore multiply each dimension by 25.4. For example, the height is 25.75×25.4 = 654 mm. For ease it would be acceptable to round this down to 650 mm.

The photograph offers further information. The legs are cylindrical for the most part, though they taper at the bottom (note the taper is not applied to the full length, only the lower quarter or so). Towards the top the legs have a square section, though it is unclear from the photograph whether the cylinder has been turned out of the same piece of timber or whether it is joined. We will assume the former since it would be a stronger joint. The legs are set back from the edges, but it is unclear by how much. Under the table top, set between the square parts of the legs, is a drawer unit with a spherical knob. Proportions, and therefore dimensions (since we know three key dimensions), can be estimated from the photograph, perhaps aided by gridding the photograph using the two vanishing points suggested by the angle of the table.

The table top is about 20 mm thick, probably planed out of inch- (25.4 mm) thick timber. The square section of the leg is approximately 160 mm tall and 40 mm × 40 mm in section. The taper begins about three-quarters down the cylindrical section of the leg. The legs are set in from the edge of the table, seemingly by about one-sixth of its width either side, thus 122 mm from each side and equivalently perhaps 88 mm from front and back.

With this information we can construct a table. Figures 5.24 and 5.25 should be referred to when creating the table top and legs as described below.

The drafting units should be set to millimetres; in general it is recommended that all projects use millimetres. In Viz, on the Menu Bar select Customize > Units Setup then select Metric > Millimetres. Remember Viz does not work in scale as such, it works in real units: since nothing is 'real' but rather points in a mathematical equation you can as easily work in millimetres as light years.

You also need to set the parameters of the construction grid, the mesh of fine lines that appear in the top viewport (normally) to aid construction. The settings for this will depend upon your project and perhaps the degree of accuracy needed. For this project we will set the grid to represent lines every 10 mm, and thick lines every 100 mm. In Customize > Grid and Snap Settings > Home Grid, set Grid Spacing to 10, and Major Lines every tenth (meaning every tenth grid line will be thicker, and if you are zoomed out too far only the major lines will show). If these facilities are not available to you it is not a huge problem, but this kind of set-up aids precision and communication at later stages.

These grid settings can be changed during the project if desired, and naturally will be set differently for projects working over larger or smaller areas.

Snap settings are a drawing aid, allowing you to asking the computer to 'snap' to the nearest pre-defined point to your cursor. This may be a point of grid intersection or part of an object. We will use this later. In Customize > Grid and Snap Settings > Snap Settings check the boxes marked grid point, centre point and end point.

Finally make sure you are familiar with how to navigate viewports. This project will require quite a lot of detailed work in the top view so you will need to maximize it regularly. You will also need to view other orthographic views and view and render the design from the perspective viewport. Set the perspective view to show a 'smooth and highlights' image and all others a wire frame image. To achieve this, opposite click over the viewport descriptor (top left of any viewport) and change the setting in the drop-down menu.

Create the table top

This should be a chamfered box from the extended primitives selection in Viz (in the Command panel, Create > Geometry (icon) > Extended Primitives > Chamfered Box). The chamfered edges round the corners in a way that suggests it has been routed. If a chamfered box is not available to you a conventional box will do but will look sharper. It is often this hard-edged quality that identifies a computer model as such – looking rather artificial and digital.

In order to aid the symmetrical placement of the legs the table is best located at an easy reference point. This might be placing a corner on the 0,0,0 origin point, or perhaps placing the centre of the table top (as seen from the top) on the 0,0,0 origin. This exercise will place the centre of the top plane of the table top at the 0,0,0 origin and build the table below Z0 (the ground plane). The reason for this will become clear as we proceed.

To ensure the proper location of the centre of the box (its pivot point) on 0,0,0 one may either build the object by Keyboard Entry (the precise method) or build it in the approximate location and move it so that its pivot is over the origin. Zooming in to the origin/pivot can allow for very precise positioning, this would be helped by switching on the snap toggle.

Keyboard Entry is the most sensible method. Activate the top viewport (by clicking in it); this will orient the construction process. In the Keyboard Entry rollout of the Command panel enter 0,0,0 in the three location fields since this sets the location of the object pivot, which we want to be at 0,0,0. In the length field enter 533, in width enter 732 and height enter –20 (minus), make the fillet 4.5. Click Create, in the Parameters rollout increase fillet segments to 6. Name the object 'table top'. Naturally, if Keyboard Entry is not available to you, the box may be created by any other method and moved to the correct location.

The drawer box

Before we make the legs we are going to create the basics of the drawer box since that will provide the anchor around which the legs are set. The box appears to extend about 150 mm below the table top, and its edges are one-sixth in from the table edges on all sides. Thus the object, a box, is 66.66 per cent of the length and width of the top. Create a box by Keyboard Entry, location of pivot 0,0,0 and dimensions 355, 488, –150. Click Create. In the front or left view move the box down (constrain the move to Y) until it is just below the table top; the top line of the box should overlap the bottom line of the top. You could have created the drawer box so that is was –170 deep, thus not needing to move it, however the former method does make a box of the right size. Name the object 'drawer box'.

Legs

(See Figures 5.24 and 5.25.) The leg will be made in three sections, each from a separate primitive. A box for the upper section, modified by a squeeze deform using only axial bulge – this will provide the detail that will make it taper into the main leg. A cylinder will make the main extent of the leg, which when copied, shortened and tapered, will provide the lower section.

Activate the top viewport. Create a box 40 × 40 × 155 with its centre on one of the four corners of the drawer box (this example placed the first leg in the front right corner – location in top view

X244, Y177.5). Create the box, and increase length and width segments to 5 each to allow for the squeeze deform. Move the box down so that it is just below the table top. Call this box 'square leg'.

Now apply a squeeze modifier to the box (in Viz selected by icon from below the Modifiers tab). Select the object and then click on the squeeze icon. We shall only apply the axial bulge not the radial squeeze. The result is a little like toothpaste coming out of a tube but without having an indent in the tube. Set the amount of bulge to 0.08 and the curve to 2. Leave all other parameters untouched. You will see the bottom of the box start to bulge downwards, stretching the box down as it does so. Knowing that this would be the effect, the box was made slightly shorter than was necessary, allowing the squeeze modifier to extend it to close to the right length. The box has now has a taper at the base that will lead into the cylinder.

One of the reasons that we are building the box from top down is that this places the pivots at the top of the objects (in most object pivots will be placed on the construction plane by default). In this case the squeeze modifier works away from the pivot; if the pivot was at the bottom of the object rather than the top the bulge would have affected the opposite end, i.e., the top. In order to achieve the effect desired we would therefore have to have turned the box upside down. The same will be true of the taper used later.

The main leg

The square section leg (made above) extends about 160 mm below the top, or 180 mm from the top of the table (160 mm + 20 mm). The next element is the cylindrical leg, extending down some 300 mm before tapering over the last 170 mm – this will be made from two cylinders, one normal, one tapered (180 mm + 300 mm + 170 mm = 650 mm, which is the height of the table).

Construct a cylinder in the top viewport, centred exactly over the centre of the square leg. This may be achieved accurately by zooming in on the area and/or using the snap function (over the corner of the drawer box). Often this can be achieved well enough by eye, frequently having made the object in roughly the correct location and then moving it using zoom views. The leg will be about 15 mm radius and should be 300 mm high (again the negative value will construct it below the top). To appear smooth 20 segments should be sufficient. Call this 'cylinder leg'. Move the leg down, using constraints to viewport Y in the front or left view so that it is 'emerging' from the bulge on the base of the square leg.

Finally copy this cylinder. Zoom out sufficiently in the left or front view so that you can see the whole leg and a large area beneath it; it is preferable to maximize the viewport. Click the move icon and select the leg. Before moving the cursor over the Y constraint arrow hold down the Shift key, then click over the arrow and move the leg down, a copy will be created. At the prompt call it 'tapered leg'. Modify the copy so that its height is 170 mm and make sure that there are at least ten height segments to allow for a smooth taper. Using a close-up region zoom in the front or left view move the tapered leg, using Y constraints, so that its top exactly overlaps the bottom of the cylinder leg object. (Region zoom is a click and drag function activated by a button normally located in the lower right of the screen.)

With the tapered leg still selected activate the Taper deformation. In the Parameters box ensure that the modifier has object axis Z as its primary, and affects XY, i.e., it will taper down the object

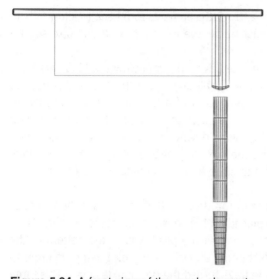

Figure 5.24 A front view of the mesh elements created for the table so far, with the sections of the leg exploded

Figure 5.25 A rendering of the table with completed leg from the perspective viewport

reducing the diameter evenly. An amount setting of 0.2 coupled with a curve of 0.06 seems effective. Never underestimate the importance of looking at the screen to see what looks right; in the end this is design, not engineering.

You now have the table top, the drawer box and one leg made of three sections. In your perspective viewport (keyboard shortcut P) orbit around the object to check it appears properly proportioned according to the photograph.

Before we copy the leg to the other three corners we need to group all three elements together to make further manipulation easier. To do this we need to select all three elements; this can be done via a select by name function, clicking on items while holding the Ctrl key down or creating a region selection. If undertaking the latter, activate the top viewport, ensure the region select tool is toggled to include only those objects wholly within the click and drag region (a button near the bottom centre of the screen showing a dotted outlined box and a sphere inside), then click and drag over the top section view of the leg.

Once all three objects are selected create a group, in Viz Group > Group and name it 'leg'. Activate the select and move function. In the top viewport (maximized and zoomed to see the whole table top) select the 'leg' and clone it by moving it with the Shift key held down – make sure you constrain the movement to X or Y for precise alignment of the legs. It would be most sensible to make each leg an instance of the original so that any modification effects all. Clone and move the leg so that there are four legs, each centred on the four corners of the drawer box.

Finally, we shall add detail to the drawer front. In the photograph the drawer is clearly recessed slightly in the front panel. The best way to represent that is to cheat and create two thin box objects sitting proud of the front of the drawer box – one at the top and one at the bottom – which will suggest the drawer itself is slightly recessed. (This is a cheat and would not stand close inspection, but for the vast majority of purposes would serve.)

The drawer knob is a spherical object, probably sitting proud of the drawer front. The detailing of this is not shown so the designer is left to create some suitable geometry, perhaps a torus

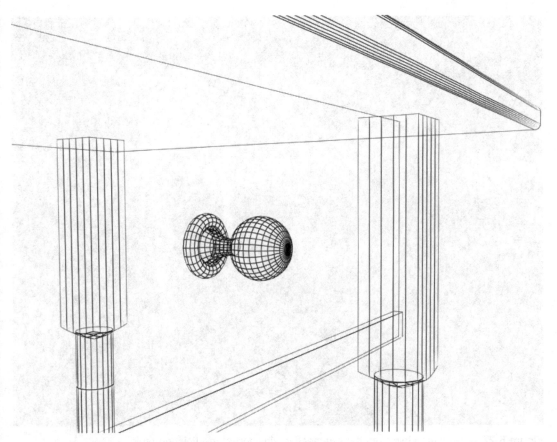

Figure 5.26 A detail of the drawer knob mesh

half-sunk into the drawer front, and a cylinder emerging from the centre of the torus with a squeeze modifier applied allowing for radial squeeze. Remember to use the snap function when creating the knob as the vertical centre-line of the drawer front is on the main grid axis.

Figure 5.26 shows the knob as it might be constructed and the lower rail that indicates the drawer recess. Group the knob elements together. Select all objects in the scene and group them together as 'Shaker table'. This final grouping will allow for the geometry to be moved and rotated as one, and easily imported into scenes. Note that for the next exercise we will ungroup the table. Move the Shaker table group up (in the front or side view) so that the bottom of its legs are at the main construction plane Z0. It is good practice to assume Z0 is stage floor level. (The table could have been made from the ground up, but this would have placed the pivots of some of the objects in awkward places for their modifications.)

In the perspective viewport try to align the view to be similar to the angle of the photograph. Your image at this stage will look a little flat since colour, texture and light have not been added (we will come to this), nonetheless your table, when rendered, should look something like Figure 5.27.

Figure 5.27 A rendered view from the perspective viewport of the finished table

Sub-object modification

So far we have considered creating primitive objects and then modifying them at the object level (i.e., changing the whole object), but as you are aware an object is usually made up of dots in space connected by lines (vertices connected by edges) and it is perfectly possible to modify an object by moving, deleting or otherwise editing these elements. To demonstrate this we are going to create and place an axe in the table top. See Figures 5.28, 5.29 and 5.30.

The following may either be created in a new file, later to be merged into the scene or made in the table scene.

In the front viewport create a box about 300 mm wide, 152 mm long (this will be Y axis in the front view in Viz, apparent height) and 30 mm high (perpendicular to the viewport). As you create this, or just after, increase the number of segments so that there are six segments on each of the longer dimensions, and two on the shorter. Since we are going to modify the vertices (corners of segments) we need plenty to work on. Exit Create mode and enter Modify mode, select the object (or select then modify). We are now going to work on the mesh itself.

From the Modifier List (next to the object name) in the Modify panel select Edit Mesh. This sets up the process of working on either vertices, edges or faces. We can now carry out a wide range of modifications on a sub-object level, some with quite unpredictable results. This exercise will keep it simple. Once we have selected Edit Mesh scroll down the Modify panel and you will find three drop-down menus, Selection, Soft Selection and Edit Geometry. The Selection drop-down specifies which sub-object we are intending to edit, in this case it will be vertices, so click on the vertex button (three dots). Each point of intersection will turn blue. Activate four standard views.

Choose the Select and Non-Uniform Scale transform (icon on the Toolbar), and in the front viewport click and drag a window round all vertices in the second and third columns from the left. These vertices, and the ones immediately behind them as seen from the other viewport, will turn red. Hold down the mouse button and scale these vertices down to about 60 per cent on the viewport Y axis. The vertices will shrink towards the middle of the object (the location of its pivot), pulling adjacent edges down; see Figure 5.28.

Once you have done this, undo it by clicking Edit > Undo Scale; the vertices should still be selected, but if not don't worry. The selected vertices only moved, thus making an abrupt transition into the non-selected ones. Return to the Modify command panel and activate the Soft Selection. Once again use the select and non-uniform scale button, and select all vertices in the second and third columns; do not drag the scale function yet. Return to the Soft Selection dialog box and increase the fall-off dimension until the fourth column of vertices is yellow and the fifth olive; this should be about 180 mm. This will create a decreasing effect on adjacent vertices. Now scale down the selected vertices on their Y local axis to about 45 per cent, and the profile of an axe head should start to emerge. In the top view do the same to scale the far right-hand side to a point, perhaps 5 per cent scale. You may have to adjust the soft selection to make the progression to an edge look effective. Next broaden the flat end, here you may need to lower or even switch off the soft selection. Switch off soft selection and move a vertex or two to take a nick out of the axe head. See Figure 5.29 for an illustration of the finished head.

The axe shaft can be made out of a cylinder (eight height segments) that is non-uniformed scaled a little to give it an oval section. One may

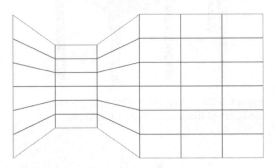

Figure 5.28 An example of scaling down selected vertices

Figure 5.29 The rendered axe-head, the shape and the nick were made by moving the vertices of a simple box

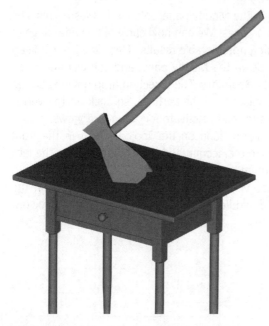

then apply a bend modifier to the whole object, offering a slight (20°) curve. Finally, moving some of the handle-end vertices, with soft selection on, in the opposite direction to the bend will provide the somewhat organic shape of many axe handles. Group the handle and the head as an axe, and place it in the table top.

This chapter has explored modelling with primitives, simple modifications and transformations and sub-object editing. A later chapter will consider some different modelling approaches including extruding and lathing 2D shapes.

However, before moving any further in terms of manipulating form we need to consider some of the basics of colour, texture and light.

Figure 5.30 A rendering from the perspective viewport of the axe buried in the table

6

The basics of materials

Texture, colour and pattern animate shape. While the use of 'white card' can offer some sense of spatial arrangement and the dynamics of space, it is absolutely true that until surface texture is applied it is impossible to understand the full effect of form. At its simplest even the most regular and measured deployment of rectilinear forms can become chaotic and dynamic when colour or texture is applied that subverts its orderliness. Or the design that seems spacious when executed in white card may look overbearing or claustrophobic when rendered in muddy browns. Even here colour alone is not sufficient; one might say that a wooden oak floor and a muddy surface both share similar colours but the sanded shiny texture of the oak with its appealing grain and appealing patina from years of use is far more inviting and warm than the uneven, slimy textures of mud. Colour, texture and form work together to give meaning to surfaces; light has a final effect and we shall return to that.

Some design tutors recommend working in space and form first, using white card to find a language of form, shape, proportion before becoming involved with colour and texture. Others suggest immersing oneself in collections of found materials, collages and palates at an early stage. Most designers, of course, move from one to the other; some projects elicit or demand one type of response, others suggest the opposite; inevitably at some point both come together. There are some aspects of working in digital space that perhaps lead to a greater sense of symbiosis between form, material and light at all stages of the development.

Firstly, nothing is real in the computer: everything including structure, effect of light, surface texture is the product of mathematics. When you view the computer image what is displayed is the function of equations considering supposed form, supposed covering and supposed lighting conditions (I say supposed, for none are real). This is of course also true in the real world; a model of a design is only perceived because of the interaction of form surface and light (light finally and most importantly). However, in the normal process of modelling certain elements are taken for granted. There is a 'working light' over the desk, probably an angle-poise, possible fluorescent tubes, sometimes the sun. A careful designer will take account of these as they work, understanding that these sources have an impact on the way the model is perceived, but nonetheless the lighting is largely a given with only limited control, and often taken for granted; because it's there it needs little consideration. In the computer there is no light, so any source has to be specified – this forces the designer to consider the impact of light. Since what is displayed on the screen is a calculation of the effect of light on a form, light is absolutely as important as shape. The computer offers a default lighting setting, but as you will have noticed in the last exercise (the Shaker table) the standard lighting is so flat that form is not well revealed. The designer has to consider light at an early stage.

Similarly most designers start modelling with mounting board, perhaps white, perhaps off-white, but almost always of a 'neutral' colour and texture. This reveals form and then goes through a process of being covered, or drawn on or painted. The white form is a base that is mechanically overwritten. In the computer, colour and texture are again only the result of a calculation of light hitting surface; the light may be red, the surface may be red, they are interchangeable. Again this is true of the real world, but we are rarely required to consider it so forcibly. There is no neutral in the computer; modelling mounting board in digital space can be written over time and time again, light, texture and form all being variable and all having a significant impact on each other. Thus the designer's explorations of space take place in light, texture and form simultaneously – the designer who does not recognize that has not grasped the profound implications of this approach; the interconnectedness and flexibility of all three elements facilitate an holistic approach.

However, for all these grand designs one must start with the basics. This section will consider how to assign materials to objects and how to make materials; in doing so we will consider some of the key variables. To do this we will work on the Shaker table project, adding some further geometry as we go.

Simple colour

You will have noticed from the last exercise that as you create geometry the computer assigns a basic colour to the mesh, usually white (mounting board for the computer). You will also have noticed that when you render your scene the objects all appear rather evenly lit (the default lighting, to which we shall return) and are rendered the same colour as their mesh with a slight shine, the objects appearing rather plastic. This construction colour (mesh colour) remains the colour of the rendered object until a material is applied to the object. Once a material is applied (see below) the mesh will still be displayed in the original construction colour, but the rendered object will be shown with its assigned material.

As you create any object you may (certainly in Viz) change the colour that its mesh is represented in; you may also change the colour at any later point through the Modify object function. This ability to colour the mesh simplifies modelling complex scenes since meshes are easily identified in the construction views.

In Viz, in the Create and Modify panels you will see a small colour button/swatch next to the object name box. Clicking in this colour box allows you to specify the mesh colour. The program offers you a number of predetermined colours and allows you to specify your own custom colours by following a further button, Add Custom Colours.

Custom colours allow you to choose from the 16.7 million variations facilitated by 24 bit colour, which as you may remember from an early chapter is determined by the fact that eight bits or a byte allows for 256 options, thus 24 bits allows for $256 \times 256 \times 256$ options, a total of $16\,777\,216$ including black and white. While here this is specifically the process for customizing the colour of the mesh it is the same process that you use for specifying the colour of light, the colour of a material, the colour of fog. Indeed any process that requires colour specification will depend upon an understanding of same selection properties.

The process of specifying colour in Viz follows the same basic rules as in many computer graphics programs. Viz offers three main methods of selecting (or creating) colour: selection from a graphical palate; selection by specifying the red, blue and green content (RGB); and selection by specifying the hue, saturation and value (HSV). All three can be used to select a colour, thus one may use the palate to point to a pale blue, decide to add a little more green to it in the RGB selector and then reduce its purity in the saturation slider.

All designers are aware of the colour wheel, the graphical representation of the components of colour. It illustrates that we can consider any colour to be the combination of three primaries (and black and white). Viz, and other graphics packages, illustrate this perfectly and are a great aid to teaching the properties of colour. The significant difference between digital colours and real pigments is that in the computer (as in light) the primaries are red, green and blue whereas in painting the primaries are red, yellow and blue. Computers deal with colour in terms of light not their surface reflectivity, thus colours are created by additive colour mixing (as is colour in light) whereas objects are perceived through subtractive colour mixing. Thus not all real-world colours can be replicated in the computer, and despite the availability of 16.7 million variations the computer palate has its limitations.

Any colour available to the computer may be constructed by specifying the proportions of red, green and blue. Shades of colours will use low values (nearer black), tints will use high (nearer white), and a colour with one dominant primary and the other two mixed in equally at lower level will create a chromatically neutralized colour, for example set RGB to 220,100,100 and you will create a dusty washed-out reddish colour – the chroma (or hue) is moving towards neutral.

The HSV model is perhaps a little harder to use. The hue slider specifies the 'colour', the saturation specifies how pure the colour is; as the saturation decreases the colour becomes more washed out and greyish but also becomes lighter. Value specifies how light or dark the colour is; the effect can look similar to saturation but here the colour (hue) remains pure, but just in more or less quantity.

Materials

Apart from the simplest exercises where the construction colour may suffice, you will want to put a material on each object in the scene.

'Material' is the overall term used in 3D modelling to refer to a collection of parameters that describe the surface of an object. A material will have a base colour (as described above) and may have properties set to indicate its shininess and its opacity. A material may have maps assigned to it, that is to say image files (or bitmaps) may be specified to provide a surface pattern or image. Maps may also specify the bumpiness of a surface using greyscale to create an illusion of texture. Further maps may provide apparent reflections and selective transparency. In addition to using found images (scanned or collected from the Internet) you may also be able to use procedural maps, images created by mathematical process; these are particularly useful for patterns such as grain, marble, noise, water.

Once a material is created is has to be assigned to the object, a process known in Viz, somewhat confusingly, as mapping. The program allows the user to specify how the material is applied to the surface of an object, its scale and orientation. More fundamentally the computer needs to 'know' the geometric form of the object so that the material can be placed correctly; placing a material on a box object but using the map for a cylinder leads to odd effects. This is similar to cutting a costume pattern in the real world. In Viz the orientation of this pattern is defined by a UVW map, a set of co-ordinates (like XYZ) that specify the alignment of a map relative to an object. Generally only UV co-ordinates are used for 2D image maps. Thus to control and modify the mapping properties of an object one selects the object and then modifies its UVW map, which instructs the orientation and layout of an applied material, often called mapping co-ordinates. In Viz the command to modify the UVW map is found in the command panel under the Modifier List roll-out menu. Once the UVW modification is activated the user may select the type of map: spherical; planar; box; face; cylindrical; shrink-wrap. Generally one selects the map type that most closely resembles the geometry of the object, however there are occasions when one might want to apply a different shaped map to an object. In Viz an orange outline will appear around a selected object indicating the form and orientation of the map; this is called a gizmo, it is not a renderable object on its own, it is a control object acting as an icon for the effect of the mapping co-ordinates. By scaling, rotating and moving the gizmo the mapping parameters may be altered accordingly.

To be able to scale the gizmo one needs to select it from the object hierarchy, which involves clicking the plus sign next to the UVW modifier on the Modifier Stack. Once clicked the hierarchy is open and you can access the gizmo commands. Further functions allow you to precisely scale the gizmo to an object or a bitmap. The computer will normally assign mapping co-ordinates while creating an object, and while these may be the most logical for the object they are not always what you want.

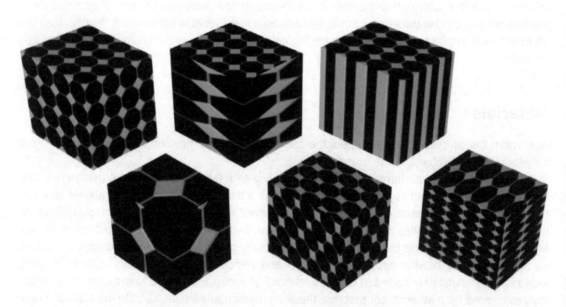

Figure 6.1 The top row shows a cube with, from left to right: box, cylindrical and planar (in the XY plane) mapping applied. The bottom row shows a cube with box mapping applied but modified in scale and rotation

Viz is supplied with a number of pre-made materials that are often sufficient for rough projects, but clearly as a project develops the designer will need to have control over the details of the object's surface. Using the pre-made materials without modification too frequently leads to a uniformity and familiarity within your design portfolio; sound designers are all too aware of the hazards of overusing BBC sound-effect CDs. We will start here by considering the pre-made materials and then examine specific properties and how to customize them.

Open the Shaker table file. When we left the project in the last chapter we had grouped the set of primitives together as 'Shaker table' and we had grouped the three primitives that made each leg. In order to work on the materials in the scene it will be easiest to temporarily open the groups. Select the table and click Group > Open from the Menu Bar, and then select each leg and do the same. Pink bounding boxes should appear around the opened groups; these can be closed later.

Select all the objects in the scene (the most efficient way is to select by name and check 'all'). We are going to assign a pre-made wood material to each element. To access the existing materials (and other image files) we need to open the program's materials and maps browser. On the main menu select Rendering > Material/Map Browser. This interface allows you to see a material or map in the location specified, remembering that a material has properties such as shininess, opacity, etc.; as well as texture maps, a map is simply an image file. The browser window allows you to navigate to material libraries (databases) and map folders. In the window select Browse From: Material Library, and click File > Open (in the browser window). You should be in a familiar file navigation interface. Navigate to the Wood database library in c:\Program Files\Autodesk Viz 4\Maptlibs\. In Viz 3 the material libraries were loaded from shortcut icons below the main menu bar; coloured spheres and boxes.

A list of woods will appear in the material browser. Clicking on any of the wood materials named should produce an image of that material in the top left of the window. You will see that this browser window will allow you to navigate to a variety of sources of materials including libraries, the design itself, the materials editor; it will also allow you to display the results in different ways. However, for this exercise we will leave the browser at its default setting.

If you do not have access to the range of wood materials then you may not have loaded the full range of materials from the CD. To do this you need to custom install the bonus materials. If you still have problems then you need to make sure that the computer is searching for the materials in the right place: Customize > Configure Paths > Bitmaps; you need to ensure that the maps folder in the application folder is selected and includes Sub-paths (a check box). If in doubt add a path to (for example) c:\3dsviz\maps and check the Sub-paths box.

Use the browser to examine the woods available. Wood-Bass seems to be the most similar to the light woods that might have been used by the Shakers for this table. Click and drag either the thumbnail or the text Wood-Bass over the table in your design (you should have all objects selected). Release the cursor when the 'no-go' icon (a circle with a diagonal slash) disappears. A prompt should ask whether you want to assign the material to the selection. Answer Yes. If this does not appear you have not selected multiple objects.

If the perspective viewport is visible and set to 'smooth and highlights' you should see the table take on a wood colour and pattern. Render the perspective viewport. (You may be told at this point that certain objects in the scene do not have mapping co-ordinates, continue rendering the scene but read further down to rectify the problem.) The table will appear to be made of wood (except any objects that did not have mapping co-ordinates, which will simply appear brown) but the grain will look rather odd, being large on some elements and small on others, and quite probably running in unnatural directions. If you created the table top as advised in the previous section (Keyboard Entry) the wood grain should be running from front to back of the table; this is an unlikely orientation. We will now explore the manipulation of the mapping co-ordinates, their type, size and rotation, in order to make the table look more real. (Depending upon the nature of the project the level of detail so far achieved may of course be sufficient, but this exercise needs to take it further.)

Select the 'table top' object only. (Note that we could have applied the Wood-Bass material to the grouped object, but in order to manipulate the mapping for each of the component parts we had to open the group.) We are going to alter its mapping co-ordinates so that the grain runs left to right along the table top and is smaller and denser. We are therefore going to modify the UVW map. Select this on the Modify list from the command panel. Grain is a difficult material to deal with: in two planes one sees the length of the grain, in the other one generally sees the cross-cut or end-grain. This level of detail will rarely be necessary but it may affect how you apply the map. In this case the table top is so thin that it will make little difference whether the map is planar (in one plane only – top/bottom, or XY in this case) or box, thus applied to each plane. Select Planar, and ensure that it is aligned to Z (which, confusingly, means that it will apply to XY). Viz 'thinks' of mapping as a projection onto the surface: the map is projected along Z in the same way that a film project is set perpendicular to the screen. If you have experimented with other buttons during this exercise you will also have to make the map fit the object.

We are going to rotate the material and scale it down. To do this we need to rotate and scale the pattern, not the object, thus we are going to operate on the gizmo. The selection level will therefore be Sub-object > Gizmo. The gizmo is accessed by clicking the plus sign next to the UVW Mapping Modifier on the Modifier Stack – this will open a tree that will include the gizmo; select it. The gizmo outline in the viewport will turn yellow. (In Viz 3 the gizmo is selected by clicking in the Sub-Object menu from the Modify panel.) The gizmo may now be modified as any other object. Rotate it, in the top view, 90° around its Z axis. The grain will now flow in the right direction, but the map is out of proportion with the table top, the planks will look short and wide. Render the top viewport to see this in detail. We need to adjust the map dimensions so that the grain is close, but also so that a repeated pattern as the map is tiled is not too obvious. This may be done either by using the select and scale modifier on the gizmo or by adjusting the gizmo/map dimensions in the Modify panel, as one would with any object. Experiment with different map proportions to achieve a convincing and appropriate grain. The example rendered below has a gizmo size of 670 length by 185 width. Moving the gizmo relative to its parent object will affect the initial location of the repeated pattern. When you are happy with the result deselect the Sub-object > Gizmo to prevent accidental modification.

Once the table top has been set each other component can have the mapping co-ordinates adjusted so that the grain is of a similar proportion (assuming that it is of the same wood) and appropriate flow.

The drawer box will need box mapping and again the gizmo is likely to need re-orienting so that the grain flows along the front of the drawer rather than up and down; the proportion should be similar to the table top, though some difference will avoid the end result looking too regular and artificial. The legs should have box mapping applied to the top section and cylindrical mapping applied to the lower two sections; if you cloned the legs as instances you will only need to effect one leg. The knob will use spherical and cylindrical mapping.

Once the table has been properly mapped close the groups and create a (stage) floor below it and place a tile material on it. Vary the scale and orientation of the tile pattern, then change the pattern. Experiment with ground materials, floor materials, etc. You will notice that there is no correct size of the map gizmo. Some patterns need large maps, some small, depending upon the content of the image file used and the intended scale of the outcome. This facility for quickly changing the pattern and scale of surface decoration is extremely advantageous to the designer. If you are working in Viz for the purposes of a later exercise, finish this experiment by placing Wood-Cedar Boards on the floor. Edit the mapping (by re-sizing or scaling the gizmo) so that the boards look reasonably realistic in scale, perhaps each 6 inches or 150 mm wide. A simple calculation that calculates the size of the map area given the number of boards in the map will provide a suitable scale. You may be able to stretch the map a little so that it only tiles in one direction. The result (achievable in programs other than Viz) should look something like Figure 6.2.

We will now examine how materials are constructed so that you can either modify existing materials or build them from scratch. A material, as noted above, is an umbrella term for a

Figure 6.2 The table with texture maps applied on a wooden floor

collection of properties that define the surface features that may be applied to an object. These features, at their most simple, define the colour, shininess, transparency/opacity and render algorithm of an object. Using these parameters alone one would be able to create a variety of surface types and colours suggesting glass, plastic, metal, paper, etc., but the surface would represent a flat colour only.

The more complex addition to a material is the use of maps. These maps may be image maps or procedural maps, and may provide surface pattern, a suggestion of texture or bumps, a reflection. Image maps are bitmap files (of a scanned image for example) whereas procedural maps are mathematical functions used to create patterns.

Editing materials

In Viz materials are best explored in the materials editor, which is opened either by clicking the icon (coloured spheres) or through the keyboard shortcut M.

The editor has a number of small windows showing material samples, set by default to grey. You will see a control panel below these sample windows that allows you to specify the material colours in ambient (shadow), diffuse (normal) and specular (highlight) lighting; ambient is normally a darker shade of the diffuse and specular is normally white, except for metals where the specular highlight is a tint of the ambient. The control panel also allows you to set specular highlights (shininess), transparency/opacity and self-illumination of the object.

The shininess is represented by a combination of intensity of highlight and size of highlight (glossiness). The shinier an object the smaller and more intense the highlight, the duller the object the larger and less intense.

Figure 6.3 shows examples of different levels of shininess. The sphere on the left has no shininess, in the middle the sphere has a low glossiness and highlight level, on the right the glossiness is high (hence a small highlight area, and the intensity or level is high). Reflections may be added (see below), which will also affect how shiny we perceive the surface to be.

The transparency setting is self-explanatory, allowing you to create effective glass and Perspex objects as well as a suggestion of gauzes. Transparent objects generally look more real when you apply refraction, which occurs when light passes through transparent objects and is affected by the

Figure 6.3 The effect of varying the shininess of a surface. Note that the smaller highlight suggests a shinier object

physical properties of light and transparency. Again, this property is changed through using a refraction index or refraction map.

The materials editor also allows you to specify the shading type applied to the material; this refers to the method by which the surface quality is calculated (the algorithm); different types are more suited to different surfaces. Blinn is a good all-purpose shader and is normally set as the default, though Metal, rather obviously, is better for metal surfaces. For full details on this you will need to consult the manual. Experiment in the editor with changing the colour, shininess and transparency of the samples. Buttons on the right of the Viz materials editor allow you to adjust the geometry of the sample (default sphere) and put a pattern behind it, which is useful for transparent materials.

Further down the materials editor window one is able to access the map controls. The number of map types available will vary according to the rendering level of the material, but the most useful to a theatre designer are found at all levels: diffuse colour; bump; opacity; reflection; displacement. Maps are child objects of a material; once applied they may be modified by clicking over the map name, but in order to make changes at higher levels you have to return to the parent material.

If you are modifying a material that already exists in a scene for use on a different object, you must ensure that you re-name the modified version. Failure to do so will affect the existing material.

Diffuse colour map – the main pattern

The diffuse colour map provides what we would think of as the main pattern or image. Assigning a bitmap here will create an image on the surface of the material. This could be the scanned image of wood grain, an abstract pattern or a clearly defined representation image, such as a painting or a photograph. The map assigned here will be reproduced once in the area of the mapping gizmo. To cover an object larger than the gizmo the map will therefore (usually) be tiled. (As is often the case there are exceptions to this – but for ease of explanation we will take it that the map is reproduced once within the mapping area of the gizmo.) Of course, if the gizmo/map area has a different aspect ratio to the map, the map will be distorted.

Figure 6.4 The material on the left-hand object has the 'speed limit 25' sign applied as a diffuse colour map, and the gizmo is sized to cover the whole object. The box second from the left has the same map applied but the gizmo has been reduced by 50 per cent and the material editor has been instructed to tile the map. Third from left, a distorted reduction of the gizmo has been implemented, planar mapping applied and the gizmo has been centred on the object, however the tile function was turned off; the result is like a label or decal. The far right image illustrates the effect of reducing the map intensity; the pattern becomes fainter

A map is assigned by clicking in the Map bar (default None) in the material's Maps rollout menu, and selecting a map, either bitmap or procedural. You will need to be familiar with navigating through Windows to find where you have located your image files (generally in a dedicated project directory, but possibly in a library), or use files provided by the program. The value selector sets the transparency of the map – a low value makes the map faint and the material colour is seen through it, a value of 100 means that the map is entirely dominant.

Bump map – textures

A bump map instructs the computer to render the image in such a way that the greyscale of the map suggests surface relief, see Figure 6.5. By default black will create indentations and white will create relief, greys generate textures between; indeed the use of grey provides the most realistic and subtle effects. The effect of a bump map can be inverted (in Viz accessible via the map parameters output dialog). A colour map may be used as a bump map but the effect will be generated on its greyscale equivalent. Very often a bump map uses the same or parallel map to the main pattern map; a good example is brickwork, where the diffuse map provides the pattern, colour and detail and the bump map suggests the rendering relief, but equally different maps may be used to interesting effect. If you are creating a bump map from a pre-existing colour file it is most effective to separate the original colour image into its colour channels.

Figure 6.5 An illustration of bump maps. From the left, the first box has the black and white file used above set as a bump map; the lettering appears to recess; the second box has the same map applied but the effect is inverted. The third image takes the map from the second and applies the original texture map (at 50 per cent intensity) to it, resulting in the text appearing to be in painted relief. The final object has inverted the diffuse map and applied an image of a rock surface as a bump map

Reflection map

While it is possible, in Viz and other advanced modellers, to give an object a surface that will calculate how the rest of the scene would be reflected in it, hence a mirror, this is a complex, time-consuming and processor-hungry activity; for most reflective objects, particularly if small or distant, it is sufficient to assign a map (perhaps a rendered image of the scene) to indicate reflection.

Figure 6.6 An example of reflection mapping

In Figure 6.6 an image of the scene was rendered as if viewed from the position of the sphere, mirroring the angle (of incidence) that the final image would be rendered from. The rendered image was reversed (mirrored) in a paint program and applied to the sphere as a reflection map. While not wholly accurate, this is a good approximation. Obviously, the reflection map may be of anything – suggesting the presence of an environment not actually seen. The cylinder on the left has a leaf texture applied to it.

Opacity map – a way to make cut-outs

Mapping opaque (and therefore transparent) areas of an object is a wonderful way to replicate the effect of a cut-out or, if applied differently, the effect of an image on gauze. It provides for quick sketch modelling and uses a visual language that does not try to deceive with an illusion of photorealism. Again based on a greyscale map the computer will render an object more or less transparent. Areas coloured black will be transparent, white areas will be opaque, and thus display the material colour or even a diffuse map; grey areas will be semi-transparent, almost misty. For best effect the material should have no shininess, otherwise there will be a slight 'mist' even in supposedly transparent areas. When combined with other image maps this facility can create some unusual and inspiring effects.

In order to make a cut-out it is usually necessary to have two image files, one that is a black-and-white treatment of the image, where the black areas are intended to be transparent and the white are intended to be opaque. Of course, if you want a mist- or gauze-like effect, a grey treatment will be necessary. The other file will usually be the full-colour original. In some cases the original may already be against a black background, in these instances the same file may be used as the diffuse map and the opacity map. For an accurate, crisp cut-out, both files will need to be the same proportional dimensions (measured in pixels) and, if overlaid, the opacity image should act as an exact mask for the chosen area of the original – this can be checked by using the layers facility in a paint program.

To achieve the accurate opacity map first scan in, download, or create the original – the image that will appear to be cut out. If the original is from a scan or digital photograph the process will be made simpler if the background is of an even colour, unlike any colour found in the main image. In a paint program crop the chosen image so that there is very little space around the part of the image you want to use. The bottom of the section required particularly should be at the bottom of the frame. Make a copy of the cropped original, naming it distinctly as the opacity file for the original, once copied do not change the size of either version. The objective is now to make one of the images entirely black and white, with the white colouring in the part of the image that will be seen, and the black occupying the parts that are to be cut away (or transparent). An opacity map will represent the black as transparent and the white as solid. Either using a magic wand selection feature or using a steady hand with the paintbrush tool, colour the background (the transparent areas) black. If the entire background was an even colour – say green – this will easily be achieved with a colour select tool.

If you have a steady hand and nerve, a lot of patience, and a pressure tablet ideally, you can use a paintbrush tool to outline the outside of the figure in black and the inside in white. Once the perimeter is done it is an easier task to fill in the rest. A zoom tool will allow you to see and colour the image pixel by pixel if necessary.

In order to prevent a distinct edge to the image it is a good idea to slightly feather or otherwise blur the edge, perhaps making the mask slightly smaller than the original. The black and white version will be loaded as the opacity map, and the original as the diffuse colour map. Of course the process does not have to result in crisp cut-outs; more use of greys and soft edges generate gauze-type effects.

Figures 6.7 to 6.10 illustrate the use of opacity maps to create a 'cut-out' of a building. A picture of a building façade was chosen (Figure 6.7) and edited to produce the necessary opacity maps to create entries through the arches. The transparent areas (including the relief of brickwork at the edge) were carefully blacked-out using a brush tool. If the colours are more even and distinctive a magic wand selection can be used; this will create the main texture map (see Figure 6.8). The opacity map (Figure 6.9; provided here with a frame for ease of viewing) was created by selecting the black area, inverting the selection and then filling the new selected area with white.

In Viz a box was created of similar XY proportions, in the front view, as these images. To obtain the precise proportions check the pixel size of the map in the image editor and divide the width by

Figure 6.7 The original image, in this case a sketch by Serlio

Figure 6.8 Areas that will become transparent have been blackened

Figure 6.9 For the opacity map all solid areas have been made white. For the clarity of the illustration a black border has been put round the image

Figure 6.10 An example of the final opacity map applied to a flat surface

the height, thus producing an aspect ratio. Use this to assist in creating the box in the modelling program. The box does not need to have much depth, since it is effectively a cut-out flat. The detailed map was applied as the main/diffuse texture map and bump map, and the black-and-white map was applied as the opacity map. See Figure 6.10 for the finished image. In summary, a material to make a cut-out needs:

- an opacity map in which the white areas will remain opaque;
- a texture map, usually of the same origin, but with the original image visible.

This principle of creating cut-outs is an effective way of representing an object if all or some of the following conditions are met:

- it is seen to the rear of a scene;
- the real-life version is quite flat but has a complex edge profile (such as a curtain);
- it does not rotate, nor does the camera rotate around it, i.e., it is always seen from a viewport closely aligned to its surface plane;
- you want to suggest a graphic or sketchy quality to the design – the intention is to look artificial and theatrical;
- you are designing a pantomime or reconstruction of eighteenth-century staging.

Assuming that a cut-out is accurately made and always seen straight on, it can stand in for very complex pieces of normally 3D set quite effectively. It is, of course, this principle that much theatrical staging before the 1900s was based upon: flat surfaces painted to look 3D can frequently 'cut' around the edges to provide the silhouette. Although there are other ways to achieve this in the computer the opacity map provides a useful technique for achieving the same effect.

Used slightly differently this map may also provide an effect not unlike a painted gauze. This involves much of the same process with two differences: when the opacity map is applied it is set to a percentage less than 100, which will allow the black areas to appear slightly opaque or gauze-like. Also, the overall surface property has its opacity reduced, thus allowing the apparently opaque areas of the opacity map to be slightly transparent; see Figure 6.11. The same effect could be achieved using a greyscale opacity map, however this approach would be less flexible. Varying the percentage strength of the opacity map in relation to the percentage strength of the surface property opacity will allow the 'gauze' to be faded in and out.

A gauze will have no glossiness but the overall area will seem slightly hazy and have a hint of the colour of the gauze. Being a matt cotton fabric it should have no shininess to speak of. A pepper's ghost is technically a reflection, but is most easily rendered using a semi-transparent image. Unlike a gauze, a pepper's ghost appears on glass and therefore should have an element of shininess, but the area around the image should be more transparent than a gauze.

Working with material and maps

In Viz the Materials Browser (the window you open when you choose a map from the shortcut icons) allows you not only to see an image of the final material, but may also be set to list or show all the

Figure 6.11 Using an opacity map on a semi-transparent surface to mimic the effect of painted gauze

maps that make up a material. Similarly, the Asset Browser (accessed from the Utilities command panel) shows thumbnail images of maps in any specified location, thus allowing for speedy and efficient identification of resources. Once in the materials editor one may either call up (load) a pre-existing material from a materials library, get a material from the scene/design or create a material from scratch. Materials provide the designer with a vast amount of flexibility and potential, both for modelling with a view to realism, and initial exploratory modelling.

Materials for realism

There is no doubt that if realism is your final goal (or rather a model that looks identical to the real-world design, even if the latter is abstract) then the ability to use materials with sophistication is an important skill. Once you are able to edit not only the material itself but also the map, you will be able to make individual and atmospheric renderings. We do not wish to suggest that the only goal should be convincing detail, but it is certainly a goal. One of the major drawbacks of using computer modelling is the uniformity of much of the output. Everything looks rather ordered and neat, and there is a danger that this may lead to neat designs; certainly the authors have observed that the computer does not easily lead designers to organic, decayed or messy products. A familiarity with a paint program is essential for effective material editing.

One of the most effective ways to achieve believable 'used' materials is to capture them from real life, using a digital camera (or conventional camera and scanner) to import selected materials directly from the world. Rather than photographing a portion of your chosen image and tiling the map (as most 3D programs do) photograph as complete a section as possible. This will result in a much more natural sample since it will not artificially repeat across the area; your design will offer as much variation as its reference object. Indeed entire building fascias or internal walls can be photographed and applied as a material to an object. Careful modelling, or good use of transparency maps, will even allow door and window cut-outs and other relief detail to coincide with the image.

Since most materials depend upon an image being tiled it is important to use initial maps that will tile well, avoiding seams, misaligned elements at the edges and obvious repeated landmarks. These can normally be anticipated in a paint program, where tools such as Offset (in Photoshop), Blur and Clone may enable you to edit the file for effective tiling. There is little substitute, though, for using high-resolution files of a scale large enough that they need not be tiled.

It is important to be able to 'mess up' a surface or to create irregular patterns over an otherwise repeated map. This cannot always be achieved by editing the original image since, if the map is to be tiled, the edit will simply be repeated also. One approach is to apply a material to a surface (perhaps as a diffuse or bump map) and then render the surface from an aligned viewport. The rendered image should be saved, opened in a paint program and edited. This will allow you to add irregularities, stains, dirt, darkened edges, etc. Using a paint program with multiple layers will aid this process. Once adapted the new image may then be re-assigned, full size, to the original object. Equally it is quite possible to assemble a tiled image from scratch in a paint program by opening the texture file and copying/pasting it across the number of times necessary to properly tile your object. As above the image may then be edited to remove obvious signs of tiling.

The skills that make a good model maker are also the skills that make a good designer: you need the ability to see the world in detail. You must be able to understand how patterns repeat and change, to see small differences of light and texture, to enjoy colour variations across a surface as it has been aged differently. The ability to see and understand these qualities will enable you to see how they can be achieved in a model, and how they might contribute to the overall design. Once identified the actual editing and manipulation of maps is relatively simple – the skill is in the seeing. However, and this is an important caveat, a good designer knows how to edit the real world; the inclusion of every element of detail (both in a material and in geometry) may be tempting but also is likely to miss the point of design. A designer selects what is important and removes the extraneous 'noise' from a design.

Bump maps are useful in realistic texturing, not only in obvious examples such as brickwork, where mortar rendering should be indented, but also on seemingly flat surfaces, since in real life all surfaces have some kind of texture. Again we should note that the same techniques that make the final design compelling will also make the model convincing.

Let us review the Shaker table project. We left it with a wooden floor applied, with mapping gizmo set to provide a realistic boarded stage. Imagine that we want to vary this material, keeping the boards but somehow enhancing the theatricality – perhaps simply making them less regular, perhaps adding something more metaphorical.

We have mapped a board material to the floor in such a way that it will be repeated or tiled to cover the surface, thus there will be obvious repeats of distinctive features such as knots, colour variation, etc. If it were not tiled, the boards would appear too big. The following stages will allow you to modify the floor pattern to look more natural.

Hide the table object group (leaving only the floor in the scene) and then render the floor as seen in the top viewport, ensuring that you save the file and that it is rendered to a reasonably high resolution, perhaps 800 × 600, see Figure 6.12.

Figure 6.12 is the render of the floor in the Shaker table scene viewed from above. Note how the pattern repeats across the floor, particularly highlighted by the three dark boards and the repeated knots. Obviously, if the pattern were tiled more frequently over the area the repetition would be more obvious still. If one simply wanted to get a more naturalistic variation across the area a simple way to achieve this is to use a cloning tool in a paint program.

Once the render is saved, open the completed file in a paint program (for this example the authors used the freely available Paintshop Pro). Crop the image so that there is no background around the floor. Work with the image as large as you can get it in the window;

Figure 6.12 An example of a repeated floor pattern

you might wish to zoom in further to complete some detail. You might start by adding some knots using the Clone tool. Identify a knot on your pattern with a reasonably clearly defined edge and use that as the source, copying it to a likely area of the pattern with a particular view to breaking up even areas. Keeping the opacity or density of the tool at less than 100 per cent will change the colour tone of the cloned knot from its original. Similarly you can clone knot-free sections of board over knots, thus removing them. The same technique can change the colour of a board, though you may wish to use a retouching tool to darken or lighten an area.

A useful tip when cloning is to work from a reference point; in this case we tended to anchor a clone from a board edge, often a top or bottom corner, which makes it reasonably easy to identify the area to clone and ensure edges are properly located.

Figure 6.13 is the result of some minor modifications using the Clone tool, which has broken up some of the repetition; some knots have been removed by cloning a similar area of knot-free wood over them; in other places a knot has been cloned onto an otherwise plain board. Some dark boards were lightened using a Clone tool with reduced opacity, cloning a semi-transparent image of a lighter board over the darker. This process results in a hybrid child that is not quite like either parent, thus avoiding repetition. There is no need to make a vast number of adjustments; your image is not going to be seen in detail and too many adjustments can create more problems than they solve, as well as being time-consuming.

Once the modified version has been created it is used as the new texture map (diffuse colour in Viz) in a new material. Since this new image is properly proportioned for the full floor area the mapping area must now cover the whole surface so that this is not tiled. In Viz this would be achieved by modifying the UVW map to fit the selected object.

The modification carried out above is useful for achieving a more natural effect but may be more detailed and fussy than many designs need, particularly at an early stage. However, a good designer should be aware of the subtle effects of repeated patterns and the advantages of dressing down a 'clean' area. This is as true for the stage as it is for digital models.

Other modifications may be made to the floor material. In Figure 6.14 the boards were rotated (we shall have to re-size the floor or the gizmo to compensate) and in a photo-editing program the text of a manuscript was applied as a transparent selection (white, the background, set to be transparent). Finally the edges were darkened using the re-touch darken tool. The image before the edges were darkened was saved to be used as a bump map. If you were using a colour image you might split the original into three colour channel (red, blue, green) and use the one with the most contrast (usually red) for the bump. These maps can then be applied to the floor object.

Figure 6.13 Modification in a paint program to mask the obvious repetition seen in Figure 6.12

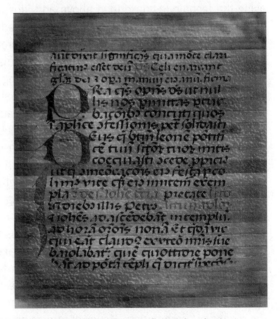

Figure 6.14 The wooden floor after further editing in a paint program

Theatrical materials

Theatre is an art-form of illusion, but also one of abstraction, artifice and the poetic re-imagining of the real world; the tendency, however, is for modelling programs to supply (or at least tempt one to use) naturalistic materials. When making models in card there can be a great looseness about the use of surface patterns and the deployment of graphics. At one extreme a model may have a sketch-like quality, using obvious graphic techniques such as cross-hatching, charcoal or pencil work; brush lines may be obvious, the texture of the base material may come through. These qualities emphasize the temporary nature of exploratory design and the artificiality of theatre. Furthermore the nature of the graphic work, the type of hatching and medium used may be a better indicator of period than the architecture itself. The use of objects that intentionally look like cut-outs also help this playful, theatrical and ephemeral view. These early choices can have a direct impact on the final product, and such an approach may help avoid unnecessary, slavish naturalism.

The use of greyscale images in this type of modelling is effective. If you do need to use photographs to provide your material consider importing the image into a paint program and using a brush or clone tool on a medium opacity to apply graphic marks to the photo. Often, one can create a textured paper effect to add to the sense of artifice.

Figure 6.15 has used three found images as the basis for all elements of the design proposal for a classical square. A drawing by Serlio that uses obvious graphic techniques to suggest a rough texture is the basis for the faces of the house stage left. The box that made the façade was distorted to bring its central section forward, roughly emulating the architecture represented by Serlio, and thus providing a slightly more dynamic and real space. The image was converted into a cut-out map using the techniques described above and illustrated in Figures 6.7 to 6.10. In a paint program elements of the fascia were copied and cloned to make a similarly textured wall without any openings or major features. This was used to provide a texture map (diffuse map and bump map) for other walls, internal and external for the mansion. The steps up to the mansion, added to separate the scenic element and create a stronger entrance, were textured with a section copied from Serlio's pillar base. Similarly the plinth that the statue stands on was a simple box textured with an extracted element from the Serlian façade.

These extracts were normally achieved by opening the original image in a paint program and using a square selection tool to isolate the chosen element, copying it and pasting it into a new image. In the case of the side wall of the mansion a new image was created in the same aspect ratio as the far-left wall object, and the same height (in pixels) as the façade. A simple section of brickwork was copied in several times and arranged to look fairly seamless. Work of this nature does not have to be too precious.

The statue itself was a found image of a Venus that was turned into a greyscale map and opacity map and applied to a flat object. In order to make this apparent 3D form look effective from a 2D cut-out it has to be rotated to be perpendicular to the line of the camera.

The baroque façade of the church (upstage right) was originally a photograph, which drew attention to the difference of style between it and the house, not just of the architecture but also of the means of presentation. However, it was chosen as providing a suitable general outline for the church entrance. To homogenize the graphic quality of the scene, elements of the Serlian façade were lightly cloned over the surface of the Baroque doorway using an opacity of about 30 per cent, just hinting at a more graphic, rusticated effect, and bringing the overall tone in line with the mansion. The box that was created as the flat upon which the church door was placed was bent slightly, apex towards centre stage, attempting to emphasize the thrusting curve of the architecture. Generic materials from Viz were used as the floor surfaces.

Figure 6.15 A scene made from found images applied as opacity maps

The model was lit quite carefully to give a sense of atmosphere to the space. It is quite easy to dismiss these graphic models if they look too clinical or not theatrical enough, so in this example it was intended that slightly atmospheric lighting should balance an intentionally theatrical style. Even though this technique would normally be applied to exploratory models its playful quality may well inform a finished design.

In Figure 6.16 two different charcoal hatch graphics have been applied as a material to the walls of this reconstruction of one of Edward Gordon Craig's screen patents. Undertaken as part of the research at the Kent Interactive Digital Design Studio (KIDDS) at the University of Kent the model attempted to illustrate how the use of Craig's own sketches gave a theatrical life to these simple screens. The human figure cut-out is an opacity map based upon a photograph of Ellen Terry.

Effective material libraries

Most modelling programs will have a range of pre-made materials bundled with them; in Viz these are stored as material libraries. These libraries may be quite sufficient for early explorations but their

Figure 6.16 Modelled by Cat Fergusson, lit by Gavin Carver, research directed by Professor Christopher Baugh at KIDDS

range is limited and in the main provide realistic or natural materials rather than the more abstract or theatrical. A working designer will necessarily build up a collection of their own materials; what follows are some pointers for maximizing the effectiveness of that collection.

Organizing

It is important to remember that a material (the Viz term) is a combination of surface properties (base colour, shininess, transparency) and images or maps applied to create surface pattern, bumpiness, areas of opacity, reflected image, etc. Thus a saved map is a combination of saved instructions and images, and it is important to organize your work in such a way that the location of both is clear and known. Moving image files after they have been used in a material may make that material unavailable to later projects; it is therefore vital that maps and materials are properly organized in a robust file structure. A later chapter will consider project organization in some detail.

Viz organizes maps and materials thus: materials are organized within databases know as material libraries, each library intended to store logically associated materials: wood, flooring, minerals, bricks, etc. Even here there may be problems since a wooden floor may be stored either under 'wood' or 'flooring'. A user can include their new material in an existing library that will also provide a thumbnail via the materials browser. This library will include information on the location of the required images (or maps) needed to construct the material, thus being able to recall them at the point of rendering (thus a moved image file will not be found at the time of rendering).

It is therefore important to create a directory/folder structure that will live past a single project, and have a logical structure. Although Viz provides its own Maps folder it is probably most sensible to create your own images folder under C:, subdividing the tree by image type such as architecture, painting, nature, etc. Further subdivisions may be necessary to allow for a growing library. After ten years' work you may have many thousands of images stored on your hard drive and, to facilitate their deployment in later projects, it might be quite useful to divide them by type, period or subject. It is most sensible to arrange this structure early on in your 3D modelling career; too much of a radical change(or unorganized and undocumented change) at a later stage may make some materials difficult to reconstruct.

Do remember that not only do materials make use of image files, but so might your more general visual research, and it is likely that a map for an image file will be a modified version of the original; identify modifications clearly.

Gathering maps

Map files may vary considerably in resolution, and there is no ultimate ideal for them since their final use may also vary considerably. If there is any rule it is simply to ask yourself how much detail will eventually be needed in the map; if it is likely to be a large portion of your scene and require close detail then a large map will be required, perhaps 600×600 (if square). If the image is only going to be seen on a computer screen there is very little point in searching out a map of a resolution higher than your monitor. If the map is to be placed on an object in the background a resolution of 100×100 may well be sufficient. If the image is to be printed or projected higher resolutions may be needed. There are broadly three different ways to gather maps (images):

1 *Internet searching*. Perhaps the easiest method is searching the Internet for an appropriate image and saving it to your computer. The problem with this process is, to a certain extent, simply the vast range of material available and the time that it would take to search for your chosen texture. This is perhaps not such a problem if your search is specific, but if you are 'browsing' for inspiration there is a danger that the amount of 'noise' compared with useful 'information' will simply overwhelm your search. Using image-dedicated search engines may help, and certainly one should have bookmarked links to the major galleries and museums. It is important to use search terms effectively and ideally start searching from a Web site or image base that is sympathetic to your needs. In general the images found on the Internet are of low resolution; in order to fit in a browser window most pictures are only 200 or 300 pixels in each dimension. This is not often a problem if you are trying to find a simple texture but it can quickly become a problem if the image is intended to be a central part of a high-quality outcome.

2 *Digital photographs* (or scanning wet photographs). This process can provide specifically selected images of patterns and textures chosen for the project, and as such it is an important means of image gathering. When taking photos try to observe some of the following guidelines:

- photograph the image plane as flat-on as possible as this will avoid distortion (or keystoning) that happens when a surface is photographed from the side. The problems of keystoning are hard to rectify at a later stage and it will often be easier to remove a small obstruction from an image than it will be to rectify a difficult angle;
- try to photograph in non-directional sunlight, i.e., on a slightly cloudy day. If you collect the image with strong sunlight you will be committed to a particular shadow/key light direction in your scene;
- keep the aperture fairly small so that you have a good depth of field (more will be in focus);
- using a long focal length lens will avoid curving verticals, but will require you to be some distance from the object;
- wherever possible, capture a large area (provided the resolution allows for some detail). It is quite possible to crop a large area down to provide a smaller map, but the larger area may mean that you need to tile less so the outcome will be more convincing and natural;
- good resolution is important but don't overvalue it; design for theatre does not normally require quite the same quality of image as published graphics. Do remember that very often textures applied to card models comes from a black-and-white enlarged or reduced photocopy!

3 *Scanning*. A common method of collecting research imagery is to scan a book or photograph, often via a paint program. Scanning can be a slow process with most cheap equipment, but nonetheless a scanner is a vital tool for a designer, and even a fairly cheap scanner will capture images to a resolution suitable for model textures (see above). Scanning software, bundled with the scanner, is usually self-explanatory, allowing you to specify what kind of image you are scanning (colour photograph, greyscale, black and white), and allowing you to zoom in on selected regions, thus increasing the final resolution of a small part of the image. A flatbed scanner is the best choice since bulky 3D items may have surfaces scanned. Generally a scanner may be accessed from within a paint program through the menu lines Image > Acquire.

Images from books, personal sketches and photographs provide the traditional material for scanning, but what is less often undertaken is experimental creative scanning. While scanning flat images is perfectly sensible for the vast amount of visual research, and will create an image archive, this is somewhat different to creative scanning in which the act of scanning is an artistic process. At its simplest this might include building a collage on the scanning plate using overlapping objects, perhaps of varying transparency; scanning cling-film is quite effective. Three-dimensional objects can be scanned on a flatbed scanner, although of course resulting in a 2D image, but nonetheless providing useful textures. Perhaps most interesting of all is using a scanner as a device for creating what are effectively the digital equivalent of monoprints. Using this approach one might, for example, cover a sheet of acetate (overhead projector transparent film) with a semi-transparent viscous medium such as petroleum jelly. One may then apply inks (or other pigmented liquid) to the petroleum jelly surface and 'move' them around using, for example, cotton buds. Other objects can be placed in the medium; cling film, water, etc. Finally a backing sheet, perhaps of coloured plastic or another sheet of acetate, can be pressed down on the surface – the applied pressure softening the edges of the image. Obviously one must be careful to protect the scanner's surface and electronics during this process.

There is nothing to stop conventionally drawn or painted images being scanned into the computer for use in a digital model. In a book such as this it is easy to overlook the importance of the interaction between digital and traditional forms, and this interaction works both ways. It is not uncommon for a designer to print a texture generated in a paint program for use in a card model; equally a watercolour sketch might be imported for use in a digital model. This hybridity certainly starts to challenge the perception of the digital version being cold or artificial or lacking in humanity. A complex process of interaction is perfectly possible; for example one might construct a model surface in the computer, perhaps including openings, arches, windows or the like. A neutral rendering aligned to that plane might be printed out and then painted or drawn on – when complete and dry this can be scanned back into the computer and applied, as part of a material, to the original surface.

It is of course possible to create an image (map) from scratch in a photo-editing or paint program, but this method is usually best confined to making simple abstract images unless you are very proficient with the tools provided in these programs. For most maps it is generally better to collect an image and to modify it if necessary.

Once an image is photographed, scanned or downloaded it will normally be processed in a paint program before being stored. It is worth, as a matter of routine, undertaking a set of procedures when importing an image for later use. Check it for flaws, scratches, pixelation, etc., and use the tools in the paint program to tidy it up. The most useful will be: clone, smudge, soften and brush using colour collected from the scene. Wherever possible, cloning is likely to give you the best results since you will be making use of natural variations in texture, colour and brush work appropriate to the image. If the image is complex it might be worth cropping a few sections of it for later use in a tiled material; these sections may need to be modified a little to ensure that they line up when tiled. If the image is one that you might apply with an associated bump map then split the image into its three colour channels and identify the most graded of the resultant images, which can be used as a bump map if needed. Thus from one captured image a designer might end up with:

- the main image, perhaps edited for clarity;
- cropped sections for tiled textures (though of course the whole image may be for tiling);
- an associated bump map taken from a colour separation.

The naming of these files is an important business if they are to be found again. It is sensible at least to begin the names of the main image and the bump map with the same letters since this should place them next to each other in a directory. Make use of multiple words when naming files; too often abbreviations or missing descriptors confuse the user at a later date. Use sensibly named folders; if under an images folder you have created a 'Vermeer' folder you will not need to identify the painter in the file name. It is a useful aid to identify the image size in pixels in the image name.

In addition to editing and preparation, a paint program may be used for full-blown image manipulation, applying effects, textures, overlays and so on to the original. This is a valuable approach for a designer, giving access to a vast range of unique surfaces for their model, however it is beyond the scope of this book; plenty of textbooks on image manipulation do exist.

7

The basics of lighting

A significant advantage of modelling programs is the facility that they offer the design team to experiment with lighting in the development stage of the design. The calculation of the effect of light is central to the mathematics of rendering. The final model only 'exists' in visible form because of calculations based on the behaviour of the virtual light's effect on the colour, shape and texture of scene objects; these features are entirely dependent upon light. Working as a designer in this space you become acutely aware that you cannot separate the manipulation of object and space from the manipulation of light.

This is really quite a fundamental observation so it is worth a little further exploration. The majority of theatre designers will build models in an environment with fairly inflexible lighting; at worst there may be a window and an overhead light, though this is usually augmented by an angle-poise or two and a torch. A well-resourced designer might have a small micro-light rig, or have access to a lighting studio, though a model will rarely be made in such a lighting lab. Thus a model is almost always seen in fairly general light while it is being made, and only at later stages (usually) is it creatively 'lit'. Thus a designer does not really have the facility to consider light as a central element of the design. Certainly many designers are sufficiently experienced and creative to imagine the possibilities and work towards them, and many lighting designers are active collaborators in this process, but the fact remains that it is very difficult to really see the effect until the set is on stage and being lit. And, of course, at this stage, perhaps a few days before the opening, it is too late to make radical changes. A lighting designer, in general, responds to the developing model; some of course do have an input into the set design, and discussions between lighting and set designer will steer the project, but as a broad rule the lighting design is reactive in the development stage. Furthermore a lighting designer does not really have a sophisticated tool for experimenting with the design. A mini-rig is a useful aid but is rarely entirely adequate, and few lighting designers have them in their homes. The key point therefore is that in a digital model there is much more scope for proactive lighting, developing the lighting environment as part of the overall scenography. A difficult question arises from this – what is the role of the lighting designer in this brave new world? In one scenario they work on the project alongside a set designer, the model is shared between them and grows by dialogue. In another scenario projects will be designed by one overall designer or scenographer, perhaps relying on a technical team to work out how to realize the design. A number of lighting-specific programs have been developed, some having useful modelling features as well, but in general these are not designed to assist a holistic design process but rather to expedite the lighting.

The role of lighting on stage

Lights can be set to cast soft-edged beams, falling on an actor from gentle angles, bathing them in a hazy soft-edged light, or it can be harsh and hard edged, with deep shadows on the floor. The stage may be evenly lit to glow as if under a gentle sun, or lit from one side only, throwing sculpted elements into bas relief. This same sidelight may be coloured to suggest a setting or rising sun, each having differences of colour and tone. A different colour and lower intensity will suggest a cold moon and if you raise the intensity and sweep it across the stage, the same light becomes a searchlight. The placement of lights, their number, angle and type is known as distribution.

Intensity, or brightness, is not only a function of the amount of electricity flowing through the filament but how the light level on one area of the stage compares with another. Our eye will always move to the brightest area of the stage, which may be determined by the reflectivity of the object as much as the brightness of the light. Contrast, then, is a key feature of lighting design. It allows us to pick out one object from another or, by virtue of shadows and highlights, it enables us to see 3D relief. An actor who is quite brightly lit when in a dark space against a dark background may still convince us that it is night.

The lighting designer will use the properties of distribution, colour, intensity and movement to achieve visibility, focus, composition, setting and mood. These concepts are often closely connected.

At its most basic lighting provides visibility. This appears to be rather simplistic but in fact the implications are far more profound. Visibility is controllable, that is to say the designer has the ability to select not only what elements are visible but also to what extent relative to other elements and from what aspect, or angle, the element is made visible. Once these considerations are applied across the stage the result determines the composition and focus of the scene, revealing, hiding or flattening forms and bringing the audience's attention to certain elements. We understand 3D objects, in part, by the light and dark shadow that is cast on their form. While the primary responsibility of a lighting designer is almost always to light the actor, there is no doubt that the way light reveals all elements of a scene influences our perception of the space. Sidelight may fall most brightly on a performer, bringing them into focus, but the long shadows that it casts, only partially revealing a set, may bring an air of suspense or mystery. If those shadows are filled in the scene may be softened. Focus is achieved by selective visibility and contrast; we have already observed that the eye is drawn to the brightest area of the stage, although sometimes an unusual colour or flickering light can take the eye away. The balance of contrast, highlights and shadows, reveals the form of set and actor in a prescribed way – this is composition.

Colour, when it is coupled with intensity, most obviously leads to the creation of mood. We have deep cultural associations with colour, some taking on symbolic qualities. Even using subtle distinctions of colour can provoke a subtle response in the audience. We can find a particular blue at a particular intensity, which seems inviting and warm, while a little variation may create a more bleak and cold space. The combination of mood and composition may also evoke location and time of day. As most books on stage lighting will illustrate, a light from directly in front of an object will tend to flatten it, reducing its apparent three dimensions. A light from the side will only reveal half the object, the other half being in shadow whilst long shadows will be cast by the object. The sidelight may reveal the three dimensions of the object but it will make the object only partially visible, which is not particularly useful in the theatre where the object, an actor perhaps, is often viewed from several sides. Lighting from above causes similar problems as only upper surfaces are lit. For an actor this often results in deep shadows in the eyes, under the nose and the chin. If the light is directly behind the performer or set there might be a halo effect. There is little bounced light in the theatre, which is unlike most real environments; as a consequence shadows remain very deep unless the designer compensates for this effect. Take as an example a light that is above and behind a performer, coming at them from 65° from the horizontal. In a dark theatre space this will possibly give them a striking halo, a kind of glowing outline, highlighting shoulders and the top of their head. Their silhouette may stand out but we will see little, if anything, of their features. If one were to look at a person in the outside world similarly lit by the sun, their features may be a little shadowy but they would still be visible, since light has bounced off the sky, a building and the ground to fill in the shadows. The angle at which the light strikes a surface relative to the observer is also important since it may vary the perceived intensity of the light.

The film and photography industry uses useful terms for the lighting effects of sunlight (or any other principal source) and bounced light or other soft source. They are known as key light and fill light; the former is the main source in a scene, the latter fills in the shadows. These terms are not so current in the theatre since there is not quite the same tendency towards naturalism in illumination and theatre faces many compromises, but this idea of key and fill is still a useful creative concept, and certainly works well in a digital model. Later on in this chapter we shall explore one 'system' of theatre lighting.

Figures 7.1 to 7.5 illustrate the effect of different angles of light on a group of objects.

Figure 7.1 Objects lit with one light from the front

Figure 7.2 Objects lit from stage right (left as we see it) at 90° to the centre line of the image, atmospheric chiascuro, but little visible detail

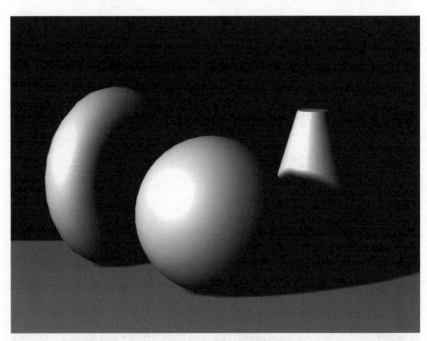

Figure 7.3 The (key) light has been moved 45° towards the front, and 45° up (the target in the centre of the objects). Objects begin to take identifiable form

Figure 7.4 A second light has been added from stage left at lower intensity, filling in the shadows, softening the form

Figure 7.5 A steeply angled backlight has been added, filling out the form, making it stand out from the background – this works particularly well on fabric and hair, creating a halo

Before we consider how theatre lighting designers think about light we shall consider the principles behind lighting in 3D modelling programs.

Lighting in the digital model

As we have noted on several occasions a key philosophy of this book is that digital modelling can assist in design exploration as much as it can assist with technical efficiency. To this end the point of experimenting with light in the digital model is to explore possibilities, not to predict specific outcomes. Put very simply the designer will create an image of what they want to achieve and then find ways of achieving it. The question is not 'what happens if I hang a 1000 W Fresnel with a 106 gel in it from position x?' but 'this is what we want it to look like, how do we go about it in the theatre space?'.

As with so much else in this discipline, technology is moving quickly. Some programs are now capable of very sophisticated lighting algorithms that will calculate the effect of bounced light (radiosity) and precisely render the effect of specifically defined real-world lighting units; other programs are more basic and rely a little more on estimation and illusion. Viz 3 and 4 utilize Lightscape lighting facilities (also available in Max and AutoCAD), which allows one to input precise data on the photometrics of the lighting unit and 'see' the effect on screen. To render these photometrically accurate lights you need a sophisticated rendering engine that will calculate radiosity. Viz 4 has this, Viz 3 does not; most budget programs do not calculate radiosity. Photometric lights offer an excellent effect, particularly when coupled with real-world inverse square decay and a radiosity rendering engine, but they do require a knowledge of the details of the lighting unit. There are other problems: not only does the accurate representation depend upon a number of other factors such as the precision with which the surfaces have been defined, but also it depends upon your monitor or printer settings. Thankfully Viz also provides a generic/standard lighting tool that is probably preferable for early experimentation. All modellers will provide some form of lighting device, and in general will have common features, the difference being in the 'accuracy' of the rendered image. In the authors' experience it is not essential to have a lighting system that calculates data precisely (e.g., bounced light) since there are so many variables between model and realization – a dirty lens on a lantern or a slightly rougher floor surface than was intended for example – and an experienced designer should know how likely their intentions are. Once design ideas are developed by the designer in a digital model these should then be discussed with the lighting designer, rather than complicating the process by attempting to produce accurate photometric predictions using difficult systems with imperfect data.

One must always remember that a computer will allow you to do things that are impossible in the real world. It is possible to set a light to a negative intensity, for example, and thus the luminaire issues darkness rather than light; or it is possible to switch off an object's shadow-casting properties. However, if one keeps reality in mind and observes some basic theatre rules the computer offers a useful environment to experiment with light and to learn the basics of lighting design. There are a number of approaches you might use when preparing lighting in the digital model, ranging in purpose from the purely exploratory in which the designer may be testing out the contribution of lighting with little regard to its implementation, all the way through to the production of schematics including rigging positions and symbols for lanterns. It may also be the case that the designer wishes to visualize the luminaires themselves in the rendered images; the rigging may be an important part of the aesthetic of the design.

Most 3D modelling programs will provide four types of light: omni-light, spotlight, direction- (sun) light and ambient light. We will explore each of these and their properties using a simple scene based on the Shaker table – if you did not make this then this set-up may easily be mocked-up using simple geometry.

Open the scene and if necessary refine it so that:

- the table is sitting centrally on a stage area about 4.5 m × 4.5 m (probably a rostrum within a larger design). To add theatricality and a greater sense of movement we have tapered our floor a little towards the back and angled the table to create a diagonal;
- the floor has an appropriate texture, wooden boards are probably best.

On the table place three objects made of simple primitives; we have created two spheres and a tube, perhaps two pieces of fruit and a mug. Set these around the table centre but some distance apart, and in the middle create a taller cylinder that is going to suggest a candle. Figure 7.6 illustrates this.

At certain points in the following exercise you may want to zoom in on the table top and objects, at other points you may wish to see the entire scene.

Ensure that the rendering background colour is black (best for theatre work) and that, if the facility is available, your renderer is set to cast shadows. Under standard (default) illumination, viewed from above the stage and slightly off the centre line, the scene will look something like Figure 7.7.

Note how flat the default light is in Figure 7.7, and that the more parallel a surface is to the viewing plane the brighter it is; the floor and table top are comparatively dim. In Viz this default light

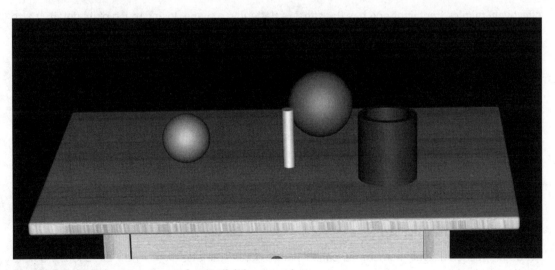

Figure 7.6 A basic arrangement for the lighting exercise

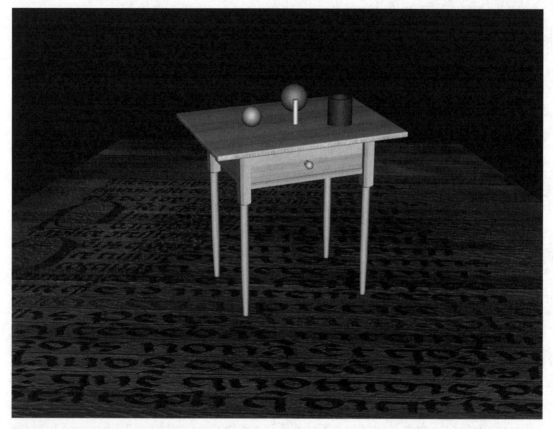

Figure 7.7 The scene under default lighting

effectively mimics front light and has the effect of flattening a scene, losing much of its detail. It also looks somewhat unnatural since we are used to light coming from above rather than eye level. The scene has no atmosphere or composition and the focus, being the brightest element of the scene, is the table front.

In Viz lights are created by selecting, from the Create panel, Create > Lights > Standard (Lightscape Photometric units could be chosen here if you wanted to use photometric data) and then the light type. The light is located simply by clicking in the desired location in the active viewport. A second click may be needed to place the light's target. The light object and target object can then be moved to refine their position in an active viewport.

In theatre design the most useful source is the spotlight. We shall consider this in detail last, and briefly look at the other light sources first.

Omnidirectional light

An omnidirectional light, sometimes called point source, radiates light in all directions from its location. This source may or may not be able to cast shadows depending upon your program. It simulates the effect of unfocused light from a single source such as a light bulb or candle. In theory it could be used for sunlight if you were constructing a scene that placed the sun at a great distance (such as a space scene), but for the terrestrial effect of sun we would need to use a more parallel source. Its most effective use for theatre modelling is either to illustrate the effect of a light bulb in the scene or to create an illusion of soft bounced light reflected off surfaces. (Some programs, such as Viz 4, provide a feature that calculates the effect of bounced light and represents it in the rendered scene, some do not. This calculation is very useful, but can be time-consuming.) You are likely to be able to control its colour, intensity and possibly attenuation, that is the amount it falls off over distance; see below in the section on spotlight for a fuller description.

Create an omnidirectional (or omni) light and place it just above the top of the candle. In the example in this book the candle is 150 mm high, the omni-light is 10 mm above it. (Remember we created the table using millimetres as the units.) Leave all other settings to their default, which should mean the light is on at a standard intensity (1 in Viz); it will cast shadows, and its colour will be white. Render the scene quite close up on the table top; see Figure 7.8.

Figure 7.8 The scene rendered with an omni-light above the candle form

The scene becomes far more atmospheric, the objects are side-lit making them appear much more three dimensional, and the half shadow on them creates a sense of form and mystery; there is something almost conspiratorial about the composition. Each object has a highlighted side from what is the key light (and only light) in the scene. The light appears to fade off as it gets further away from the candle, however this is (probably, depending upon your software) an illusion created by the calculation of the angle of incidence. As the light 'reaches' the further edge of the table the angle of incidence (the angle at which light strikes a surface) decreases (becomes less than 90°) and thus the calculation of the effect of light reduces its intensity. A surface created in the distance but struck by the light at 90° would appear as bright as a surface close to the light. Light in the real world is not only affected by the angle of incidence but also falls off, or attenuates, over distance; we shall return to this. The effect of this omni-light mimics the effect of a candle well, the shadows radiate away from the source, the floor cannot be seen of course since it is shadowed by the table. Note also the reflected highlight on the table top, a function of the shininess of the texture. There are some faults in the scene: the shadows appear too dark for normal conditions, and the reflection of the central sphere in the table is too bright. In real life, of course, light would bounce off the table and illuminate the lower portions of the sphere; this will only be shown if you have a render capable of calculating radiosity (the effect of bounced light). However, there is no doubt that this scene communicates the essential qualities of candlelight. Experiment by moving the source, or changing its colour or intensity. Return the omni-light to its location above the candle after any experimentation.

Note – depending upon the size of your table and the position of the omni-light you may find that some of the floor in your scene is also lit and appears unnaturally bright. This can easily be remedied by either applying an exclude modifier to the source, instructing it not to light the floor, or perhaps more effectively applying an attenuation or decay modifier (see below or the instructions for your software) so that the light falls off before it reaches the floor.

Ambient light

Although not a light source as such this sets the general level of non-directional 'background' light in a scene. It can be a quick way to suggest a general sense of bounced light and light from sources such as emergency exits lights, etc.; no theatre is ever truly dark! The ambient light in Viz can be set from the Render drop-down menu, selecting Environment and clicking in the colour swatch for ambient light. This should normally be a low value, around 10,10,10 on the RGB scale, perhaps emphasizing green or blue a little to suggest the normal spill from blue lights. However, if your design is of a particularly bright and reflective nature then you might need to increase the ambient light to replicate the amount of bounce that such a set would create.

Directional or direct light

This function replicates the light that we experience from the sun, where the source is both so large and so far away that to all intents and purposes the light beams are parallel. This phenomenon is easily seen by observing shadows in sunlight: all shadows fall in the same direction. This would not be the case if the sun was a nearer point source such as a street light, where as you pass it the direction of your shadow changes. As such this function is not overly useful to the theatre designer unless they are either preparing for an outdoor production or researching the effect of sunlight in historical open air playhouses. Some software operates a sunlight system that will provide precise data about the angle of the sun at any given location, on any given time of day and date, extremely useful for research purposes when considering historical open air theatres or planning an outdoor event.

Spotlight

The spotlight, as its name suggests, functions like a theatre light, effectively a zoom profile (ellipsoid). It is a point source with a confined but adjustable beam, which can be given a hard or soft edge. It will cast shadows, take on any colour and may be used to simulate a projector. Indeed it is such a flexible source that it is the only light type needed for most work, and it can adequately duplicate the effect of directional and omni-lights.

A spotlight may (depending on your software) be created with or without a target, the latter being referred to as a free spot. Both function in similar ways but the target spot is directed by moving its target around, thus rotating the light, and a free spot is pointed by rotating the light object itself. The authors prefer the target spot, and that is what will be illustrated below. As noted above Viz allows the user to create standard spots or Lightscape spots with photometric data used to replicate specific real-world lights. We will principally deal with the standard spot since it is the most similar to functions available in all 3D programs, and is quite sufficient for most purposes.

The spotlight is the most useful light for the purposes of the set designer and familiarity with its use is essential. With a click and drag method you can create the light source and its point of focus or target. Two different symbols will represent the source and the target and both can be moved as separate objects. So, you can point the light in different directions, or keep its focus constant but move the source. There may well also be an indication of the beam spread, which is symbolized by a cone. As with any other object it will be created on the construction plane active in the viewport. It is important to note that this creation method will not create a mesh for the light object; the source will be invisible when rendered. If you want to include an image of the light source you will have to create an object. The spotlight has modifiable properties, On/Off, which is a straightforward tick box. The colour of lights, like the colour of objects, is set with Red, Blue and Green (RBG) sliders, each one having any of 256 possible values. These values may be entered by keyboard, or picked from a swatch. Value 0,0,0 will result in a black light, basically no light, whereas 255,255,255 will provide a pure white light that will not alter any of the colours of the objects that it lights. Any of the other 16.8 million combinations are shades and tones of all the colours of the spectrum and learning how to create desired colours is a great educational feature of the software. Note that the computer replicates the colour of light much more closely than it does the colour of surface pigments.

It should be apparent from this description that the colour of the light is also a function of its intensity. A dark blue will let through less light than a light blue, which may have some red and green in it. Most programs will offer a separate intensity or multiplier control but by keeping the intensity control constant and adjusting the colour values you will have less variables in the scene. You may also pick the light colour from the hue, saturation and lightness value sliders. Using these controls you select a spectral colour and then adjust its purity and the amount of black or white in the colour. It is possible to select a colour for the light using the RGB method and then pull the value or lightness slider down towards black. This will result in the same colour appearing dimmer, that is, of lower intensity. Remember that as theatre lights are dimmed they actually become a little more orange in colour (the colour temperature decreases). To replicate this you will need to 'warm' the colour a little, adding a little red and green (thus orange).

By default the intensity is likely to be 1 but may be adjusted to any positive value, and in some cases negative values to project darkness. Increased intensity will increase the amount of whiteness in the light. A value of 1 will mean that the colour projected will be that chosen in the colour variable box. As it increases above 1 the colour moves towards white and eventually at high values the computer will calculate a bleaching effect on the object lit. A light with a high intensity shining on a red object will eventually bleach out the object's colour and show a white object. Similarly, a red light will be bleached to white. High intensity therefore produces an unnaturally bleached and hard-edged effect that is undesirable.

The higher the multiplier the nearer to an over-exposed, bleached-out scene the render will become. Furthermore the render calculates the values for all lights falling on any given area of the scene, thus two lights hitting the same area may also bleach out an area, or make it look unnaturally over-lit. Although intensity is a useful function for tweaking lighting levels without adjusting the colour swatch, be careful not to introduce too many variables and it is preferable to adjust intensity via colour value than multiplier function. Note that a light with intensity of 1 and colour value of 250, 250, 250 will look the same as a light with an intensity of 10 and colour values of 25, 25, 25.

In Viz we find that light with an intensity of 1 and RGB of: 225, 210, 170 looks sufficiently like an uncoloured 500 W lantern if rigged at about 5 m. If you are using Lightscape units (requiring photometric data) the values would be a halogen bulb with an intensity of about 15 000 lumens or 53 000 candelas. This is, of course, an approximation since there are a number of variables including beam spread, age of the lamp, lens type, etc.

Here is a rough guideline to help colour and intensity balance. An intensity of 1 and colour values 255,255, 255 in one light is, in the computer environment, neutral; a surface lit with one light set to these levels will show up with the colour intended for it. Thus the sum of the colour values is 768 (including the zeros). An equation can be proposed that apparent illumination = intensity × total colour increments. So as the total value of intensity × lighting increments increases beyond 768 the colour of the objects in the scene will be overcome by the colour of the light, a white light of high intensity on a red surface will turn the surface white and the lights will not fade out at the edge. We have found, using standard lights in Viz, the general principle should be to not let the apparent illumination of any one part of the stage exceed 1500 of these units. By the time the intensity multiplier is set to a value as high as 10 the effect is very unnatural indeed.

The best way to get a controlled look to lighting is to keep the number of lights low; do not use multipliers over 1 if it can be avoided, and make adjustments based on a common-sense knowledge of how light behaves. Photorealistic rendering engines will avoid this problem to a certain extent since real rather than arbitrary values are used.

The beam spread, or light cone (in Viz under Spotlight Parameters in the Create and Modify command panels) describes the angle at the apex of the cone of the beam. Most programs will in fact offer a hot-spot beam spread and a fall-off beam spread, the latter sometimes called the 'field angle'. The light will be at full intensity within the hot-spot cone and then fall off to 0 intensity at the edge of the fall-off cone. Between the edge of the hot-spot and the edge of the fall-off, the light will therefore fade. If the fall-off and hot-spot cones are almost the same angle the beam will be hard edged, the more they differ, the softer the edge. This is extraordinarily good news for theatre designers since this function allows the replication of the optical performance of almost any theatre light (more discussion on this follows below). Although the default is likely to be a beam with a circular cross-section it may be possible (it is in Viz) to change this to a rectangular beam, and in this case not only is it possible to adjust the overall angle, but also the aspect ratio of the beam. This function can quickly mimic the effect of using all four shutters on a profile.

Casting Shadows (a simple tick box in Viz) will allow you to specify whether the light should cast shadows (objects can also have shadow receiving and casting properties set). Although for the most part this should be on, it will increase rendering times. Where the shadows are unlikely to be significant this should be turned off. If this is off then an object with protruding surfaces will still cast shadows on itself and create relief but not on other objects. Depending on the rendering options available different qualities of shadow will be cast. Raytracing produces very hard-edged shadows, calculated by the way a light beam passes by the object. It is the only method by which to see the effect of light through glass or other transparent surfaces, as lesser rendering techniques may estimate shadows but will not pass through glass. Shadow-mapped shadows render much more quickly and can often look more realistic as they are softer-edged than those that have been raytraced. They can sometimes be slightly off-set from their source, noticeably where one shadow-casting object is in contact with the shadow-receiving object (a table on a floor). This can be adjusted by altering the bias settings.

Attenuation (or decay) is an effect that recreates the fall-off of a light over distance, acknowledging that as the distance between light source and target is doubled that amount of light falling on the same (constant) area is reduced to 25 per cent or one quarter (the inverse of the square of the distance multiplier). Depending upon the software it may be possible to prescribe no attenuation, a user-defined attenuation, a linear decay or an inverse square decay. At its simplest, attenuation functions in a similar way to hot-spot and fall-off, but down the axis of the beam rather than across its section. In other words light falls off to zero between the start of the attenuation and its end. Viz provides near and far attenuation parameters; far attenuation is the more useful for theatre design. Viz offers a decay function as distinct to the attenuation function; decay is less easy for the user to manipulate since it affects the light output across the whole length of the beam, reducing it according to one of three formulae along the length of the beam. Since you are unlikely to be using full lighting data this is not a necessary function, and it is likely that the 'faking it' approach of attenuation will be easier to use. Given the rather large number of variables governing intensity it may cause you problems. We have found that a light source some 6 m above the stage may need an intensity of nearly 1000 in Viz to cast a realistic light using inverse square decay. For the purposes of set design, with most programs this attenuation modifier should only be used in limited circumstances:

- where you are using fog in the light (see below) in which case you will control the amount of fog by controlling the attenuation parameters;
- where a low intensity source (a light bulb) is illuminating a number of objects across the stage and thus would illuminate those further away less intensely (as with the candle above);
- where a spotlight is coming from a low angle (a sidelight, perhaps for dance) and thus may light an object very close to the location of the source, and one much further away. Here the variation of intensity may be important and noticeable.

The majority of lights, hung above the stage, will not decay in a way that will noticeably (for design purposes) affect the intensity of their illumination of one object relative to another.

Lightscape lights (or other photometrically based system) will automatically include decay in the rendering calculation, thus it is not set as a separate parameter. This makes the use of fog (volume light) slightly different, see below.

The projector parameters allows the user to specify an image file to assign to the light, which will be projected onto the receiving surface. These images may be black and white (the equivalent of a gobo, perhaps), colour and, if desired, moving. Clearly this is an important feature for exploring the possibilities of light in the design (experimenting with movies and gobos has always been difficult) and particularly allows for the anticipation of keystoning problems and the effect of projecting onto an irregular surface.

Photometric lights

Most of the information given above for standard lights will also hold true for photometric lights. The following are the key points of difference:

- rather than selecting a spotlight or omni-light one allocates the distribution parameters after the light has been created: 'spotlight' behaves like a theatre light, 'isotropic' is the equivalent to an omni-light;
- Photometric lights do not use multipliers, they ask the user to input the light output in lumens, candelas or lux at the distance (in metres) required. Decay is calculated;
- the user selects the bulb type or colour temperature, which will define the base colour of a light source. After that the user may define a filter colour;
- hot-spot and fall-off are called beam and field.

In Viz, therefore, to create a theatre light using a photometric source, follow the Create > Lights path and select Photometric (rather than Standard) from the menu box. Select Target Point as the object type. In the Intensity/Colour/Distribution menu select Spotlight for distribution and Halogen as the bulb type (or select 3200 degrees Kelvin as the colour temperature). Set the Intensity to a value of 15 000 lumens for a 500–650 W light, or around 30 000 lumens for a 1000 W unit. You may also select the percentage intensity of the light. You now have parameters to insert a theatre light using the click, drag, release method in the viewports. Please note that the luminosity of a light depends on many factors; straightforward specifications of lumens are not useful.

The basic premise is that the user can input exact data on their lighting units; while useful for a lighting designer this may rather impede the playful exploration that a designer/scenographer needs. If Lightscape units were chosen for the exercise below (which is based on standard units) then you need to specify the type; target point simulates theatre spots best. You use these slightly differently from standard target spots in that once a target point is selected you have to specify the distribution, bulb type/colour temperature, and power; for further details consult the software reference. However, to get you started using Lightscape units:

- a target point with spotlight distribution, a halogen bulb, and a light intensity of 20 000 lumens works as a general theatre spot – since beam angle, lens type, lamp age all affect this there is no point in greater accuracy for set design;

- a target point with isotropic distribution and a lower brightness (approximately 1700 lumen) makes a bright light bulb;
- a target point with isotropic distribution and a much lower brightness (approximately 15 lumen) makes a candle.

Before you render a scene that includes photometric units, and intends to display the effect of bounced light (radiosity), you will need to instruct the program to carry out the radiosity calculations. The details of this are beyond the scope of this book, however, just to note, in Viz this is activated from the Radiosity command below the Rendering drop-down menu. For details check the reference for the software.

Spotlight view

Viz will allow the user to view the model from the position of the spotlight, by assigning it to a viewport. (Opposite click over the viewport label and select Views > Spot.) Once thus assigned the beam parameters may be adjusted using the viewport navigation tools, which are at the bottom right of the window in Viz. This is effectively carrying out virtual focusing and allows for the prediction of focusing problems. This is a useful tool for the lighting designer to experiment with before arriving in the theatre space.

Lighting the table scene – some design considerations

We have created a scene using the earlier Shaker table on a wooden floor (in our example tapered towards the upstage end), we have placed some objects on top (two spheres/fruit, and a tube/mug) and created a cylinder/candle. We placed an omni-light above the candle to suggest candlelight. Apply (far) attenuation parameters to the omni-light (select it and modify it), setting the parameters so that the light fades off after it has lit the table.

If this were a theatrical moment we might be aiming to create something rather intimate, perhaps conspiratorial, certainly private. Nonetheless the scene does need to be lit in such a way that an actor or actors might be seen as they move around the space. Remember two rules about theatre: (1) very rarely do directors or actors allow for such stillness on stage that one tight light is sufficient, (2) the theatre cannot sustain real darkness for long so it has to be achieved by contrast and visual cues.

While the candle may provide the key light for the scene – it provides the atmosphere and setting – it will not provide most visibility; additional lighting will be required but it should support this overall mood. In the theatre, of course, the candle is almost certainly going to be a small flickering bulb, possibly enhanced by a light coming directly from above it, but for the purposes of setting the scene the omni is sufficient.

Create a spotlight, locating the source 5 m above the downstage right corner of the stage; locate the target over the centre of the table. We have undertaken this using standard (not Photometric) sources, but very similar effects would be achieved with Lightscape. Move the light further off stage until the angle at which the centre-line of the beam hits the table is about 60° from the horizontal.

In our example, with the datum point (centre-line/setting-line) at 0,0 (XY in top view) we have the light object at –3000, –400. Our mind tends to accept light from above the scene and to the viewers' left as the normal angle for the dominant or key light in a scene. It is the basis for the trick effect whereby a negative mask of the face, a plaster mould for example, when lit from below and to the right will look like a positive mould. As with any system if it is applied too rigidly it will lead to unimaginative lighting but it is a good and safe foundation.

Set the intensity and colour to be an uncoloured, undimmed 500 W lantern. Either input figures suggested above, or render the image and do this by eye! Adjust the beam angle so that the hot-spot and fall-off are enough to cover the table and fade out before the edge of the stage (in our example a hot-spot of 15° and a fall-off of 30°). The steep angle and the narrow beam will mean that the light is contained within the stage space, fading to black before the edge – this will help the idea of darkness; if we lit evenly to the edge there would be no sense of intimate focus on the table. See Figure 7.9.

Leave the 'candle' omni-light on (if necessary attenuate it so that it only lights the objects on the table, perhaps fading out across the table), and render the image.

Note the following in the scene:

The 15° difference between hot-spot and fall-off creates a soft-edged beam, allowing the pool of light to blend into darkness – the scene 'feels' dark. The candle still creates focus.

Figure 7.9 The table lit with a spotlight focused on a small area around the table. The light is coming from above and to the left as we look at it

The objects on the table are 'formed' by two light sources, neither is necessarily dominant (or key), but each have their own qualities; more importantly this use of two sources allows an object to take full shape. The sphere on the left of the illustration has two defined highlights, the one on the left being created by the spot, the one on the right by the omni, this really reveals its form. The sphere in the middle is being lit 'straight-on' by the candle–omni, and thus looks rather flat. The simple cylinder/mug to the right is lit from one side only since both sources come from the centre of the scene compared with it. This makes it a slightly harder form to distinguish.

The candle source casts longer shadows than the spotlight, given its position 'lower' than the spot. These shadows, though, are lightened by the presence of the other light. Areas of full shadow, where neither light reaches, are extremely, perhaps unnaturally dark; in real life, even in the theatre, some bounced light or ambient light might reach them. This can be achieved in this scene either by slightly increasing the value of the ambient light or by creating another light source on a very low level to fill in some of the shadows.

While this is effective we do not really have a sense of what the light from the spotlight is. Is it from a window (thus the sun or moon), another candle, etc.? For this scene it seems apt to suggest that it is moonlight from a window. This will require the setting of two parameters. The light should be made a pale moonlight blue, and we need to set up a gobo (projected silhouette) to suggest a window. Select the spotlight and modify the colour; if you are using Lightscape units you will be modifying the filter colour as distinct to the initial filament colour.

RGB 65,200,255 should give a paleish moonlight blue that might translate as something equivalent to a Lee 144 gel. Please note that we are not advocating trying to find exact gel matches, there are so many variables at work in a system such as this that we believe exact matching is neither desirable nor possible. In our system the designer finds a colour that works and then works with the lighting team to achieve the same or similar effect on stage. Do be wary of the over-use of strong colour.

Once the colour is set we shall assign a gobo to the light. This is achieved using the 'projector' parameters. In Viz the projector is assigned as a Spotlight parameter (standard light) or an Extended parameter (Lightscape), and one selects a bitmap or procedural map as one would for a material, selecting the map type and choosing the 'new' option. One then navigates to the map location and selects the file.

As with all image files these can be pictures that have been downloaded, scanned, digitally photographed or created from scratch in a paint program. In this case we need a window gobo and these may be captured by either scanning them, downloading them from the Web site of a gobo supplier (such as DHA lighting at http://www.dhalighting.co.uk), or creating them using simple forms in a paint program. You should create a gobo folder on your hard disk and establish clear naming conventions. An image can be downloaded from a Web site by opposite clicking over the image and specifying the location that you wish to save it to. You may have to undertake some minor editing of the downloaded image to prepare it for use in the scene. The authors have contacted DHA and they are happy for designers to use their Web gobo catalogue images in this way; if you choose to do this you should navigate to the larger image of the gobo on the Web site. It is extremely useful to keep on record the supplier and model number of a gobo so that this information can be passed on to the lighting designer.

Thus, for our example, a DHA Regency Gobo image (model 135) has been assigned as a projector to the spotlight, see Figure 7.10. In order for the light to be even it is sensible to adjust the hot-spot and fall-off so that their values are close. Once projected the assigned light can be moved, re-sized and rotated to achieve the desired effect – that of moonlight coming in through a window and falling across the table. Note this might most easily be achieved by setting a viewport to present the scene as it appears from the light's position – a great aid to directing the light. The light size, position and rotation parameters may be changed by the viewport navigation controls. In a scene where light comes through a window one should normally attempt to rotate the gobo (or roll the light) to ensure that the shadow of any object in the scene lines up with the supposed line of the window (i.e., a shadow of a vertical object would appear parallel to vertical elements of a frame), although sometimes rigging positions make this impossible. Remember this light has two functions: to help set the scene in time and place; to assist visibility, augmenting the candle. From the point of view of the latter, either the window needs to be quite large, or one might use two window gobos.

Figure 7.10 shows the effect of a gobo on the scene. This now gives a very strong sense of location and time of day (of course this is reproduced in greyscale, so the effect of the moon colour is lost). However, the shadows are still deep and the performance area is quite confined. Audience in the right of the auditorium (stage left) would be confronted with a lot of shadow. We will add a low-level soft light from the stage left side, providing a general fill light. This will be placed so that it more or less mirrors the spotlight with the gobo in it, but will be at a much lower level. The location will be about X 2500, Y –400, and about 4000 above the stage floor. The colour is likely to be a slightly murky warm tone, perhaps Lee 156, hinting at the candlelight, wood and shadow.

Figure 7.10 A detail of a window gobo spilling on the table and floor

Figure 7.11 The table with candle, gobo and fill light. Note the slightly illuminated curtain in the rear – this adds a slight sense of depth to the stage and provides a useful 'stop' to the scene

Finally, in order to develop a slight presence upstage and above the main scene we will add an object with an opacity curtain material applied, and very softly front-lit with an omni-light, restricted by attenuation. This combination will suggest a gentle sidelight in the final real-world performance, but given that this is a flat surface, effectively presented as a trompe l'oeil it need only have soft front illumination; this is a little like a floodlight in theatre.

Therefore, in this scene we have used:

- localized light, in the form of a candle, creating focus. This was represented using an omni-light with restricted attenuation, on stage this would probably be a small effect unit;
- a larger key light of moonlight through a window, setting the scene as an interior at night and supporting the localized light – its purpose is really to open up the light across more of the stage. In practice this would be a zoom profile with a gobo, and a pale blue gel;
- a fill light downstage, lighting in some of the shadows and giving a general stage wash without losing the overall effect;

- a low light on the upstage scenic unit, just framing the piece and introducing some background (of course this is not necessary), on stage this would be a low-level soft light illuminating a curtain from the side to create the chiascuro effect.

Faking bounced light

A sophisticated radiosity renderer will calculate the effect of bounced light, but normal, scanline renderers will not. However, the effect can be easily duplicated using an omni-light. Light a scene using spotlights and render the scene. Identify areas of the scene that are brightest, i.e., planes that receive the most light. Create an omni-light just above or in front of the centre of those planes (multiple lights may be necessary), and set the colour of the light to be the colour that the area looked when rendered. Exclude the surface that the light is supposed to be bouncing from (if you don't you will overlight it); you may have to exclude a few other nearby objects if they burn out too much. Carefully set attenuation so the bounced effect fades out across the stage, as a rough guide we find that the attenuation should start close to the source and fade to black halfway across the stage or up the flats. The multiplier will depend upon the colour, but the light level should be low.

Three-point general cover

In the exercise above we lit the scene with a view to atmospherically lighting the model, providing focus, setting, visibility and composition. We did not have to pay too much attention to translating this to stage use, nor to systematizing it. Theatre lighting designers often work from a basic set of rules called a three-point general cover, loosely based upon the idea of key light and fill light. This set of rules, usually intended to be broken, sets up a formula for creating a flexible efficient lighting environment.

It assumes that we break the stage down into manageable units, usually about 3-m diameter circles, and light each one from three angles. As we have noted above, light straight on to an object flattens it, but as light moves around towards the side it reveals the 3D surface qualities of the object. A three-point cover therefore places two lights at the front of the area but to either side, the centre of their beam hitting the area at about 45° to the horizontal and 45° to the centre-line of the area. Light comes from above since it both looks more natural and is really the only practical solution in most theatres. These angles are obviously flexible and will vary depending upon the nature of the scene and the location of rigging points. One of these lights will tend to be the brighter, providing the key light, the other softer, providing the fill. Often the colours will vary somewhat between the two.

Therefore one of the two lights is either dimmed, or coloured more deeply, with the end result that the form is revealed with the shadows less extreme. The actor may be seen from anywhere in the auditorium. The addition of a third light slightly behind and above the actor will give them an outline and make them stand forward of the background. This backlight also has the advantage of reducing the floor shadows cast by the front lights and may provide colour to the scene without unnaturally colouring the actor's face. This system proposes that an actor facing directly into the audience is lit by one light 45° up and 45° to the left. One light is similarly placed to the right and one light above and a little behind. The two lights from the front may each have a different colour but often this is reasonably subtle, whereas the light from the back may, if desired, have a deeper colour. Independent control over the intensity of each of these lights allows for the creation of numerous lighting variations.

This set-up is repeated across the stage, each area overlapping with the other. A stage 9 m × 6 m will therefore need six of these areas, each with two front and one backlight. To add to the flexibility additional lights may be rigged into each area, perhaps having two from one side and one from the other, providing a wider range of colours, should the lighting equipment be available.

This system can be effected by considering where light in the real world would come from for the scene in question. For example, the backlight might suggest the sun; if this were the case this would also be the key light for the scene. The two front lights replicate the effect of the bounced light coming off nearby walls. On occasion it will be sensible to only use two of the three lights into each area. In a street at night the backlight might take on the pinky-orange of a street light, while only one sidelight is used to fill in the shadows, as if from the moon perhaps, or local ambient light. The third light is left off, allowing the contrasting shadows to evoke a dark night.

A complex general cover system can be difficult to reproduce in a modelling program; the number of lights required would significantly slow down rendering times and, unless you are using advanced lighting functions (for lighting source and rendering), you may have difficulty where the lighting areas overlap – overexposure will occur all too easily. This is less likely in Viz 4 if using Photometric units. Generally in the computer the designer will create a lighting cover with broader strokes than the lighting designer will for the theatre, and the thoroughness of a conventional general cover will not be necessary.

A lighting test box

Every time a designer constructs an object they may explore its relationship with light. This may lead the designer down the route of simply lighting each individual object for best effect and paying less attention to the coherence of the lighting design. The following guidelines should not be taken as prescriptions but do serve as a useful working practice. Once a very basic design has been established, even simply a box for the stage, a very simple version of a general cover may be set up. Since you have to have some light on when modelling it might as well be something equating to a theatre set-up rather than the flat light that some programs provide as their default. For the computer model one area can cover the entire stage. Remember at this stage you are simply setting up a modelling environment. This is an indicative working light, not a finished lighting plot.

If you construct a stage 7000 mm × 7000 mm, with the datum point halfway along the front of the stage edge at stage floor level 0,0,0, this stage may adequately be lit by three lights positioned at: spotlight 1 (in mm): −4500,−1000,6000; intensity 0.8; hot-spot 22; fall-off 40; target centre stage. Spotlight 2: 4500,−1000,6000, intensity 0.5; hot-spot 22; fall-off 40; target centre stage. Spotlight 3: 0,7000,6000, intensity 0.6; hot-spot 20, fall-off 50; target slightly upstage of centre. Use no attenuation but set all lights to cast shadows. (In order to see the effect you will have to place an object in the scene.) You will note that the light from stage right is of a higher intensity than the other two. This gives a sense of direction. Overall the intensities add up to 1.9, any more than this and there is a danger of creating a bleached hot-spot. The beam angles should create a hot-spot over the central acting area, fading out towards the edge of the stage, though still allowing visibility. If this is not the case, slightly adjust the angles or the target location. Colours for each light may be changed as the scene demands and should be set to something other than white, which will result in bleaching. A good configuration for general use might be: spotlight 1: 255,250,200 (RGB) making a straw-type colour. Spotlight 2: 215,245,255 making a pale blue. Spotlight 3 may be the most variable and the colour should be set for the overall tone of the scene. These colours and intensities may be changed at will to suit the scene. Most modelling programs will have a light control panel that allows a quick change of these modifiers, showing all lights in one scene in the same control panel. Remember that colour and intensity are functions of each other; if the colours are left white the above configuration may be very bleached. If the colours are deep the intensity may need to be increased. The latter can also be achieved by decreasing the saturation of the colour. This set-up can be merged into any scene created.

This configuration, like a general cover, is a basic foundation for lighting but is fairly unimaginative and not specific to any scene. However, it will model the sort of general lighting that a design is likely to be seen under. It provides the front light that actors will need, and offers a difference of intensity and colour that will properly model 3D forms.

Fog

Volumetric lights imitate the effect of fog or smoke in the light beam, and may even allow shadows to be projected through the fog. This is an effective aid for the designer since it has become quite common practice to give lights form and to include the beam as part of the sculptural component of the piece. One is reminded particularly of Joseph Svoboda's experiments with ionized water particles suspended in the performance space to give an even mist to lend form to the lighting (see Svoboda, 1993: 59). Many lighting designers now make use of some form of hazer or fogger. The use of fog both on stage and in the digital model can be an extremely overused, clichéd effect. However, it does have some important functions; it gives presence to light which may underline an sense of the spiritual, holy or otherwise supernaturally powerful in a scene. It may also provide strong verticals and height where they may be missing from the scenic objects. This effect is therefore best deployed in scenes of heroic scale, dramatic moments elevated from the everyday. By contrast, smoke can also suggest a decayed, dusty or quite literally smoky atmosphere.

In Viz this function is either set in the individual light's dialog box under Atmosphere & Effects, or it may be set in the main Rendering > Environment menu. In the latter case it has to be assigned to each required light, which also means each light in a scene can have different quantities of fog assigned. In the modification menu for the light the user can select the effect required, and then highlight it and click set-up to change the parameters. Using the main Rendering menu one selects the effect desired (Volume Light), highlights it and clicks Set-up; the user must then add the lights to this effect using the Pick Light function. The variables provided allow the user to change the density of the fog, the amount of light reflected (the brightness), the rate of decay of the fog (as a proportion of the decay of the light) and the addition of noise to the fog, i.e., a system that breaks up the regularity, giving the impression of wisps of smoke or clouds. Volume light can be difficult to use as there are a number of variables, including the type of light; its colour and intensity; its

Figure 7.12 A simple suggestion of fog/smoke illuminated by a spotlight beaming vertically onto stage. This is known as volume light

attenuation or decay; the volume light parameter settings. An important process to observe when experimenting with complex elements such as these is to only change one variable at a time, that way at least you will know what each does. Volume light is featured in the later Steps project, but below are a few basic considerations.

In summary, to add fog (volume light) to a light, select the light, click the Modify icon on the command panel and scroll down to the Atmosphere & Effects panel. Click the Add button – an options window appears – select Volume Light, click OK. To set the parameters (see below), click on the effect in the Effects list and click the Set-up button.

In general, in the theatre, fog rises towards the lighting units, and normally the design team will wish to keep the effect high, nearer the rig rather than obscuring the stage. In order to replicate this effect and keep the fade-out subtle, a light will need to be assigned a long attenuation. Since attenuation not only fades the quantity of fog but also the quantity of light the attenuation range of a light volume light must be far further than the object that it is lighting. For example, if a light is 5 m off the stage, pointing straight down, the following settings (for a standard light in Viz) will provide an effect similar to high-level haze. The end product of this exercise is illustrated in Figure 7.12. Create a spot directly above a stage floor, about 5 m from floor level – this example has given the floor a simple wooden texture to create a theatrical feel. When you finally render it you will have to use the perspective or camera viewport to see the effect.

The spot is set to colour 255,255,255 (thus white) and multiplier 1, hot-spot (beam) is 20°, fall-off (field) 50, perhaps a bit high for a normal theatre light but it will better illustrate the effect in this example. Far Attenuation is set to start at 5 m and end at 10 m; don't use Near Attenuation. This will mean that the light intensity will only start to fade after it has hit the stage, thus keeping our illumination intensity constant. We can change the fog intensity relative to this.

In the Volume Light Parameters dialog box (accessed either from the Effects menu in the individual light's Modify panel, or from Rendering > Environment drop-down menu) we shall keep the default density and maximum light (although sometimes it is necessary to reduce the maximum light to avoid an over-exposed effect in the fog). The important parameter is the Attenuation element; we want a smooth fade, with the fog finally clearing about 1.5–2 m above the stage floor. The Start box specifies where in relation to the Far Attenuation modifier the fog starts to fade; in this case 100 per cent would commence the fade 5 m from the light, thus below the stage, but 0 per cent will commence the fade at the light; set this to zero. The Far Attenuation modifier does the same; we want the fog to have faded out about 3.5 m from the light, so in this example we have set the far attenuation setting to 35 per cent. (You might want to set this a little higher, as the fade-out may look a little high.)

As a final example of what can be achieved by the addition of the noise function we have allocated a volume light effect to the window gobo in the table scene that we worked on earlier, see Figure 7.13.

Digital light sources and their theatre equivalents

A contemporary zoom profile may have a field angle (possible beam spread) between 20 and 40°; light may spread wider but the intensity will be reduced below a usable level. This beam may also

Figure 7.13 Fog added to the Shaker table scene. Note the shadows of the window in the fog

vary from hard to soft edged. Thus a sharply focused narrow profile can be created by setting the hot-spot (or beam) of a spotlight to 19 and the fall-off to 21. Settings of 25, 45 will roughly equate to a zoom profile such as the Silhouette 30 set on a wide soft beam. Fresnel lanterns have a soft beam, which fades gradually through its beam. At its narrowest the settings of 6, 18 should work, at its widest 45, 80. A Pebble Convex lantern is similar to a Fresnel and has slightly less distinction between fall-off and hot-spot, so about 5, 10 for the narrower beam and 36, 58 for the wider would be appropriate. The beams of Pebble Convex lanterns are also generally a little narrower than a Fresnel. The Parcan has a fixed beam angle, which is only variable by changing the sealed bulb unit. A Parcan beam is more difficult to emulate than other lanterns since it is slightly ellipsoidal and irregular in intensity. However, an intense beam with a few degree variations between hot-spot and fall-off each set either side of the bulb beam width should provide an adequate approximation. We have found that by assigning a greyscale image to the light as a projector one can emulate the filament effect from a Parcan.

While the standard theatre lantern is likely to have a circular cross-section to the beam, this may be able to be converted to a rectangle by the use of shutters. Once converted the aspect ratio and the ratio of the length of one side to its adjacent side can be adjusted. This is the shape created by the aspect ratio and it replicates the effect of using all four shutters in a profile lantern, or if the hot-spot and fall-off are far apart. It will roughly equate to barn doors on a Fresnel or Pebble Convex lantern.

If you are using photometric data for light sources the lantern and lamp specifications can usually be found on the manufacturer's Web site. The details should include beam and field angles (maximum and minimum) and light intensity (in lumens or lux) at various beam angles.

The set designer's and lighting designer's work comes together with the composition, moods and metaphysics of the design, the way light plays in the space. As Appia acknowledges (various papers contained in Appia, 1989) light unifies the actor, the set and the space. It is the responsibility of the set designer and lighting designer to understand how light will work on the design proposals and how light will affect colour, intensity and distribution. These features of the design will provide the best means to communicate and evoke the mood and themes of the production and under-score or through-score the developing action.

For each scene in the piece the set designer should provide an indication of the lighting in a 3D program. The purpose of this should be both to communicate their intention for the scene and to illustrate how the lighting will accommodate the actor, the space and the architecture in a coherent way. For each scene the set designer and lighting designer should have considered the dominant mood of the scene or environment. The lighting might reflect this dominant mood, or it might play against it. The light might follow through the scenographic metaphors discussed by the whole team. Questions of pace of change and actor placement will come later in the process and during subsequent meetings with the whole team and, of course, through discussion with the director.

8

The rule of change – scenographic improvisation

The previous chapters considered some of the practicalities of basic modelling and the application of materials. Although the examples offered were focused on theatre, the chapter did not really reflect upon the poetics of the process. The authors believe that it is as important to understand the metaphysics of the creative process as it is to understand the practicalities, and that an intelligent designer must see the significance of their working methods as much as the efficacy of their design choice. We do believe that the process by which one chooses to approach a project will have an effect on the result of that process. This chapter will reflect on the process and attempt to understand how it differs from the conventional approach to modelling.

The designer in the digital space is working in a void, free from boundary, gravity, intrusion and clutter. It is the idealized essence of the black theatre space, which may have to deal with tedious mechanics but aspires to a more transcendent state. In order to make a statement in this space a designer has to engage with the clutter of the interface, a space laid out with boundaries, buttons, boxes and intrusions. Nonetheless, the first object made, whatever it may be, is placed in dark nothingness. This has a number of immediate repercussions. This first mark has no context. It is free of both theatre space and workbench space. Does one create a concrete space first, possibly constructing the theatre, its walls and floor in some detail, or does one start with a detached object, or an actor? It is not inconceivable that the designer might spend some time building a highly realistic image of the context in which their design is to be located. Through the process of modelling the theatre there is the potential for the designer to come to understand it quite intimately. Here, architectural detail, rather than a volume of air, might put into context the scenography. Although this practice is the same as when using a card model, the total nothingness of digital space requires the designer to transform it into a theatrical space. To paraphrase Svoboda, this is the process of making the production space, a process that moves the significance of the space from the frame of the scenography, to a part of it (Svoboda, 1993: 30).

A designer may simply start with an object in space, free from the debilitating presence of gravity. The black non-space becomes a place to dream and get lost in. Without the understood physical representation in a 1/25th-sized world, the proportions of digital space are quite disorientating, as indeed are co-ordinates, since up and down have no real meaning other than by relationship to the point of viewing that space. This lack of registration may work to the advantage or detriment of the design. On the one hand it is an illustration of the freedom from substance facilitated by a computer. It requires an experienced designer to be able to discriminate between such results that are achievable in the theatre and those that are not. A real model inevitably requires the designer to engage with physical laws. An object is placed on the table top wide-side down, or it is hung with cotton, or propped up, or it falls over. This may force a designer to engage with practicalities but they are the practicalities of model-making, rather than the theatre space, where illusion is a stock in trade. Such practicalities do not encourage speculative play. The drawback of this digital freedom is obvious and most precarious to an inexperienced digital designer.

Confronted with this realm of possibility, how does the designer start? We will examine a very simple, typical activity. For example, an initial tentative visual response might be swiftly generated in a graphics program and applied as wallpaper to a simple structure – perhaps, an architectural piece derived directly from scanning a sketch of the item and using that outline to generate a simple 3D form. The form might be lit and include a simple cut-out figure. There are several key differences between this process and a conventional equivalent. In both examples a similar initial chronology is at work. The swift 2D responses are made more theatrical by applying them to simple solid geometry. In the example given there is probably little gain of speed if a computer is used. It is not necessarily the initial act of creation that is substantially altered but the act of re-creation. The process we have described is infinitely repeatable or disposable. Minor or major modifications are far easier in this domain than in the conventional studio. The changes need not be linear, one need not go back to the beginning of the process, or complete it to the end. The other significant difference in the digital version is the presence of controllable light, which must be engaged with in order to work in the space at all.

The making and unmaking of an error is an entirely different proposition in a digital space. The complexity of the programs, coupled with the significance of apparently small acts, make errors a common occurrence. They are, however, entirely recoverable. This factor inevitably leads to the use of error as a means of exploration and the construction of objects not by design but by result. Indeed many programs have randomizing capabilities built in. The designer quite literally can ask the computer to make errors defined by particular parameters. At its simplest, you do not need to decide how big a cube needs to be and then build it or decide what texture it will have and then paint it. You can change the elements until they are right. It is an amalgam of graphic sketching, model making and fortuitous accident. This flexibility prompted Darwin Reid Payne to suggest that, 'it promotes nothing less than a radically new approach to scenographic design' (Payne, 1994: 177). This is perhaps completely apparent but the repercussions are quite fundamental. A computer model, unlike its solid sibling, is not the product of a series of mechanical processes but is a collection of mutable design *ideas* of scale, shape, texture, colour, position and illumination.

The proposal that a digital design is an arrangement of ideas is not a fanciful metaphor. An idea exists as nothing other than electrical impulses waiting to activate its means of communication. A computer model complete with light and texture is nothing other than an arrangement of electrons in a circuit. Its logical and visible outcome is dependent upon how the designer defines it, not upon mechanical laws of model construction. An imaginative vision, right or wrong, is immediate. It may be forgotten or modified but is not dependent upon a period of construction. The somewhat time-consuming process of making a conventional model must therefore come after the visualization of a design idea. While there is certainly a feedback between model and idea, the model cannot change as rapidly, nor can it change in the same way, as the internal imaginative vision. Furthermore, as the design process comes closer to completion, the mechanical model tends to minimize change since it is becoming an increasingly complete and detailed reproduction of the vision. This is the very stage when a designer is increasingly familiar with the conceptual concerns of the project and it is the point where informed change might be most necessary. The non-mechanical and speedy nature of digital modelling allows for a much closer alliance between the manner of envisioning design and the manner of its exploratory realization.

There is an equivalent in word processing. While text may be entered as a string of letters, spaces and punctuation, it may be re-visited and edited in a wide variety of ways. The writer may rearrange paragraphs, remove all references to the term 'scenography', automatically update indexes, databases or footnotes. Whether these changes are cosmetic or fundamental, they exemplify a different relationship between the author and their text than is facilitated by pen and ink. 'Change is the rule in the computer, stability the exception, and it is the rule of change that makes the word processor so useful' (Bolter, 1991: 5). Unlike conventional rewriting, Bolter suggests that the computer allows the user to deal with and edit topics rather than words. We are enabled to deal with whole units of meaning simultaneously and thus organize and re-organize our writing in blocks of thought rather than strings of letters. We propose that the same is true of visualization technologies. We may deal with our exploratory model by topic rather than as a physical entity, which it is not. We are less beguiled by its substance and more interested in its idea. Bolter has further insights into the process of electronic writing that might be applicable to the design paradigm. Although he discusses word processing, the main subject of Bolter's study is hypermedia, that is the interactive electronic text that allows the reader to follow various trails within the document, constructing their own pathway through it. Bolter's point is that this form of writing creates a dynamic relationship between the reader and the text in which the order or type of information received depends upon the action of the reader as they follow the links from place to place. An authorial voice is absent and the reader is active and the text polyvocal. Let us return to our hypothetical model and assume that it is to be shown to a director. It is not a complete object, it is a text containing a collection of ideas that may be interrogated and reassembled during the course of discussion. Ideas, unlike objects, are indestructible, forgettable and debatable. They do not achieve the same difficult status of artefact or product and are easily disposed of. Given the entirely digital nature of our example, the manipulated image superimposed on form, we can suggest that it is an arrangement of ideas within an illusion of space that almost demands change and plasticity. In a sense, the physical model is authoritative, the digital equivalent is compliant. Change is the antithesis of monumentality and monumentality the enemy of responsive creativity. Of course, every phenomenon, if it is not to be a mere static fact, must be observed in the flow of time. And time is expressed through change. Not mechanical change but change as the flowing current of a lively imagination, like the clouds above a landscape that never acquire substance, never become a solid spatial form (Svoboda, 1993: 21).

A computer is good at exploring changes throughout the procedural time of making a design but, more fundamentally, it allows the exploration of the changing scenography over theatrical time. The movement of objects, light or actors may be represented and played with as easily as their form. Visualization programs allow and encourage animation. The designer's storyboard may come to explore and represent not moments of stasis but moments of transformation. The digital model may animate lighting, falling fabrics, trucking, flying and the movement of actors, indeed every element of the scene may be choreographed and accompanied with sound. In a digital space a static object is not privileged above its ability to transform or describe space over time, nor its ability to be described by the moving actor or the play of light. This is a scenographer's work space, providing the opportunity for the exploration of rhythm, tempo and life. The replication of movement in a conventional model is difficult, often impossible, and where it is achieved it often serves to demonstrate an end result rather than assist in a process of exploration. Fewer opportunities are explored and the design may be left standing. Since the only time that the interplay of all scenic elements normally occurs is perilously close to the final production, their interaction is necessarily determined through careful plotting and mechanical prediction rather than holistic experimentation. While the actors have been allowed to explore the possibilities of their kinetic interaction through improvisation, the interaction of other scenographic elements has had little such opportunity. The digital space allows for something more akin to improvisation than progressive rehearsal. Colin Beardon has made a particular point of pursuing this correlation. 'Being able to manipulate the whole stage space instantly gave this visualisation process an improvisatory quality. Improvisation [. . .] is fundamental to all Western theatre training and all live Western performance. The correlation, therefore, between using improvisation in the drama studio and in the virtual space of the computer is fascinating' (Beardon and Enright, 1999a: 8; www.tees.ac.uk/cade99/ beardon.doc).

9

Peopling the stage

Why use human figures?

Any designer will know that scenography revolves around people. A design is both a practical space that must be used by actors and a world that must respond to the lives of the characters who inhabit it. Scenography often begins with the consideration of the actor in space and many design classes ask the student to begin by creating characters in scale. The human maquette has several functions. It communicates to the viewer that this is an inhabited and live space. It gives a sense of scale without which a model can be quite difficult to read. It makes the performer/body a central part of the design and, most importantly, it allows for experimentation with arrangements of actors, investigating scenographic and practical possibilities of the performance space. Without some kind of human representation a model may be a rather lifeless artefact that does not really do justice to its intended end result. This is no less true of a digital model.

The designer working with conventional materials has a number of techniques at their disposal. The simplest representation may be to make the silhouette of a character cut from a piece of card, perhaps with details drawn on, or pasted from a photocopy. One might use wire or pipe-cleaners that will achieve a 3D representation ranging in style from a Lowry type stick figure to something slightly resembling the Michelin man made by wrapping wire to achieve a stylized organic form. Plasticine or low temperature hardening modelling materials often applied over a wire armature allow for a more realistic form, which may be painted.

Before we examine techniques that might be applied in the digital model it is worth giving some consideration to the semiotics of these figures and how they affect the way that the model communicates. Towards the later stages of the design process most designers strive to make their model as much like the version that will appear on stage as possible. While the design itself may be abstract, theatrical, minimalist and so on, the model always presents an illusion of reality. This suggests that the model people should also aim for this level of verisimilitude. However, some designers choose to be far more impressionistic in their representation. The advantage with this approach is that it alerts those who work with the model to the fact that it is not the end product. The model is simply one of the routes by which the final theatrical presentation is arrived at and the sense that there is something missing or incomplete keeps us alert to the contingency of the model. Furthermore the designer should be careful not to go too far towards specifying character if costume designer or director have not been involved. Their principal interest will usually be in form and scale. Finally, an actor is frequently moving, from small gestures such as facial expressions to large journeys across the stage; all of these offer an energy and image that is far from the frozen snapshot that a realistic model may offer. Artfully coiled wire may suggest more about the human form in space and time than a perfect plasticine figure. However, there are times when the life-like is necessary or appropriate. If your first vision of the scenography is a crouched figure over a simple bench in a dusty beam of light, then simply producing the bench and the light may not be sufficient. Realistic figures may also be important for exhibition models after the event, which do offer a miniaturized record of set, costume and actor arrangement. As these are after the event this is a record rather than an indication and so may properly be more realistic. In the digital world the same issues should be considered, however there are two particular and peculiar aspects to the digital model that should inform your decision as to which style of model to make.

The digital model can be made as an incredibly photo-realistic model. A final render, seen on a monitor that resembles a television, is in danger of becoming a medium detached from its purpose. Using extremely realistic figures may enhance this view, making it hard to see it for what it is, a process in the design and production journey. The use of clearly artificial figures therefore will always remind the viewer that this is a temporary and exploratory iteration and not complete until it is built on stage.

The digital model also allows for movement in the design and, since for many projects the most kinetic element is the figure, it may be necessary or desirable to animate it. This requires a particular approach to its construction. However, the point above remains: if a figure is animated realistically, which is actually very difficult on desktop set-ups, then one is in danger of working to the aesthetic of an animated film rather than a designer's model. If the initial explorations lack the subtlety of real flesh there is the potential danger that this acts as the paradigm for the final event on stage.

Practical application

There are three main methods of putting people in your scene.

Method 1: building with primitives

This is the simplest and quickest method, using techniques covered in Chapter 5 on basic modelling. The assembly of primitive objects can create a more than adequate representation of a person. At its simplest a sphere for a head on top of a cylinder may be sufficient as an indication of scale, but with a little more sophistication a good generic form can be created. A slightly more complex version using stretched spheres or capsules, an extended primitive in Viz, or similarly deformed ellipsoids may create lower and upper legs and arms, pelvis, torso, neck and head. The adult human form is eight times the length of the head measured in front view from chin to crown. Thus the head makes one of these sections, the torso from chin to groin is three units, and the legs are half the body length, comprising four units.

We will now make a simple human figure, a little like an artist's maquette; however, for ease of construction this version is wearing clothing along the lines of a long sweater and trousers. Using different materials and slightly altered deformations this basic form may suggest a variety of character types. Explore your program for the following features: Move Vertices in a mesh; apply

Non-uniform Scale. Knowing how to move the Object Pivot, Create Groups and use Squeeze and Taper modifiers will also help. Set the units to millimetres.

From the front viewport create a box the height of your actor, 1800 mm is about 6 foot; this box can be seen in Figure 9.1. The width (world X axis) should be about 25–30 per cent of the height, which will be the shoulder-to-shoulder dimension. Body shapes do of course vary. The depth (world Y axis) of the box dimension should be perpendicular to the front viewport plane and will be the guide for the front of the chest to the shoulder blade. This should be between 200 mm and 250 mm. Of course one should adjust these accordingly; a child will have very different proportions to Falstaff. Set the box to have eight equally spaced segments in the height. These will guide the proportion.

Working between top, front and left or right views create a sphere, inside and centred to the box. This should be approximately 200 mm in diameter for the head. This should be slightly elongated using scale functions to be a little longer on the world Z axis (chin to crown) than on the X and Y, as a head is bigger chin to crown than ear to ear or front to back. Rotating the sphere in a side view around its local Z axis, world X in such a way that it tilts backwards by a few degrees, will give it slightly more life. The sphere should be moved and scaled so that its dimension from top to bottom fits in the top segment of the box. Now name the sphere 'head'. A neck is a simple cylinder placed, rather obviously, below the head. Check that they align well by switching to a right or left viewport.

The torso is the most difficult but practice makes it reasonably straightforward. Create a sphere with 32 segments and a diameter approximately 400 mm, radius 200 mm, in the top viewport. The alignment is important because it determines how the vertices are placed and thus how easy it is to edit. Choose a distinctive colour for this and all other primitives since the scene will become full of overlapping meshes. Seen from the front the sphere should have 15 lines of latitude between the poles. If your program provides more, recalculate the instructions below; less will not work well. If your software allows it, a capsule (an Extended Primitive in Viz) may be easier to use but here we will illustrate the process with a sphere. Scale the sphere using non-uniform scaling to make it wider (world X) than it is front to back or top to bottom (world Z). The curvature from the top axis is going to be the shoulder, so they should gently slope. All the following steps may be done by simply moving vertices but, if it is available, use a squeeze modifier as this will do the same. This modifier simply moves vertices in much the same way.

Move the modified sphere so the top is just below the head, connected by the neck, and align its central axis with the head's. From the front viewport modify the vertices in the mesh. In Viz, select the object and open the Modify command panel. From the Modifier List select Edit Mesh and then select Sub-object > Vertex – in Viz 4 this is an icon representing dots. Select and move all the vertices in the bottom five lines of latitude so that the 'south pole' is about a third into the fifth segment of the box, counting from the top. Once the vertices of the lower five lines of latitude have all been moved down, move the upper one of these lines of latitude up a small amount, somewhere near the line separating the third and fourth box. Move the lines of latitude until you are satisfied that you have a (rough) outline of a torso. The two lines of latitude above the equator may be moved down a little to even out the spread. Naturally the proportions of body form that you require will mean that these vertices may be moved rather differently. Once the head, neck and torso are created within your proportioning box, and the vertices of the torso moved, the resultant mesh should look a little like Figure 9.1.

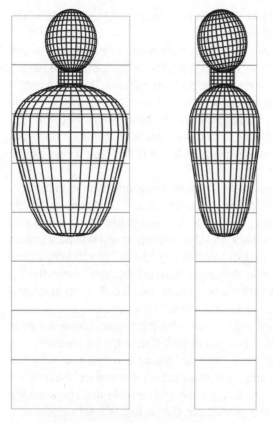

Figure 9.1 The head, neck and modified torso and the box used to guide proportions

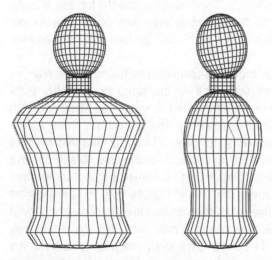

Figure 9.2 The torso after vertices have been moved and scaled to sculpt the form

By moving selected vertices (either individually or in groups) or by applying a non-uniform scale, the mesh can be sculpted to suggest waist, chest, hips, etc. (it is probably a good idea to identify the gender of the model and the nature of their top clothing – in the example illustrated here we have a male in a sweater). For best effect you need to work between front and side views. You need to be comfortable with sub-object modification to do this.

Using these techniques you may sculpt quite an acceptable generic torso. It should be given a cylindrical UVW map or surface map co-ordinates. The scale should be appropriate to the material applied.

Legs are created in a similar way by breaking them down into upper and lower sections. Make the upper section first. Start with a sphere (or capsule) of a similar diameter to the top of a leg, 20 mm. Stretch its length so that it is the equivalent of two box sections but scale its cross-section so that it is longer from the front to back than side to side. Experiment with modifications until a slightly tapered, slightly flattened capsule is made. Locate it so that the top of the leg disappears under the torso. For ease of use later on, move the object pivot to the top of the mesh, where the hip joint would be. Copy and move this to make the other upper leg. Copy each of these again but this time scale down their cross section, X and Y, leaving the length as it is. Move them down to make the lower leg, overlapping with the top leg at the knee. The pivot should also be at knee height. Each leg in both sections can now be copied and re-scaled to make arms. With properly set pivots each limb may be moved and set in different poses. Ensure that each part of the form is named and if desired grouped into parts of the body. For ease of use make each section a distinctive colour.

Depending upon the level of detail required you might also add modified spheres or other primitives for the shoulders, knees, hands and feet, buttocks and even groin. A simple full figure, seen from front and side as a mesh, and front as a textured object may look like Figure 9.3. Here, the arms and legs have been moved to suggest life.

Material may then be assigned to provide costume suggestions. Remember that if the arms and torso are to be given the same material their UVW map should be the same scale. It is also possible to import the figure into a program such as Mesh Paint, which facilitates real-time painting directly onto the object surface, much like painting a real figure. Ensure you always save the grouped mesh of every figure you make into a library file for later use. Pre-made meshes of human figures are commonly available for download from the Web, although these tend to be more oriented to a video games aesthetic than to the theatre.

There are more sophisticated ways of making figures in a modelling program. Processes such as metaballs and NURBS (Non-Uniform Rational B-Splines) both make effective organic figures but are by no means necessary for modelling for the theatre. You might like to

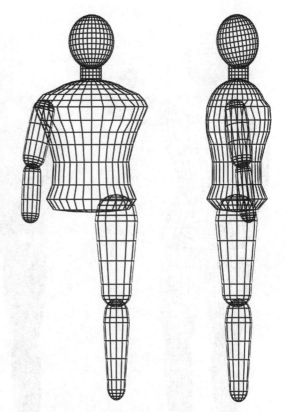

Figure 9.3 The torso with examples of upper and lower legs and arms

experiment with these tools if your software has them; see Chapter 11 on advanced modelling for an introduction to NURBS.

In order to animate the figure, or to create poses easily without having to re-align every limb each time, it will be necessary to use linking and inverse kinematics. In brief, one selects an object, for example a lower arm, and links it to a parent object, the upper arm, which is then in turn linked to the torso. In Viz this is achieved using the Select and Link icon. The torso becomes the terminator of the chain so it doesn't move when an arm moves, set in the Hierarchies Panel > IK, checking the Terminator box of the selected terminator object. When Inverse Kinematics is switched on, if you were to move the lower arm the upper arm would follow but the torso remains fixed in place. Equally, moving the upper arm will move the lower. The torso can be moved itself, thereby moving its children, but it cannot be moved by its children. Without a terminator, or fixed object, the process can become rather surreal. This is not a vital process but does aid positioning.

The process above has been described using polygonal models (i.e., 'standard' meshes). One could use NURBS, probably creating elements as polygons first and then converting to NURBS for joining the parts together. This will make a more organic form, but the added complexity (if you are not comfortable with NURBS) is probably not warranted; this is a theatre model not an animated film.

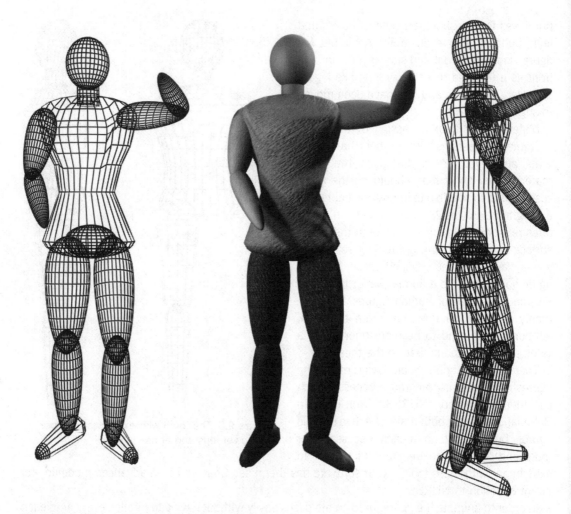

Figure 9.4 The completed human figure seen from front and side; the central form has been textured

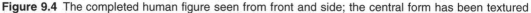

Method 2: using a figure-generating program

A number of stand-alone or plug-in programs support the generation of 3D objects to represent the human form. One of the most complex and expensive of these for the desktop market is Character Studio, which will allow for reasonably realistic animation, jointing the body properly and generating character motion based on its footprints. Once the footprints are set for a particular body size the program calculates the movements from the ground up. This is really beyond the requirements of the theatre designer. A simpler program, such as Curious Labs' Poser offers an easy interface from which the designer may select a range of body types and poses, and then position the arms, legs, head, etc. These forms have facial features and clothing detail. After being created in Poser they may be merged into your model as .dxf files. However, remember that there are frequently problems in merging such files and complex meshes such as those generated by Poser may appear to lose mesh, becoming less anatomical! This problem can frequently be solved by ensuring that all the faces have their normals pointing out from the mesh. A normal tells the computer which side is out. If it thinks a surface is facing in, it will not render it. However, this problem seems to be diminishing with every new release of the software. A simple way to scale figures or other objects after importing them is to create a simple primitive such as a box or cylinder of the height that you require. Apply a uniform scale to the imported object so that it matches your place-holder. This will ensure its proper size.

Poser figures provide reasonably realistic, flexible and easy forms. It is worth noting that a rendering of a figure such as one made in Poser and set with neutral colours may be imported into a paint program and used as the template for a costume design.

A free working demo of Poser is available to download from Curious Lab's Web site, http://www.curiouslabs.com. Other software that deals with figures includes the cheap and cheerful Digipeople by Digimation Inc. and People for People.

Method 3: using cut-outs or opacity maps

This process has its nearest equivalent in the card cut-out of the conventional model and is a very suitable method if you wish to illustrate the theatricality of your model. It allows for the easy incorporation of existing costume designs into the model but does not allow for realistic animation. The process, which was covered in detail in Chapter 6 on materials, has four stages: selecting an appropriate image of a figure; modifying the image in a paint program; making a flat surface in the modelling program and applying the image to the flat surface as an opacity and texture material. This process requires your modelling software to support opacity maps, also known as transparency maps. Examples can be seen in Chapter 6, Figures 6.15 (of a statue rather than a living character) and 6.16.

If you wish the lights to cast a shadow of the human form (rather than of the box that the map was applied to), then the lighting has to use raytraced shadows. Standard shadow maps will cast the shadow of the box as if none of it was transparent. Naturally, the light also has to be reasonably straight on to the cut-out for this to work, because if it were coming at an angle the shadow would be distorted. Remember that a cut-out such as this needs to be perpendicular to the line of the camera in order to work effectively.

The choice of an obviously sketched image for the cut-out can emphasize the fact that this is an exploratory model rather than an attempt to deceive the viewer that this is a 'photograph' or exact representation of the end result.

This opacity map technique may be used to create a variety of other cut-out type images and is an extremely useful feature for including existing images in your design and cutting down on the construction of time-consuming and memory-hungry polygons. When you can control the viewing position you can convincingly use this approach for almost all objects in a scene but a camera moving around the space will expose the illusion. We have usefully used opacity maps to represent crowds in animation, you have to ensure that the cut-out is always parallel to the camera plane and this can be achieved by rotating it when it is not on camera.

Other methods

A recent development in the architectural modelling market has been the launch of RPC from Archsoft, a plug-in for 3D Studio Max and Viz, with future plans for support of other modelling programs. The libraries contain images of real people or any other 3D object, either static or moving, which may be viewed from any position around the Z axis. A place-holder (a non-renderable object) is located in a scene and, when rendered, will appear to be 3D, that is when it is seen from the appropriate angle. Since they are photographed at eye level they are of little use when viewing a scene from much above 30° to the horizontal. Simpler versions have only a limited number of viewing positions and the render will include the image from the nearest available location. The drawback of these, aside from the cost of buying the libraries, is that for architectural purposes only contemporary figures are needed, hence there is a lack of historical characters. We understand that services are being started that will provide the same product from the customer's photographs, so theoretically it would be possible to include your own costumed actors in these scenes.

Once a model is made and rendered as a still image or animation it is possible to include video of live actors using a process not dissimilar to the opacity map. This is an advanced technique of limited use to the theatre designer. However, it deserves a brief overview. The actor needs to be filmed from the same camera position in the Z plane as the model. You must use the same focal length lens placed in front of a distinctive single colour screen (green or blue is often used) and the actor must not be wearing any clothes of that colour. Green or blue blocks can stand in for props, chairs, tables, etc. The video and rendered 3D model then need to be imported into a video editing program, which allows for colour separation overlay. Here, the two images are overlaid and the coloured background is removed from the video, leaving the moving actor on the digital set. Needless to say any digital animation should not include camera movement unless it is paralleled by real-world camera movement.

Summary

Whatever process is chosen it is important to decide how the people will fit into the scheme of design management. Cut-outs and opacity maps neatly cross over from costume design in a paint program to the model, whereas meshes may work more easily the other way round by exporting a rendered form as a .jpg into a paint program for costume detailing. Very realistic forms, such as the use of real people, may assist publicity images but it may give a false impression in an otherwise exploratory model. Figures for animation must be more complex and the creation of these is more time-consuming than for still figures. In this case many rules about character animation need to be followed.

It is always useful to keep characters, from whatever source, on separate layers from the rest of the design and it is imperative to ensure proper scaling for your model. The use of meshes, either self-made or imported, will create a lot of complex geometry; this may potentially slow down the re-draw times and make editing difficult. It might be sensible to hide them during some parts of the process, either using the display function or the layer controls. It is certainly wise to lock their layer once they are created.

10

Composition, cameras, rendering and resolution

As has already been described, rendering is the process by which the computer creates a detailed image of a view (or animation) of the scene, usually including the effect of light, textures and reflections, all of which are not generally shown in the interactive part of the modeller. It is the means to check the detail and effect of models as you make them and produce the final images for showing to the production team. More importantly the creation, placement and use of cameras is a very important tool for understanding the dynamics of how a scene will be viewed, a vital part of the design process. When one is composing a render one is also considering the composition of the whole design.

We shall now consider some practical details about rendering and scene composition. When starting any render we need to consider what is its purpose, what will be the function of the final image. The image may need to show objects clearly and accurately so that alignments and sight-lines may be checked. It may be designed to show the scene from a number of places around the auditorium, it may be designed to sell an atmosphere or moment. In other words the rendered image may be analytical (even critical, seeking to identify weaknesses) or dynamic and persuasive.

A render taken from any orthographic viewport (top, front, side) will tend to be analytical, it will represent the scene using a parallel projection and thus will tend to look more like a working schematic than a dynamic, lived-in space (see Figure 10.1). It is also quite likely that the rendering engine will not render certain effects, such as fog, on an orthographic view. These views therefore may be used to check alignments and arrangements and will simply provide a clearer, more detailed view than a working viewport. It may also be that outcomes from these renderings are used to provide the workshop with construction information. The nature of this kind of outcome will probably mean that rendering from these views uses fairly even lighting so that details may be seen (but not too flat to appear 2D). In these instances the default lighting will probably provide a very suitable option, but this can be augmented. A well set-out three-point cover with light from one side being brighter than light from the other will do well.

A render taken from a perspective, or better still custom camera view, may be either analytical or evocative, usually both towards the end of a project.

A camera object is placed in a scene a little like a spotlight. In Viz a target camera or free camera may be chosen, the former being pointed by moving a target object, the latter pointed by moving and rotating the camera object. We favour the target camera (in Viz, Create > Camera). Once the camera and its target are located the lens size (or field of view, both functions of each other) may be chosen, the camera moved, orbited and panned and, of course, a viewport established that sees the scene from the camera's position. Once the viewport is set up (opposite click over the Viewport Label and select Camera) the camera view may be manipulated via the viewport navigation tools. Note that you should not edit geometry from a camera view; in most cases you will not be given the option.

There may of course be multiple cameras in a scene, perhaps positioned in the centre of the auditorium, one at each extremity seat, one at the stage manager's desk, etc. Of course, the more cameras there are the more complex the scene is to work in, so it may be preferable simply to create one and move it.

Focal lengths and framing

The focal length of the lens really specifies how wide the camera's field of view is – the shorter the focal length the wider the field of view. However, as the field of view becomes wide the perspective begins to distort rather too much, looking rather unnatural. A long focal length (of 85 mm or more) is like a telephoto lens: it can offer a close-up on objects while the camera is some distance away and, rather than distorting perspective, a long focal length tends to minimize it.

In general of course a theatre designer is mimicking the way an audience member will see a design, although there are always reasons for wider or narrower views. A person has a peripheral range of view that allows us to roughly identify forms across an arc of almost 180°. However, we make little sense of images across so wide a field and certainly cannot focus on them. A field of view of about 40° comes close to mirroring human vision when we are focused on an object or scene, and this is achieved with a 50 mm lens, but anything as wide as 55° (35 mm) will not look too unrealistic if you are imagining an audience member taking full view of a stage. The only reason to use a lens narrower than 50 mm is to pick up on a detail for evocative 'selling' purposes. It is unwise to over-use impossible camera angles and fields of view since this will misrepresent the product both to yourself and the director. Since the location of audience members is a given we can use a standard 50 mm lens to appreciate their field of view from various seats in the auditorium.

Low camera positions, and indeed low audience positions, will offer a view of the design quite different from high ones. From below, the floor may well not be seen, instead scenic objects stand out against back walls, cycloramas or even blackness. There is something monumental about the setting, it may even feel as if it towers over you as you look up from the pit; see Figure 10.2. Frequently, objects are seen from unnatural angles, making them somewhat strange. It is dynamic, powerful theatre. Often, of course, the lower view will also be a close view, increasing the sense of presence on stage, and restricting the field of view. The design is not seen in context but rather as strange, almost abstract, dominating forms. People may be seen to be more isolated.

A viewer higher up and usually further away will see more, and therefore will see objects and performers in the context of each other, and will often see them against a floor. Backgrounds will be smaller and a slightly more natural view will be offered (we are more used to seeing most things from above rather than below). This gives the audience a more distance-critical perspective, seeing 'the whole' from a safe and familiar place, often with audience visible between them and the stage. The dynamic of the relationship is very different and the camera gives the designer access to these differences. Camera placement is not simply about viewing a design for presentation, it is an active part of the design process.

It is tempting to place a camera targeted directly at centre stage, and certainly this will give a fairly full view of the scene. However, the audience will tend to be focused on either the point of action in a scene or on the brightest part of the scene (the two will normally be the same), thus it makes sense to focus the camera at that point. And here we identify a problem. These renderings will tend to be lifeless visions of toy boxes, they do not have the energy of a live performance, and this metaphysical or abstract quality can create a great absence in the images. There are ways to cheat this absence of life and the following are worth considering:

- include human figures in your model; this is extremely important since it gives a scene life and provides a scale reference – see Chapter 9 on peopling the stage. Figure 10.2 illustrates the advantages of using a human form;
- make use of dynamics of line if appropriate. Rather than framing a shot (render) neatly so that all the stage is contained within the frame and the camera focuses on centre stage, consider allowing certain elements to continue out of shot, thus creating a sense of openness or movement;
- diagonal lines create movement in the scene. If possible view the scene from a slight angle as many audience members do, thus creating diagonals and bringing a sense of energy. This is of course the reason why many designs have their main units on an angle to the front of the stage and auditorium, or why thrust auditoria are favoured;
- use lighting to full effect to create atmosphere and to reveal sculptural forms; this will normally mean bringing in light somewhat from the sides rather than the front;
- allow the edges of the stage and upper levels of flats to fall off into darkness: lighting designers do. This darkening edge will give a sense of enclosure, focus, distance and mystery; it will also avoid showing the generally artificial-looking edges of objects;
- pay attention to effective use of materials (see Chapter 6 above);
- focus on something in the scene other than empty space – the audience will never focus on empty space.

Not all renderings are intended to communicate this metaphysical dynamic dimension. Too many done this way may obscure problems with the design, but creating a few will indicate that the space can have a life and atmosphere appropriate to the play. Needless to say these processes are particularly useful if you are considering videoing your production since these will provide important information about camera angles.

Where the design changes through the course of the production (either in spatial configuration or lighting composition) a sequential series of renderings will provide a storyboard that describes the evolution of the design. Although the process by which you create and show a storyboard will vary depending upon its purpose and your working methods, the following guidelines may be helpful.

- Where a storyboard image shows the design for an act or scene (or other distinct scenographic moment) save the model file separately from other acts or scenes. Do not be tempted to make changes in an existing model to produce the new render – inevitably you will need to go back to the previous version at some point, but if you have adjusted it confusion will ensue. Therefore, if scene 2, for example, is an adaptation of scene 1, save scene 1 and then open a new file, call it scene 2 and merge the appropriate elements from scene 1. Alternatively you can use the Save As command to save a new copy of scene 1 under a different name; you would then work on the new version. There is a more sophisticated but also more complicated method that is prone to mistakes. If you have an animation function in your software each scene or variation to the design can be saved as a new frame in an animation sequence. You need not render the sequence as an animation, simply deal with each frame as a complete design. However, unless you have a good grasp of the implication of making changes to a scene in an animated sequence this method is best left alone.

- Always clearly label each rendering when it is saved as an image file.
- Unless you are intending to show different points of view, render each image from the same position with the same focal length lens. Since the model does not exist in real form in front of us it may be quite hard to orientate oneself to the image if the point of view has moved and the design itself has changed. Since there may be no fixed reference points it may be hard to understand the changes and orientation.
- Render each image to the same size/resolution. Changes in resolution may affect the clarity of the image, making changes, particularly to lighting, difficult to compare.

Figure 10.1 A rendering of the front of the table scene, using default lighting. The scene is flat and gives little impression of the dynamics of performance (note, although this is the front orthographic view you can see the table top since the floor is on a slight rake)

- Include human figures to illustrate how each moment of the scenography is used. Indeed, a storyboard may be far more about the changing relationship of the performers to a space than about the changes to the space itself.
- You might think about showing this sequence of image in a presentation program such as PowerPoint, in which a keystroke will advance from one image to the next. Text and music can also be included.

Rendering environment and effects

Your software may provide added effects that can be introduced when rendering, particularly (sometimes only) from a camera or perspective viewport. We have already considered volume light (an atmosphere effect), which is perhaps the most often used, bringing an architectural element to

Figure 10.2 The same scene lit as described in the previous chapter. Atmosphere has been turned on and it is viewed from below and to one side (stage left). These new angles, with the addition of a human figure, give the scene a necessary theatrical energy and focus

the lighting. General fog is a simpler version whereby fog fills the entire scene (at specified density and depth) but is not tied to a light. This is adequate for uniformly lit scenes but will rarely work to advantage in theatre design where there are areas of darkness. One use of general fog can be to fade a scene to black in the distance. A volume fog is similar to volume light, but in this case the fog is assigned to a gizmo object (Create > Helpers > Atmospheric Apparatus); once assigned, the fog is 'contained' within the gizmo. Of all of the atmosphere effects settings, volume light is certainly the most useful to theatre. In Viz these effects are set from (among other places) Rendering > Environment.

Of the other rendering effects perhaps one that affects the depth of field is most useful. This effect simulates the blur that occurs to objects in front of and behind the focal point of the scene. It is by no means essential to a design, but in an image that is intended to convey a sense of action and movement it can be a useful aid.

When rendering it is usually possible to turn off atmosphere and effects to speed up the process.

Resolution

When rendering an image you will have to specify how big it is in terms of its pixels (the dots that make up an image). We have already considered the theory of resolution in Chapter 3 on hardware, so now the practical application – how big should you make the image? This question can be answered when considering what the image is to be used for. Several guidelines can be applied:

- the higher the resolution the longer it will take to render;
- the higher the resolution the more detailed the final image may be (unless you have to compromise the resolution in order to display it);
- the higher the resolution the larger the image can stand to be, i.e., if the image is to be projected via data projector or colour slide it will need a higher resolution than if it is going to remain on a computer monitor;
- too low a resolution will make an image indistinct, too high a resolution may show errors of modelling material (not of design);
- generally, unless you are aiming for projection of print, keep the resolution within the resolution of the monitor so that it can be shown one image pixel per monitor pel (dot);
- images with low contrast, fewer colours, softer tones, faded forms, etc., will generally need higher resolution than images with bold contrasting forms.

Thus if you are rendering an image simply to have a look at it while you work, then render it to a comfortable size to view within your monitor and of a size that renders quickly, probably 640 × 480. Indeed, this size will be suitable for most designer audit purposes. The resolutions of 720 × 540 and 800 × 600 also serve on-monitor viewing well since in general they will be within the boundaries of any monitor they are viewed on, and show enough detail to offer a convincing image (indeed higher than video). Once resolutions of 1024 × 768 and above are reached it is likely that the image may be reduced for showing on a monitor, which can create problems of clarity – the other alternative is only to see part of the image at any one time, scrolling across it to see specific sections.

It is, of course, quite possible to render an image to a larger size than the monitor can support, though to see it, as above, you will have to reduce it or scroll across it.

If the image is to be projected or printed the resolution will need to be higher than if it stays on the monitor. The resolution for print will normally depend upon the size of the final image, since a print is made by putting dots on paper (measured in dots per inch (dpi), an annoying use of units for metric users). Print methods can utilize a huge range of dpi so there is no hard and fast rule. A moderate print quality begins at 150 dpi, but many printers can now print well over 1000 dpi (often more than necessary). Since it is always a good idea to keep the number of pixels the same as the number of dots to be printed, we can work out a sensible print resolution formula along these lines:

> If the print is to be of moderate quality, say for circulation to the director for comment, a print resolution of 300 dpi (118 dots per centimetre) should be more than satisfactory (150 dpi would normally be fine). Assume you need the image to fill the centre of a sheet of A4 paper, thus about 20 cm × 15 cm, the required resolution will therefore be 2360 × 1770. Size multiplied by print resolution per unit; i.e., 118 dots per centimetre × 20 cm.

An image to be printed for publicity purposes may well require a far higher resolution, but may often be smaller, thus perhaps needing the same overall resolution. Since these large images take a long time to render, particularly if reflections or fog are present, it is frequently worth setting off a high resolution render of a scene at a suitable work break, knowing that a render with a resolution in the region of 2400 × 1800 will suit all but the most exacting purposes, and will therefore be available if called upon.

Finally if the image is to be turned into a 35 mm transparency for projection, the resolution will need to be very high (generally 3027 × 2048) to sustain the expanded image size.

The problem of credence – reading the digital model

The rendered digital model, even an early exploratory one, may look like a moment of theatre (if effort is put into its realism). The realism or credibility of the digital image creates a paradoxical problem. Despite the contingency and plasticity of the digital design, the image that it presents may be so convincing that it seems to leave no space for alternatives. If the political problem of naturalist scenography was that it left no space for change, offering a complete picture of how things are, then surely the same monolithic finality is offered by the photo-realistic rendering on the computer screen, even more so if it is projected to a large scale in a conference room. Once an image is so complete and credible, how might we engage with it and critique it? If this stage can be reached early in the process, are we not confronted with an under-developed design masquerading as the complete and final image? In order to maintain exploratory simplicity and disposability, Beardon's Visual Assistant project consciously resisted the production of complete and realistic images. However, Beardon also notes the necessity of being able to produce work within a believable theatrical world (Beardon and Enright, 1999a: 7). There is no easy answer to this conundrum, though we must be aware of the potency of the image and learn how to read it.

Let us compare the relationship of digital model to the stage with that of the card model to the stage. The card model undoubtedly has more obvious interference and requires specific decoding; some of those codes are quite clear and generally well known. Scale is perhaps the easiest of these and, while difficult to unscramble precisely, most theatre makers are skilled in seeing objects for what they represent, multiplying their size by 25. However, scale creates certain less easily overcome problems. Fabrics do not hang the same way in reduced scale and thus are either represented through the use of different material, held in shape with gesso or sometimes they are verbally excused. Paint techniques do not always scale down effectively either and might be represented in model by an approximation, while a more precise simulation is set up in full scale alongside the model. It is rare for even the most proficient model maker to produce an object that precisely mimics an industrially produced artefact. When the referent is known the translation is easy. A model Bauhaus chair, for example, will rarely be a precise copy but its decoding is straightforward. The model simply refers to a piece of furniture that will be bought or borrowed. The situation is complicated when the referent is unknown.

The propensity toward environments that include decay and roughness as an element of their visual language is, in part, determined by the propensity of the modelling medium. The frequent appearance of this idiom can largely be attributed to the need to give history and habitation to an environment, coupled with the textural richness that it provides; nonetheless, the techniques and materials common to conventional model making are sympathetic to a slightly rough visual metaphor. It is possibly the case that this look does not demand such a precise decoding because it does not use a language of visual precision but of designed chaos. Random factors and imperfections become intentionally integrated and consciously produced in the design. In addition, such rich use of textures perhaps compensates for the general absence of the atmospheric contribution of light and possibly framing architecture from the final model, an absence which plays a major role in the decoding process. The point is that creator and viewer of conventional designs implicitly know that they are working in a form that approximates the final stage version, but the designer might compensate for some of the differences by building solutions into the model and such augmentations may find their way on to stage.

The differences between a finished card model and its referent provide much of the discursive material of later design meetings. Phrases such as 'of course in scene 3 it will be lit in blue', 'that stuck-on photograph is actually a projection' or 'that element will be somewhat different when scaled up' are common, and provide a framework with which to critique the model and the design. In enquiring whether an element will translate to stage effectively, you are implicitly allowing discussion on the more fundamental merits, or otherwise, of that element. Thus, these imperfect models provide ways into the discussion of scenographic elements, their relationship to each other and their relationship to their intended execution. Furthermore, these differences clearly illustrate that the model is not the same as the performance. Its representational flaws insist that we acknowledge that a set on stage is a wholly different thing from a model and the need to account for movement, the architecture, the music and the audience is constantly present.

The major problem with decoding a digital model is that there would appear to be no problems of interference in the reading. The computer simulation moves into the territory of the photograph. It is almost, in Barthes' terms, a perfect analogon (Barthes, 1961: 17) of the reality, a message without a code. It is easy to assume that the image or animation that one is viewing is that which will appear on stage. The difference between computer image and stage is masked by the program's in-built tendency to hide the imperfections of its representation. In the sense that it inclines toward the photograph it assumes the character of truth, albeit subject to the designer's manipulation, in the same way as a photograph is subject to the editorial role of the photographer. Unlike the conventional model, it proposes that it is complete. The messy business of performance in a half-full auditorium and flickering exit lights are removed from the debate because their absence from the image is not apparent. The fact that the images are presented on a flat screen does not seem to cause many problems in terms of reading scale or depth, particularly when references such as human figures are included. Perhaps our familiarity with the similar window of the television screen enhances the credibility of a digital model. The apparent coincidence of screen and stage seems to remove the topic of difference from discussion. It is therefore not the difference between model and execution that forms the subject of critique but the difference between what is currently proposed and what else might be proposed. These alternative models may be substantially similar to each other or radically different but the ability to swiftly construct alternate worlds potentially focuses the discussion of difference on the appropriateness of the world to the dramatic text, rather than the difference between model and production context. However, unless such alternative worlds are forthcoming the apparent lack of difference somewhat guillotines discussion.

11

Advanced modelling

In the chapter on basic modelling (Chapter 5) we considered the creation of primitives and their modification using standard deformations and transformations. We also considered creating Boolean objects. In this chapter we are going to introduce:

- creating 3D objects from 2D drawings using lathe and extrude commands;
- creating arrays;
- creating NURBS surfaces.

Using lines and shapes

So far we have worked with 3D geometry that is represented as a wire frame and is visible when rendered. The process that we are about to undertake begins with shapes, which are (generally) 2D forms. The term 'shape' usually refers both to a closed set of lines (a square, a circle), a line (straight or curved) or an open connected series of line segments. Viz offers two types of shape: splines and NURBS. For the moment we will concentrate on splines.

By clicking Shapes from the Tab panel, or from the command panel Create > Shapes > Splines you will have access to shapes such as line, arc, rectangle, star, etc.

Of these, three commands create open line shapes (Line, Helix and Arc), and seven create closed line shapes (Rectangle, Star, Ngon, Circle, Donut, Ellipse, Text). The eleventh shape command is Section, which makes a shape from a specified cross-section of an object.

All but the line tool and section tool are quite simple to use, and create their shape in a straightforward manner – we will follow this in detail below. However, the line function is less easy to pick up. In essence the user creates vertices that are connected by a line, but the manner of the creation of the vertices (click and drag, click, etc.) and the options selected from the creation dialog box will allow for the creation of complex curved shapes. There is no substitute for experimenting with drawing a series of lines using different settings. Enlarge one viewport, Create > Shapes > Spline > Line, and examine the options in the Create parameters. The Interpolation parameters set the way the curve is calculated (adaptive is the most efficient) and whether the line can be rendered, but it is the Creation Method parameters that are the more important. The Initial creation method specifies how the line behaves if a vertex is created by a mouse click, the Drag group specifies how the line behaves if you drag a vertex. The effect of Smooth and Bezier methods will result in organic non-symmetrical curves, but the control over these curves takes a little practice to master. Before embarking on the exercises below it is worth creating some lines.

Making an 'S' shaped line

To explore the use of the line spline it is worth taking some time to understand the different creation methods.

Method 1: Create > Spline > Line and set the Creation parameters to Initial: Corner, Drag: Corner. At its simplest this setting will create straight lines connected at vertex points. In a viewport click – release – click, etc., to place vertices to indicate a rectilinear S shape; using this method you will get a squared result looking like LED letters. Right click in the viewport to exit create mode. In order to achieve a more rounded, organic shape we will fillet each corner. Select the shape and choose Modify or, from the Modifiers tab, select Edit Spline (by now you probably realize that there are always several ways to skin a cat!). We are intending to fillet the shape at each vertex location, thus we are operating on (or selecting) vertices, therefore at the Selection level in the Modify command panel select the (icon) dots that represent vertices, or choose Sub-object > Vertex if working in an older program. You will now be able to select a vertex, rather than the entire shape, and edit it. Select a vertex and then scroll down the Modify panel to Geometry. Select Fillet and adjust the fillet value; you will see the corner become curved as the fillet radius increases. This tool can be used to create very precisely specified curved (filleted) corners. Figure 11.1 illustrates this.

You should also observe that, while you have the selection level set to vertex, you could move and rotate any selected point independently of the others. It is also possible to insert new vertices on a segment by selecting the segment level, and inserting a 'break' on any segment.

Method 2: create a line, as before, but this time set Initial to Corner and Drag to Smooth. Try to create an S shape. This time you will find that if you click for the first point, let go, click for the second but then hold the button down and drag the mouse, you will create a curve. Let go of the button and the curve will continue. Click the mouse again to fix it. This takes some practice to control. Again, once this shape is completed, opposite click to finish the shape. You may now edit or move vertices or segments by modifying the object at the vertex or segment (sub-object) level.

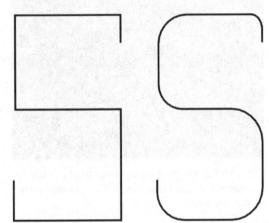

Figure 11.1 A line made into an S shape using corner creation method; the line on the right has had a fillet modifier applied to each corner/vertex

Finally, make the S shape using Initial: Corner and Drag: Bezier. The effect is similar to the smooth version above, although the dragged curve behaves a little differently. When you modify the vertices of a bezier curve it is also possible to adjust its 'handles' (you will see two squares appear either side of a selected vertex); moving these will adjust the tension or curve at the vertex. Bezier splines can therefore have the tension in the curve adjusted after construction.

A further experiment could be undertaken using the smooth initial setting. The important point is that you should become familiar with these creation methods; any one of them may be used to create a line needed to make a larger object or shape. In the exercises below you should generally choose your preferred method, although the first exercise, making a book, will introduce one other.

Making a book

The first practical exercise will be to use simple straight lines and predictable curves (arcs) to create a shape that will be turned into an object. In this exercise therefore we will not make a single curved line (as above) but add arc segments and line segments together to create a more complex line (an outline in this case). Once we have the outline we will loft it, or extrude it to make a 3D shape. Lofting or extruding is the equivalent to drawing a section or plan of an object and then 'growing' it out of that line. Although an obvious function for this process would be the creation of a run of flats, we will use it to make a book (to lie on the Shaker table). The book will be closed and will look like a rather large antique volume. Figures 11.2 to 11.5 illustrate this project.

Imagine, therefore, a book lying on the table in front of you, its outside front cover facing upwards. We can consider it to be made of two component parts, the card covers and spine, and the paper

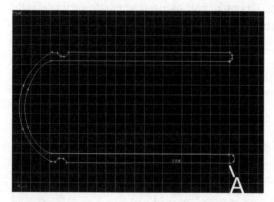

Figure 11.2(a) The closed shape that makes the section of the book cover. The starting point is indicated

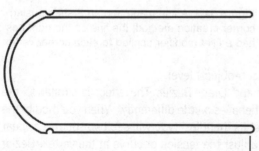

Starting point

Figure 11.2(b) A clearer schematic of the section of the book cover, see also Figure 11.2(a)

pages. The former element is the larger, and in front view or section might look like a U on its side. The pages are smaller, sitting within the cover. The book will be about 150 mm wide and 60 mm high (relative to the front view); exact precision is not important. Set units to millimetres.

The book cover should be created in the front viewport, which is best maximized. Zoom in so that the origin 0,0 is at the bottom left of the screen, and the screen X axis (which in Viz is also world X) offers at least 200 mm. Figures 11.2 and 11.3 show how we will create the section of the book cover for extrusion.

Snap Settings need to be set to snap to the end point of a line. Thus, select Endpoint only. The Snap function should be switched on with the toggle button, bottom centre of Viz.

The grid should be switched on (the grid toggle towards the bottom of the screen, or opposite click over the viewport label and select Show Grid). The grid should show lines every 10 mm, set this in Customize > Drafting Setting > Grid and Snap Settings > Home Grid. Open the Create > Shapes > Splines command. We are going to make the shape from lines and arcs, and each spline we make will be connected to the previous one, thus making a closed shape that should look something like Figure 11.2(a) and 11.2(b). Be sure that the tick box next to Start New Shape is off; as all of our lines will be part of one shape we will only click Start New Shape when the outline is complete.

Select Line and adjust the creation methods to be Initial: Corner, Drag: Corner. This will create straight lines with sharp corners, which is what this project needs. In the front view click the mouse to set the first vertex at X200, Y0 (viewport axes). That is to say the first point should be point A as identified in Figure 11.2(a). Move the mouse 150 units to the left (the relative co-ordinate will be −150) and click at X50, Y0. Once this second point has been created we must complete that section by opposite clicking (you will note the line is continuing until the opposite click is applied). A straight line has been drawn.

We will now insert the arced recess that is found on many volumes where the cover meets the spine. Select the Arc tool and make sure that the creation method is End-End-Middle. Click over the end of the line that has just been drawn and hold the button down. The Snap function (which should be on) should activate to snap the cursor exactly over the end of the previous line. Move the cursor about 5 mm to the left and let go of the mouse button. Moving the mouse will now generate a curve. When you are happy with the curve (which should arc up the screen) click again. The curve is created. For ease we will insert a short straight line again from the end (snap) of the arc to X40, Y0. From the end of this line an arc needs be made to represent the spine, thus click over the end of the previous line and hold the mouse down and then move the cursor up to X40, Y80. Let go of the button and move the mouse to create the arc. If you've kept to the dimensions so far a radius of about 42 mm should be about right. Keep adding lines and arcs until the section of the book looks like the illustration; once you have completed the top edge of the front cover you will add an arc (the edge of the cover) and repeat the shape on the inside. Make the cover about 4 mm thick. The final point on the last arc will finish over the first point created.

Throughout this whole procedure we have been working on the same shape – we have never selected Start New Shape, and each point was started directly over the previous, so there should be no gaps. If you have not cleared the Start New Shape box you will have made ten distinct lines.

Opposite click in the viewport to exit the creation mode, activate four views (Top, Left, Front, Perspective), select the shape and name it 'book cover'. If you are unhappy with the shape you can modify it just as you would any other object (see the chapter on basic modelling, Chapter 5). Equally you can move any of the component vertices or segments (connecting lines). You achieve this in Viz by selecting the object and then, on the Modify panel, set the selection level to be Sub-object: Vertex or Sub-object: Segment. With either of these selected one may move, scale or rotate vertices or segments. You also have access to the tension handles so the parameters of the curve may be changed.

Once the shape is set we will extrude it into an object. Select the shape (making sure that sub-object is off) and activate the modify menu. Select Extrude from the Modifier List. This is also available from the Modelling tab, which will provide an icon with the fly-out title Extrude. Once this icon is selected you enter the parameters in the Modify command panel.

In the Extrude parameters set the amount to 280 mm. The book cover will become three dimensional. Figure 11.3 illustrates this. The other parameters should be kept at their default settings for this exercise, though you should ensure that the operation has capped the start and end (tick boxes).

Figure 11.3 The extruded book cover as it might be seen in the perspective viewport if the view is set to show a shaded image. This example has had a dark grey colour assigned

Figure 11.4 The book made from extruding two shapes, one for the cover and one for the pages. This image is viewed from a perspective viewport

We will now create the pages by a similar method. In the front viewport (maximized) create another set of lines, using the cover as a reference, that suggest the section of pages in a closed old book. The curve of the pages should perhaps be little irregular, and you might try a curved line with bezier curves rather than an arc. Alternatively, you could move the vertices to create an irregular curve. Once constructed these lines should be extruded to an amount a little less than the book (270), and then the pages moved to sit inside the cover.

You should now have the basics of a hard-back book with a single object representing the pages, see Figure 11.4.

Warning: there will now be a large number of polygons in the scene so editing processes may be a little slow.

Embossing the book – using fonts to chisel forms

One of the shape functions available in many programs is the generation of text shapes, a closed spline in the shape of letters using specified fonts. When extruded these therefore become text objects, which can be used as any object might.

Create > Shapes > Spline > Text or, from the Tab panel, Shapes > Text (icon). The parameters allow you to choose the font type, letter spacing and size. Enter the text in the box provided and click in the creation viewport. Choose a font (Times New Roman will work), set the size to 50, and enter the title of your book; keep it simple since the next stage will create more geometry. In the top viewport click over the centre of your book to locate the text. Modify the text to Extrude it by about 10 mm.

In the front or left view, position the text so that it crosses into the top of the front cover by about 3 mm but does not go all the way through it – it should act like a stamp. We will now Boolean the text out of the book. However, on this occasion, we will want to keep a copy of the text operand to provide an inlay for the cover.

We shall now use the text as a Boolean tool to emboss the cover of the book (this could be done as a bump map to save polygons, but that's not what this exercise is about). Select the book and then Create a Compound Object > Boolean. Before picking the text operand to emboss the book cover set the effect of the Boolean to copy rather than move the operand. Check the Boolean function will remove B from A and pick the text as Operand B. The text will not disappear since a copy was made in the Boolean process. Opposite click in the viewport to clear the Create function and select the remaining text object (move it up if you wish to see that the Boolean did work). If this is scaled down so that it is only 1 mm high it can be embedded in the embossed text space, thus allowing for a different colour and texture from the book cover. It could perhaps be gold. If you choose to do this you will be working with a fairly complex object, so modifications will be slow on an older computer.

A leather texture can now be applied to the book cover, and a creamy white grained texture for the pages. The example here used the Viz textures 'Wall-cling' from the Wall library for the pages (totally unmodified, the stucco effect was fine for the paper) and a modified 'Skin-Orange Leather' for the cover itself. The latter was modified in a paint program; the map was imported, the whole image copied and pasted below the original, thus doubling the vertical size (height on screen),

effectively undertaking a simple tiling. This double map was then retouched with a clone tool to move some scratches around and a 'darken' tool to age the edges. The new map and material were re-named to avoid writing over the original. The map was applied to the book cover using a UVW box map, scaled to fit the book cover object. This will compress the map for the spine face (being a different size) so it will not really appear to repeat. Adapted organic materials are effective for a distressed or aged look. Save the file.

The book may now be 'placed' on the shaker table by merging the table object into the book scene (or *vice versa*). This is achieved by opening the file into which you wish to merge the object and selecting File > Merge, then navigating to the target scene and selecting the objects required. The problems that you might encounter in merging are:

Figure 11.5 The book made from two extruded shapes. The text was embossed with a Boolean function. The material was standard leather edited in a paint program to give it a more distressed look

- the scenes use different units, thus a merged object will be too big or small. Advanced planning solves this, if all scenes are created with the same units (millimetres, ideally) there will be no problem, otherwise re-size or scale the merged object;
- merged objects share the same name as objects in the original scene. Usually overcome in advance by careful naming strategies. You should have the opportunity to re-name as you merge;

- merged objects have materials with the same name but different properties. The solution is to always re-name customized materials.

More complex extrusions

The previous example illustrated a simple extrusion; the original shape was simply 'lofted' in a straight line to make an object. A large number of more sophisticated versions of this are available. We will simply consider a few here.

As we observed in the chapter on basic modelling (Chapter 5) a large number of objects (in some ways conceivably any object) can be made by assembling primitives; a pillar illustrated the point. The extrude function can work in much the same way: an object can have a cross-section taken in a number of places and each of those sections extruded and then assembled. There are, however, slightly more complex extrusions that may speed the process.

Bevel and Bevel Profile scale the original shape towards or away from its pivot as it extrudes, see Figure 11.6. In Viz the former requires numerical values for the bevel, while the latter uses a shape as a template – it is chosen as an operand during the bevel process. The simple Bevel command is adequate for fairly straightforward variations, but the Bevel Profile can make quite complex extrusions. One has to take care constructing the profile operand, making sure that the profile does

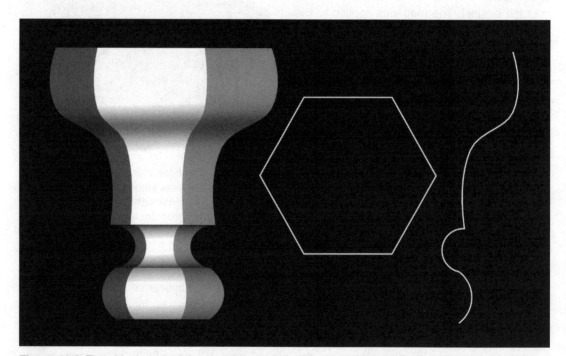

Figure 11.6 The object on the left was made by Bevel Profile, extruding the hexagon (centre) using the spline (right) as a bevel template

not cross the centre of the shape. The commands are chosen from the Modelling tab, or the Modify panel (from the Modifier List). If Bevel Profile is used do not delete the profile splines, or the effect will be lost.

These functions are useful for symmetrical extrusions and represent pillars, pots, pedestals, furniture legs, etc., well. A circle so extruded can look like a glass or a pot. We will return to a different method of making these objects by lathing them.

Lofting on a path – a chandelier

So far we have explored the extrusion of one shape along a straight path, albeit with the object's section scaled as it builds (extrudes) along the path. Now we will both change the shape and use a curved path. Of course, one could keep the same shape on a curved path, or change shapes on a straight path. Please read this whole exercise and check illustrations before attempting it. Figure 11.8 illustrates the finished object, Figure 11.7 illustrates a halfway point.

We will make a simple two-tier chandelier with swan-neck type arms and a hub made of simple primitive shapes. Select the Front viewport and maximize it (for visual illustration of the following instructions see Figure 11.7). First we need to outline the path, that is to say the profile of the arms. Using Arc and Line tools (ensuring that you are working on the same shape and not starting a new one) create the line of an arm (see Figure 11.7). The overall width should be

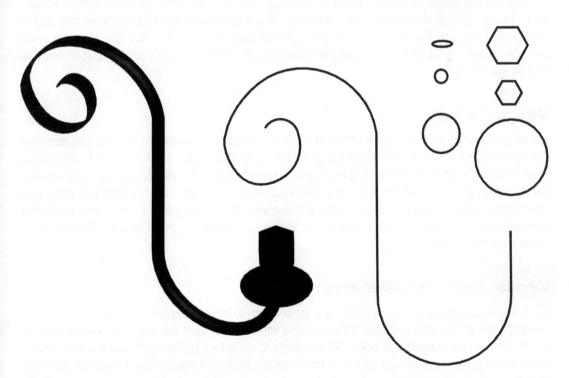

Figure 11.7 Chandelier arm: on the left is the complete, lofted arm; on the right is the swan-neck path (made as a spine) and the shapes that were lofted along the path

about 400 mm. Once that is done we will detail each shape that appears along the path. Our arm will transform from a hexagonal section candle holder to a circular section main arm, eventually becoming a flattened circle towards the inner end of the path. Create a series of shapes including a large circle, a medium circle and a small circle; a small and large hexagon and a small ellipse. Each of these should be new shapes. We will now make a loft object, placing the shapes along the path. Select the path. A loft makes a compound object, so select Create > Geometry > Compound Objects > Loft. Click Get Shape, and select the large hexagon; a hexagon will be lofted along the entire path. Now, under Path parameters advance about 4.5 per cent along the path (a yellow asterisk will appear – this proportion will depend upon the length of your path). Select the small hexagon as the next shape; the shapes on the path will scale down. Every time you put a new shape the section will transform. Following the small hexagon place the small circle at 5 per cent and again at 5.5 per cent. Place the large circle at 5.51 per cent, medium circle at 6 per cent, small circle at 6.2 per cent (all of the shapes selected so far make up the candle holder and should be on the initial straight vertical). If you want a shape to exist continuously and untransformed along a section of a path then the same shape needs to be inserted at the start and finish of those sections, thus insert the small circle again as the arm starts to curve at the top, and then finally insert the ellipse as the arm begins to spiral. Experiment with you own locations and place your shapes along the path until you have a simple chandelier arm as illustrated in Figure 11.7.

Once the loft object is created make a small cylinder or chamfered cylinder (or even sphere) from the left view, and line it up with the apex of the innermost curve of the arm; this will be where the arm joins the hub. It is not an essential part of the model, but will help the visual balance. Make a group of the arm and the joining piece. You can see this piece between arm and hub in Figure 11.8.

Making the hub

Activate all four views. The centre of this style of chandelier is a number of spheres and stretched spheres or extended primitive capsules aligned on top of each other, see Figure 11.8. You should experiment with cylinders, toruses, spheres and capsules. The upper section will be a profile bevel. Create these, ensuring that the two main sphere capsules are about 100 mm diameter (the upper one a little smaller) and that the outer edge of the lower main sphere just intersects with the joining element of the arm. For the top section of the hub use a circle and a bevel profile template. Group all hub objects as hub.

Circular array – the other arms

Once one arm is complete we can create a circular array. It is probably best to do this in the top viewport. Isolate the arm and then zoom out and reposition so that the arm is off-centre with the candle holder end towards the edge. We are going to have four further copies of the arm created automatically, arrayed around a central cylinder object. Firstly we need to set the centre, which we will do by moving the object pivot to the place where we want the chandelier centre to be. On the command panel select Hierarchies > Pivot and click Effect Pivot Only. Now select and move the pivot of the arm group so that it is exactly over the centre of the main capsule in the hub (about 100 mm directly to the left (negative X) of the inner edge of the arm). Deselect Effect Pivot Only, but keep the object selected.

Select from the menu bar Tools > Array and enter values for a Total rotation of 360° around Z axis; make sure the Re-orient box is checked. Set the total number of the Count to 5. You can also set this by incremental rotation, each therefore being 72° round Z. Note this will not work if the pivot has not been moved (see above), or if the array is rotating around the wrong axis. The array will create five arms (original plus copies) rotated around a centre.

The chandelier has two tiers, the arms of the higher tier being a little smaller and closer together than the lower. We could either select, copy and scale the entire array, or select copy and scale one arm group, position and then array it. The former is quicker, the latter more accurate. Select an arm (the original will be at the easiest alignment), clone it and move it to the position of the next tier, keeping move constraints on. Scale the arm so that it is visually lighter than the lower arms. Move it or re-set the pivot so that the inner edge connects with its capsule, and the pivot is over the centre of the hub. The arms in the upper tier need to be offset from the lower tier, so rotate the arm in the top view around its pivot Z axis by 36° (to bisect the arms below). Then a second array can be made. Group the entire object as chandelier. The 'Metal-Orange' pattern (if you are using Viz

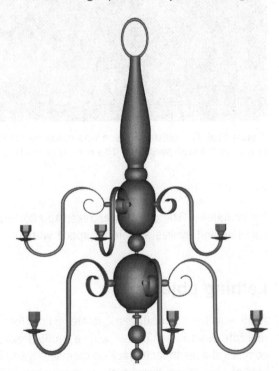

libraries) is quite an effective material, otherwise find or make a metal-based material with a brass look to it. There is no doubt that this would be a fiddly item indeed in a conventional model and will rarely be achieved to best effect.

A loft is a useful device for creating picture rails, cornices and the like; see Figure 11.9. The path is a line, following the intended line of the detail of a run of flats – this is easy to draw after the flats are constructed. The section of the architectural detail is then made using line tool to create a closed shape, and lofted on the path. If you have problems with orientation of the shape on the path try moving the shape's origin or pivot.

Figure 11.9 shows a ceiling piece with a cornice, made by lofting its section along a path. The chandelier (see above) has been 'hung' from a rose made by lathing (see below) the same outline. The chandelier was lit with three omni-lights placed among its arms. Each light had different intensities and attenuation to give a textured light. An omni-light placed halfway between floor and ceiling lit the room; this latter light was set to exclude

Figure 11.8 Chandelier seen from front viewport, thus some arms obscure others. Hub made from various primitives and extended primitives, top tear shape is a bevel-profiled circle and the arms are lofts

169

Figure 11.9 The plaster cornice was made by creating a section that was then lofted along a line indicating the wall perimeter. The rose was made with a lathe

the chandelier. The ceiling was raked to offer the audience a clearer view. A design such as this specifies and evokes an interior space without the need for flats.

Lathing objects

A lathe, as the name suggests, rotates a line (template) round its pivot, thus carving a shape. It can replicate what is achievable with a profiled extrusion of a circle, but a lathe can produce more complex shapes that cut back on themselves and is a little more predictable (to these users) for this kind of work. It also has slightly more variables in its editing process, for example it allows a variable rotation of the lathe. We shall make a vase; however this process is effective for almost any conceivable turned object, including machine parts, table legs, etc.

Using lines from the Create > Spline command create a halfsection of the vase, see Figure 11.10. This example has included an outline for the interior as well, however that will often not be necessary for theatrical models. Indeed it will also not often be necessary to create a base either, so this is included here for example only. Ensure that the line is one spline shape. Modify the spline as necessary. Move the spline pivot to a point that will become the centre of the lathed object (in the command panel – Hierarchies > Affect Pivot Only).

The object may now be lathed. In Viz lathe is applied by selecting the spline and then choosing Lathe from the drop-down Modifier List in the Modify command panel, or from the Lathe icon below the Modelling tab. Lathe parameters include rotation of lathe, capping of ends, interpolation and output. The output specifies what type of object will be produced by the Lathe function, and here we have our first view of NURBS. The Output may be selected as Mesh (the polygonal model object that we have used to date), Patch or NURBS. For most work of this kind a mesh output is fine, and theatrical models can generally be made entirely from polygonal meshes, thus the user becomes

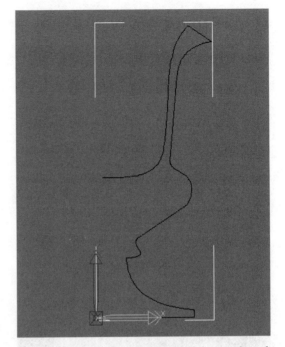

Figure 11.10 A spline, suggesting the section of a vase created in preparation for a lathe

familiar with them. Though we will continue this exercise to produce a NURBS output, more or less the same effect could be achieved with a mesh output, and the process would be simpler.

NURBS and Patch objects make models that tend to be far smoother and more easy to edit into organic or curved shapes. Lathing is one simple way to create NURBS out of splines (or NURBS curves). Adjust the Lathe parameters > Output type and render the results to see the difference. You may get an unusual effect when lathing this object, appearing to see the inside but not the outside of the object. This is remedied by selecting Flip Normals in the Creation parameters, or Render Two Sided in the Rendering dialog box. This effect is caused simply by the computer not fully 'understanding' which is the outside of a complex shape (indicated by the surface's normals).

Lathe the vase shape, setting the output to be a NURBS. Finally we need to collapse the object so that we can deal with it as a NURBS object. Select the vase (it may already be selected) and in the Modify panel opposite click over the Lathe in the Modifier Stack. From the drop-down menu select Collapse All. A prompt will inform you that you can no longer deal with the previous commands, i.e., you cannot change the shape of the line to change the shape of the vase, click OK. Now not only will the object look smooth, but it has to be edited in a different way from polygonal meshes. You may now assign a material to the vase if you wish.

Note: you could have lathed the vase with a mesh output; it would be slightly less smooth, and harder to edit to produce an organic form (see below) but the outcome would be quite acceptable for theatre modelling.

A little more about NURBS

Figure 11.11 The vase, lathed from the outline (see Figure 11.10), and output as a NURBS object

NURBS surfaces and curves are controlled by points away from their surface (almost like magnets); this means that the effect of modification tends to be less abrupt than it is with polygonal shapes and objects. A number of polygonal shapes can be converted into NURBS, and this is perhaps the easiest way to start creating NURBS surfaces.

This book cannot cover the details of NURBS modelling, other than to give one brief example. If you have made the vase above, create two torus shapes to make two handles either side; create them large enough to see them clearly. Move them so that they are just embedded in the sides of the vase (hole facing forwards). View the scene in the front viewport, as large as you can. Select a torus and then opposite click over it, and look for the Transform dialogue box (in the Default Quad menu that appears). Select Convert to: NURBS. The torus is now a NURBS object, which we shall attach to the vase NURBS object with a chamfered, natural, join. With the object selected the NURBS Modification command panel for the NURBS torus will be live. First the torus handle will be attached to the vase. Select General > Attach and click on the vase. Now select Create Surfaces > Fillet. As the cursor moves over the torus surface it turns blue, indicating it can be connected. Click and move the cursor over the pot; viable surfaces will also turn blue. Click again to make a filleted join. By varying the fillet amount, the thickness of the join may be altered; a fillet of 1 or 2 mm should be sufficient if the vase is of a standard size. Render the vase.

This is a brief introduction to NURBS; they are of enormous value, but a full introduction would take this book into far more complex territory than it is designed to go.

12

The design over time: storyboards and animations

An introduction to animation

Animation has two definitions. The first is part of the language of cinematography and represents the common understanding of the word. It relates to the technique of filming successive drawings or objects, each illustrating a small incremental change from the previous one, creating an illusion of movement. This effect works since the eye and brain hold the first image briefly, even while it is being replaced by the next; this is called persistence of vision. Provided each image is shown quickly enough the whole will appear as a seamless movement.

The second, both broader and more traditional, sense of the word means simply the state of being alive, and of moving. Animation–life–movement, in the broadest sense, can be seen in early examples of ancient cave drawings where a wild boar is depicted with eight legs. It is drawn in this way to create the impression of movement. Not only have technological developments such as computer animation widened the possibilities now available to the animator but they have facilitated the use of animation in other media, notably the Internet. It is important to remember that whilst computer animation has changed the entertainment industry, it is used in many other fields, such as space exploration, defence projects, medical research, forensics, Internet development and education: each with their own aims, formal requirements and aesthetics. The formal requirements of animation as an aid to stage design are far simpler than those of film or television presentation, and aesthetically one is being driven (hopefully) by the needs of live performance, not feature film.

A wholly separate activity, not covered by this book, is the generation of animations to be projected on stage as part of the performance event, an exciting development aided by the fall in price of reasonably high-performance data projectors. In this book, though, we are concerned with animations to aid the design process.

Animation (in both senses) for the theatre designer

Theatre design exists in time; whether apparently static or changing the scenography is seen over time, it facilitates action over time (movement) and reflects time in response to the text or themes of the piece. The designer must consider time as much as space. Look at Edward Gordon Craig, whose seemingly monolithic screens are designed to be fluid and flexible and to offset the plastic body in motion – they both move and set off movement. His woodcut 'studies for movement' (1906), and illustrations of 'steps' (1905) (both illustrated in Walton's (1983) *Craig on Theatre*) all express motion through a combination of line, human form and architecture. Although rendered as still images, movement (and stillness) are central to them.

Indeed, since the Renaissance the ability to change scenery, and the spectacle thus provided for the audience, has been a central feature of theatre. It celebrates the ability of humanity (and art) to control its world and it signifies the importance (political and cultural) of transformation. Additionally, the delight of witnessing clever or spectacular transformations has always been a crowd-pleaser, whether for the audiences of nineteenth-century pantomimes and melodramas or twenty-first-century high-tech musicals. The ability of scenery and space to change has been one of the cornerstones of scenography.

However, often in the process of producing theatre the designer is forced by their working methods to consider the design as a static space, or at best one that changes only sporadically at key and necessary moments in a performance. Ironically of course a director may be working in a rehearsal room dealing very specifically with time (and performers in time) but not necessarily with space.

In working on a project the following may be of concern to the designer:

- the changing physical setting, either in detail or in whole;
- the changing atmosphere and lighting environment;
- the changing look of characters;
- the rhythm and pace of movement and change;
- the development of theme/metaphor over time;
- the balance between motion and stillness;
- different groupings and dynamics, developing a scenography of the actor in space;
- the fact that nothing changes;
- the compression or expansion of time.

There are two ways in which a designer can explore the design in time during the design process: the storyboard and the animation. Both are in some ways related to each other. We have used the term 'animation' here to refer to any moving element(s) in the design presentation (not simply animation in the 'movie' sense); a storyboard can bring life to a design as much as a moving sequence might. Storyboards and animations have two useful, related, purposes. Firstly and most importantly they are tools with which the designer can visualize time/change, and having the means to visualize it the designer may then experiment with it – in essence they can *design* it. Secondly of course these are communication and presentation tools, devices by which the designer can illustrate to the director and production team what their intentions are. As with all aspects of design it is important to know why you are using a particular tool or approach.

The storyboard

A storyboard is a simplified animation; it illustrates key moments (or frames) from the complete drama. In a few images it sums up the scenography of two hours' passage upon the stage. It illustrates key moments in the production, traditionally as still images, often selecting one or two moments from each act or scene. Movement will generally be illustrated by showing the beginning and end states that bracket the change. In traditional approaches a storyboard may be a set of drawn or painted images, perhaps each occupying sequential small boxes on one large sheet of paper (like a cartoon strip), thus sketching the production over time in a method that is easy to see. At its most impressionistic, at the very early stages of design, these may well be scraps of found material, research images, abstract washes of colour, written metaphors, a suggestion of music. These can be quite rudimentary in presentation but the idea is to plot through the developing scenography as it changes and develops. A small series of sketches may help the designer visualize the whole project prior to embarking on detailed designs of each scene. In these early versions the designer may not illustrate the whole stage but may sketch important details, derived as much from an emotional or dramatic response as a spatial one. Generally speaking this stage is best achieved using conventional sketch methods (pen, paint, collage) as most computer systems are too cumbersome and do not allow the speed and freedom of a handmade artefact. However, a scanner and paint program can assist the process, and the Visual Assistant package, referred to in Chapter 2, is a very useful scenographic storyboard tool.

At a more advanced or complex level the storyboard may consist of a series of more fully rendered (realistic?) images. These may suggest, in some detail, costume, lighting, scenic arrangement and set dressing but, more importantly perhaps, sum up a sense of the production. Although usually created weeks or months before rehearsals begin it is not unusual to find these images closely replicated in the production. Finally a storyboard may be a series of photographs of the model(s), sometimes taken under a miniature lighting rig, illustrating at least an impression of changing light. Storyboards can of course act as useful sketches or scripts prior to a full animation. In essence the storyboard is a simple format consisting of a variety of usually sequential images – each image is constructed using the means described in the preceding chapters, thus we will only give it brief attention here.

Digital tools serve the production of the more advanced or finished storyboards well. A storyboard, even of the conventional kind, can easily be displayed on a computer; the sketches, painting or photographs can be digitized, perhaps imported into a presentation program such as Microsoft PowerPoint, and even projected onto a large screen during the presentation. Similarly a sequenced order of annotated images can easily be emailed to colleagues. This approach is reasonably well suited to the final showing of a photographic storyboard to the assembled cast and crew. However, in the end this is simply a presentation solution, drawn from conventional techniques, and does not use the full advantages and resources of digital modelling.

As has been described in several places in this book one key advantage of using a computer to model a design is the facility for change; the ability of a designer to make transformations and modifications (small and large) to all aspects of the design, and to see the results swiftly, often alongside the original. No change need overwrite the previous version, as each may be saved as a unique (and clearly labelled) outcome. Not only may the designer easily transform the design over time but may of course view multiple possibilities for each transformation, or view it from various view-points.

The series of 3D 'sketches' illustrated (Figures 5.14 to 5.20) in Chapter 5 provides an example of a simple storyboard. They show a number of different stage configurations, which could suggest changing scenography over time. At an exploratory stage simple geometry with minimal use of texture and lighting might be quite sufficient to offer a sense of the effect of time and movement. At a later stage the ability to make significant changes to setting and light fairly quickly, and to render still images of those changes, makes the production of a series of final, lit and textured images far more efficient than the process of using card models. Needless to say rendered images can be printed, even framed, and displayed in sequence, thus making an exhibition of the storyboard. Chapter 10, on composition, cameras, rendering and resolution, includes some guidelines on rendering for storyboards.

In a computer a storyboard may include animation as easily as still images. In PowerPoint, for example, which is a simple but flexible presentation tool, the designer may advance from one 'slide' to another, and each slide may contain either a still image or an animation. It may also have titles and annotations. Thus certain scenes may be illustrated simply through still images, while others may be shown by animation. It is also possible to assign sound to the slides, a particularly useful feature for plotting changes to music.

Digital animation

An animation, of course, shows the movement/transformation itself – as movement. It is quite possible to construct models that 'do' what is required of them. For his 1963 production of 'Romeo and Juliet', for example, Joseph Svoboda built a complex model where every piece moved as it was intended to in production, thus he could plan the changing environment as part of the scenography (rather than leave it as a technical necessity). Only by experimenting with scenic choreography in real time can it be perfected. The kind of resources required for this are beyond those available to most designers, but even the act of lowering an object on a piece of fishing wire into the model gives insight into movement. Light can be one of the most fluid elements of scenography and it is perfectly possible, though again a little expensive, to equip a design studio with a miniature lighting rig, and explore the effects of lighting changes in real time. Failing this, a couple of torches and a gel swatch-book works.

Through the use of animation tools within computer modelling programs the theatre designer can take the production team on a walk through the set; they can set up a series of shots or frames which can then be played as a sequence to show the movement of scenic units such as flats or a revolve. The theatre designer can illustrate dynamic scenic features to be viewed by the production team in real time on a virtual stage. The team can then discuss the mechanics by which this movement might occur. Thus, in the pre-production period animating the flying pieces of a set design can enable a sense of time for the movement of these features and allows the designers, director and production team to fully understand the type of look and movement of complex flying sequences.

For the purposes of the theatre designer we are rarely looking for a faultless animation technique but rather an indication of the way in which objects or light move in the 3D space. Furthermore, animation is time-consuming and generally very processor-intensive – so one must account for it in planning a project and identify elements that will really benefit from animation rather than storyboard treatment; animation can sometimes be used more as window dressing than a useful design process.

How digital animation works

Animation in the cinematographic sense depends upon producing a large number of images (frames or cells) each showing a slight change from the previous one. The trick is to then show these individual frames one after the other quickly enough to deceive the eye that the movement is smooth/continuous. There are many standards that propose an ideal frame rate for smooth animation (frames per second – fps), affected by optical, technical, physiological and neuro-logical variables, but for our purposes a frame rate of about 25–30 frames per second shows a smooth animation. However most theatre projects will not depend upon this level, and even 15 frames per second can illustrate movement reasonably well, albeit slightly jerkily. (You must ensure that you both make the animation at 15 fps and play it back at the same rate, otherwise it will appear to speed up or slow down.) The higher the fps rate then the smaller each incremental move will be and each static image will be on screen for less time; both these factors contribute to smoother movement. The number of frames required in an animation is therefore the fps rate chosen multiplied by the number of seconds needed. The European video standard (called PAL) is 25 fps; it is easier to carry out mental arithmetic using 25 rather than 30 fps (the American standard, NSTC), and animations at 25 fps take less memory and less rendering time than NSTC (since they have fewer frames), so for most exercises we advise 25 fps. For exercises using very complex geometry you would be wise to use fewer frames still. In animation, frames and time are functions of the same thing. If something happens over fewer frames it happens more quickly (assuming it is played back at the same fps rate as it was made). To slow an action down, make it happen over more frames. Your program should allow you to specify frame rates.

Before the advent of computer graphics, film animation was generally founded on one of two techniques. In one a new drawing or painting was made for each frame (sometimes only elements were changed and drawn on a transparent sheet placed over the original); this image was then photographed, the next frame was prepared and shot and so on. This process, with variations, produces typical 'drawn' animations. In the stop frame motion technique a model is fractionally moved between each frame, a technique familiar to viewers of old monster movies or Aardman Animations. The computer removes much of the tedious repetition of these systems. The designer/animator specifies key points in the sequence (called keyframes) and the computer calculates each in-between position (tweenies) depending upon the selected frame rate. These keyframes may be the start and end points of a simple movement (a cloth flies in, a light fades to blackout) or they may be important interim points of a complex sequence (the apex of a bouncing ball, for example). Essentially the user maps an animation sequence, identifies important points (keyframes) and sets those in the computer; the computer does the rest.

In essence then, to create an animation the designer sets the initial arrangement (usually in frame zero) advances to a frame where a key moment has been identified, activates the animation tool (in Viz a large button bottom right of the screen – labelled Anim) and then sets the new position(s) or parameters. This process is repeated until the sequence is complete. Thus the designer simply specifies moments during the animation where movement starts, stops or reaches some other kind of crux, such as a change of direction or speed.

Different software allows the animation of different parameters, Viz for example is more limited than Max in what it can animate. For most theatre uses (to explore changes on stage) the following are the parameters that one may need to animate:

- object position and angle (move and rotate) thus enabling the visualization of truck movement and flying;
- light intensity, illustrating lighting fades. A computer lighting fade will not precisely mimic a stage fade since the dimming curve on stage is not usually linear;
- moving light targets will mimic follow spots and intelligent units, further enhanced if beam and field are animatable parameters;
- light colour is useful but not essential as two lights of different colours can be used;
- the ability to project animated flies from lights is potentially useful but by no means essential for most work;
- human figures can be animated through extremely simple means such as moving an opacity mapped cut-out across the stage, more complex means such as animating the sub-objects that make a simple human maquette, or extremely complex character animation systems.

Computer animation is technically a fairly easy process; the hard part is planning the sequence and keeping movements accurate. Having modelled the scene as it will appear at the beginning of the sequence we need only tell the computer how long the sequence will be (in frames or seconds) and then specify the position of objects and cameras or the properties of light either at the end of the sequence or at key points within it. The computer will calculate all the frames between these keyframes. The keyframes of course are like images for a storyboard if used without interim animation.

Some tips for effective animation

For the most part a designer will use animation to identify and solve technical and aesthetic issues related to the timing of changes. It is therefore more important to identify movement accurately than to produce a polished end result. To this end a designer should have some knowledge of the mechanics and speed of trucking and flying systems; a change that does not depend upon these is unlikely to benefit overly from being animated in a computer. That being said it is likely that the designer will intend for the pace of the change to reflect the nature of the dramatic material (and possibly accompanying music), and the ability to visualize this dynamic alongside mechanically sound scenic movements may save a significant amount of precious time in the technical rehearsals. Chris Dyer's OpenStages project specifically aimed to address this pre-emptive need. See http://www.openstages.com, from where a free, save disabled, download is available.

Keys (or keyframes) indicate the start or end of any movement, or a change of direction or pace in a movement. Understanding the function and manipulation of keys is vital to successful animation. For example, if an object flies in, remains on stage for a period and then flies out again there are four keys involved: the first sets the initial position of the object in the flies, the second indicates the time and location of the object as it completes the fly in, the third (often ignored) sets the time for the object to fly out (and thus remain in stasis between key two and three), the fourth sets the final location back in the flies.

In Viz create a flat box for the stage floor and a simple primitive as a flown object (you could use the chandelier from Chapter 11 if you completed that exercise). You might wish to add an indication of the height of the proscenium opening and masking.

Establish the scene so that the chandelier (or substitute) is in the flies, out of the sightline of the audience. The exact location will depend upon the size of the theatre, but for this example assume 10 m is sufficient. In Viz, below the viewports there is a slider (called the Time Slider), which should currently read 0/100. This indicates that you are working on frame zero, and currently there are 100 frames set as the maximum length for the animation. Below this slider is a ruler measuring off frame numbers. Near the bottom right of the screen is a set of buttons that look a little like a video recorder control. These control the animation playback, and are called Time Controls. Click over the button showing a small clock face and a window (called Time Configuration). The Time Configuration window opens, select PAL (or Custom 25 fps) as the frame rate. In the End Time dialog box type 250. Upon closing the window you will see that the frames ruler has now changed to a maximum of 250.

Flying speed varies but 1.5 m per second is a good guide for a fairly fast movement. Let us assume that the chandelier needs to fly from 10 m above stage floor to 5 m above, at about 1.5 m per second, that will be 3.33 seconds (5/1.5). To set the 'in' position for the chandelier advance the slider to frame 83 (25 × 3.33), click the large Anim button (bottom of the screen near the animation controls): the button turns red. Move the chandelier down to its 'in' position. Click the Anim button again, you have now set the second key. Press play on the animation controls, the chandelier should descend from its position in the flies (key 1) to its 'in-dead' on stage (key 2) – you may find that the animation only plays in the active viewport. Stop the animation and, if not already selected, click the chandelier (or dummy object) to select it. Underneath the Time slider you will see a graphical representation of the keys (red blocks in Viz 4, white ellipses in Viz 3). These can be moved and copied as an object can, they also control some of the key parameters, accessible by opposite clicking on the key icon – see below.

Most mechanical objects (including people) appear to accelerate from standstill and decelerate before coming to rest; this is particularly true of mobile scenic units. In order to replicate this and avoid objects unrealistically keeping a constant velocity from start to finish most programs provide a command to 'ease' the movement in and out of keys. This allows the designer to specify how abrupt or linear the change of pace is. Each key has a control to ease in and out from it – a little like a car taking a corner. To ease out of the starting position in the flies opposite click over the key in frame zero (the red marker on the animation slider when the chandelier object is selected). Select Chandelier: Position (it may say Box: Position or other object name depending on your naming protocols). A dialog box will give you information about the keyframe, including a graphical representation of the speed into and out of the key; as this is the first key we only need speed out (unless the cycle was important). Click and hold over the Out graph; you will see a number of options appear. The option that indicates a curve starting quite flat and then dipping down steeply (like going down off a hill top) represents an easing out, a motion that will start slowly and get quicker; select that option.

179

Still in the Chandelier Position dialog box there are arrows either side of the In and Out graphs. These allow you to apply the same easing parameters to the next key in the series. Click the arrow to the right of the Out graph; this will assign an easing in to the next key, slowing down as it approaches the key. To check this we will advance to the next key. At the top left of the dialog box there are two arrows with a number next to them: these select keys before or after the present key. Click the right arrow to advance to the second key (chandelier flown in). You will see that the In graph shows a slope becoming more gentle, hence the movement slows down towards the key.

Close the window and return to the main program and play the animation; you will see a slight change in speed to the descent.

Now copy the key from frame 0 to frame 250, and the key from frame 83 to 167. To copy a key hold down the Shift key, click over the key indicator on the track bar, hold the cursor down, and slide the duplicate key to its location. (To move a key you simply slide the key without the Shift.) This will result in a 10-second sequence with the chandelier flying in for 3.33 seconds, staying on stage for 3.33 seconds and flying out. However, it is likely that as the chandelier flies in it will bob below its dead (a dead is a theatre term for the pre-set location at the end of a flying event).

Between two keys that set the start and end of a period of stasis, such as the chandelier/object in the example above, a computer may try to insert some movement, often a gentle curve. In the case above this may manifest as the object gently flying below its set position and returning to it just before it flies out, looking a little like a bounce. This is because of the observation in point one above: the computer is easing the object in and out of the keys. To avoid this key 2 (above) needs to be set in such a way as to ease in to the position but to have no movement out, similarly key 3 should have a flat line in but ease out. Opposite click on key 2, select Chandelier Position and click over the Out graph; one option shows a graph with three vertices connected by bold horizontal lines and dotted verticals – this indicates that the object does not move between keys but snaps to the next position when the next key arrives. To remain static between keys we need to apply this to the Out of key 2 and the In of key 4. Select this linear/snap option and then click the arrow to the right of the out graph, thus assigning the same dynamic to key 3. Key 3 needs to ease out gently, as described above.

As with mechanical movement, lighting fades are rarely even; often a change of light is not particularly noticeable near the start and end of a fade in the theatre.

To render an animation in Viz activate the desired viewport (normally camera or perspective) select the Render icon on the main toolbar, and in Time Output select Active Time Segment. Select a fairly low resolution and then click to save the file, either as an .avi or .mov. It is vital that you instruct the computer to save an animation as, unlike a still image, it will not remain on screen after the render. Once saved it can be played through a media player. If you have selected .avi you will be asked to select a codec, a means of compressing and decompressing the animation data for ease of storage. We tend to use Indeo Video. See the Viz reference for further details on rendering animations.

We shall explore the animation of a slightly more complex sequence, based upon the flying chandelier. If you tried the exercise above, keep the file as it can be modified for this exercise. This exercise is not specific to Viz and simply explores animation planning rather than operational detail.

Let us imagine that as a scene ends, a bed, with the main character on it, trucks to the back of an otherwise empty stage (ending up behind a drape, or otherwise off stage). As it does so the stage fades from a moonlight state to black and a chandelier flies in. As it reaches its dead (the pre-set lowest point) the lights fade up to a general warm interior. It must all happen within a specified phrase of music that lasts a maximum of 15 seconds. It is worth noting that although music can be added to animations in a film editing program (such as Adobe Premier or, at the free end of the market, VirtualDub) it is generally easier and more flexible to play a CD or tape completely separately, alongside the animation. This gives far more scope for quick changes to cues.

Set the animation length to 375 frames (25×15). To allow some slack in case you have to extend the animation you could set the overall time for 450 frames which would make room for some experimentation; one need not render the whole lot. (If you carried out the last exercise you will need to move the keys, or delete them and start again.)

The scene consists of a stage floor, a 'truck – bed' object and a 'flown – chandelier' object. You can make the lighting and geometry as simple or complex as you like to test this sequence, however animation generally takes a long time to render and creates large files, so the simpler the better. Initial experiments to test timing and movement flow could be done with very simple objects indeed and only one light for each state – this will still suggest the rhythm. Once fixed the scene may be fully made from more complex geometry and animated.

For keyframe zero set:

- the bed in the middle of the stage;
- the chandelier (or other flown object) in the (imaginary) fly gallery above the stage and out of sightline. It is important that it is a 'real' distance away – approx 10 m would be sufficient in a small theatre, more in a larger one.

We will assume that there are two lights, one for the moonlight of the first scene, one for the daylight of the second. In a computer you could achieve this with just one (changing the parameters) but for clarity we shall use two. In the default frame zero set:

- one light as moonlight onto the centre of the stage, diameter of beam approx 7 m, a blue light (perhaps even a gobo);
- one light for the warmer second scene, set the colour to an amber, but for frame zero set the intensity to 0.

Generally the speed and flow of such a change will depend upon the pace of the piece. A set-move or fade to black after a comic punch-line is always likely to be more abrupt than it is after a tragic ending; the speed of the movement of lights or set must follow the tempo of the play unless a deliberate attempt is being made to juxtapose it. Normally a slight pause (a beat) will be given after a final line or action and before the closure begins, equally a beat is often (though not always) taken after the lights come up on a scene and before the first line or movement. This pacing, or the disregard of it, is vital to the flow of a piece. For this animation, however, we will start from the first movement, and end as soon as the final one is complete. This saves animation time and does not fix the beats – the pauses can be added with still images later if necessary.

Sketch out the action as follows.

The truck should move fairly slowly, say 5 m per 10 seconds (approx 1.8 kph), or 0.5 mps. Let's assume that it needs to truck back 7 m until it is off-stage (perhaps hidden by a drape), but at 3.5 m it is out of light. Thus in approximately 7 seconds it leaves the lit stage area (3.5 m/0.5 mps), at 14 seconds (7/0.5) it is obscured.

The chandelier will fly at around 1–1.5 m per second.

The lighting should be dipped cross-fade, never quite reaching blackout, and perhaps fading up a little quicker than it faded down (this fancifully assumes that scene 2 is a little more up-beat than scene 1).

A sequence may be mapped out a little like the table below, of course each one of these key points may be experimented with, and the following is for guidance only.

Time/frame	Bed	Chandelier	Moonlight	Daylight
0/0	**starts to truck**	out	on full	blackout
2/50	*trucking*	out	**starts to fade**	blackout
6/150	*trucking*	**starts to fly**	*fading down*	blackout
9/225	*trucking*	*flying*	*fading down*	**starts to fade up**
11/275	*trucking*	**completes flying**	**completes fade**	*fading up*
14/350	**completes truck**	in	blackout	**completes fade**
15/375	off	in	blackout	on full

The notes in bold are key points in the sequence, otherwise an object or lighting state is either at rest, or moving between these key points (indicated by italics in the table). In an animation program these key points become keyframes.

Frame 0 is generally considered to be the default setting and sets the first key for all objects and parameters. Thereafter the user advances to the next desired keyframe, activates the animation facility and moves the object (or rotates it, or scales it) to the next location. In this example, the bed/truck would be set centre stage for frame 0 and then the designer would advance to frame 350, activate animation, and locate the bed far up stage. The computer will then move the bed incrementally for all frames between 0 and 350.

Where the movement starts at frame 0 this is all fairly straightforward – one sets the end position and away it goes. However, when the animation has to start later than frame 0 this needs to be specified. Taking the chandelier, for example, if we simply set the end point at frame 275 the flying cue would begin at frame 0. To ensure that the cue starts at frame 150 it is necessary to copy or move the chandelier 'position' key from frame 0 to frame 149 (or then delete the key at 0) and set a new position (the lowered in position) key at frame 275. To ensure that no unexpected animation occurs it is usually also a good idea to copy the key for the final position or parameter of any object to the final frame. Ensure that the keys are set to avoid 'easing' movement between fixed positions – see above.

In Viz, as in most programs, more detailed editing of keys can be undertaken from the Track View – where all keys for all objects and parameters may be accessed, moved, copied, edited and so on.

The lights are animated in a similar way. The desired frame is selected, the animation button activated, and a new parameter for that frame entered.

In Viz, for the moonlight for example:

- in frame 0 the moonlight is set to its normal intensity (1) and colour (e.g., RGB: 40,110,230);
- advance to frame 275, activate the Anim button and take the light's intensity down to 0 (or RGB to 0,0,0).

Similarly for the warmer light (RGB: 255,190,85) frame 0 should have intensity 0, frame 225 should also have intensity 0, and frame 350 should have intensity 1. (A tip is to set frame 0 and 350 first, then copy or move 0 to 225.) As with animated objects it may be necessary to ensure that between key 1 and 2 the transition is set to a snap (in Viz set by opposite clicking the key icon on the track bar and selecting Spot: Multiplier), then easing out of key 2 to 3, otherwise the light may fluctuate in level between keys 1 and 2. Similarly the light should not ease out of 3, but stay static.

As the keys are being set the effect of the animation may be seen in the construction viewports and the Light Parameters dialog boxes. Once you are happy with key placement, render a number of still frames to check light levels before setting the full animation to render. An animation such as this, with 375 frames, will take some time to render. Make sure the model file is saved before rendering.

Careful key management is essential to preserve the correct movements (and the designer's sanity). A pen and paper will always help – keep one by the computer; however if you intend to do significant animation it is important to fully understand the key editor. Keep a copy of the file saved prior to assigning any animation, as sometimes it is the only way out of problems.

Managing the animation and storyboard project

Rendering an animation, particularly with full materials and lights, is a very time-consuming business, so always render a low resolution version first, possibly using placeholder objects with simple geometry and texturing. Render a few frames from the whole range with full lighting and textures before you render the final animation to check for any obvious errors.

It is far better to investigate timings using simple animations than complex textured ones. If one of the advantages of a computer is the speed with which it deals with changes, this is one place where that does not hold. Moving bits around a card model is quicker, if less convincing! If you want to make changes after showing an animation to a production meeting you may need to undertake a complete re-render, tying-up your computer for hours or days. Unlike a big production company an individual designer is unlikely to have networked rendering, or other load-sharing capability.

Where you are undertaking a project with one static scene file management is fairly clear (see Chapter 13 on project management). One model file will contain your work, perhaps with a regular back-up made. There may of course be older versions saved previously, but in the main the material is clearly stored and easily accessible.

Once a project has multiple scenes for a storyboard, including some animations, design management becomes a major issue. A change to elements in act 1 may have a knock-on to act 4 and vice versa.

One option is to keep all material in one model file, this certainly simplifies change management. Even if you are not intending to render animations keyframes can be used to define moments of change. An entire production of multiple acts can be modelled in one file, provided every act or moment of significant difference is located on a new frame. If this method is used, set each new 'moment' a number of frames apart to allow for interim changes. However, this is fraught with problems. It is very easy to re-set earlier scenes, and mismanagement of keys can have unpredictable and devastating effects. Far better to have a new file for each scene, and a different file again for each animation. In general of course the opening and closing arrangements of an animation will represent the status quo of the scene each side of it. Thus one animation file may hold the layout for two scenes. If you wish to open a new file to work on the final state of an animation as a static view, then re-save the animation file as a new scene, copy all final keys to frame 0, delete all keys after frame 0. Meticulous logging and record keeping are necessary to avoid confusion.

Fly-bys, walk-throughs and complex movement paths

Above we considered simple linear movements of items of set. It is possible to construct much more complex movement paths for objects and to animate the camera on a path. The latter procedure can produce the effect of walking through a design. It is debatable how useful this is for a conventional performance, but it is of undoubted value for site-specific and installed work where the kinetic element will be provided by a mobile audience rather than mobile set. Creating a smooth walk-through is difficult, first-time animators tend to move the camera and its target too much, too quickly and slightly haphazardly. As with all work of this kind, ask what the animation is supposed to show; will two or three still images that can be annotated or spoken to do better? If a walk-through is animated do try to keep the camera field of view constant throughout.

However, if a complex path is needed, either for camera movement or scenic movement, a spline can be created and assigned as a path to the object. In Viz, once the path is created from a spline, select the object or camera, and from the menu bar select Animation > Follow Path, and when prompted select the path. The object will move to the first vertex of the spline, and animate along the spline for the duration of the set fames. Start and finish position keys can be moved in time.

Summary

There is no doubt that being able to view the design over time has great advantages, but given some of the potential problems of using cinematographic animation the designer would be wise to consider whether a series of static images are preferable; certainly it must be borne in mind that the aesthetic of animations is likely to be different from the aesthetic of still images unless a lot of time is available for the project. There are cases where kinesis is vital of course, or when the animations thus created will be projected on stage. This is an important tool, but must be used with caution.

13

Project management

To digitally model, or not to digitally model . . .

While it is appealing to think of the design process as simply one of accessing creative flair, all designers, in every discipline, are aware that their task is as much about problem solving and accurate decision making as it is about artistic vision. At the commencement of and throughout any project the parameters must be known and an environment and context established that offer the most suitable tools for making and assessing decisions. The first of these, in the context of this book, is to establish to what extent digital tools may assist the process. While it may be that their deployment is reviewed and changed as the project progresses it is unwise to simply start by sitting in front of your favourite program and assuming the creativity will flow.

Two apparently conflicting attitudes need to be addressed throughout the design process and kept firmly in mind by the designer. In his excellent overview of digital modelling Peter Weishar (1998) observes that in creating virtual worlds for many purposes (product design, games creation, etc.) a digital designer must think like a set designer. We have been at pains to point out that the creator of imaginary realms is not making them to be lived in for real but rather to offer the appearance or illusion of reality. You must consider what is and is not seen, what needs to be 3D and what can be falsified. A cut-out of a pillar with a texture applied, for example, rather than a fully rounded object will still look like a 3D pillar in the image. This is useful for the set designer as the approach required by modelling virtual worlds for the computer is equivalent to the approach needed in creating worlds for the stage, which are of course equally unreal. However, it is also possible for a designer using the computer, as it is for a card model maker, to become involved in their creation to the extent that they may forget that its purpose is to illustrate something that is to serve a different purpose. The computer model is not an end in itself, rather it is a means to test and communicate visual and spatial ideas ultimately designed for a different medium. These positions should be constantly in the mind of the designer. While this book focuses on creating digital models it is not our intention to suggest their use to the exclusion of more traditional approaches and, in planning a project, an initial assessment of the value of the computer and traditional methods of working should be made.

So the theatre designer needs to consider the experience of working with the digital tools versus the pressure to complete the project. Most modelling programs, even the simplest, take some time to learn and certainly require practice to use with any sophistication and ease. Inexperience may not only restrict and frustrate creative development but at worst it may create errors that are not easy to recover from. The designer is in dialogue with the computer but if the conversation is stilted it is unlikely that poetry will be made. Therefore the first few projects undertaken using computer modelling should be free of unnecessary pressure – perhaps there is an extended development period, or you are working with a text or director with whom you feel comfortable. Ideally, a computer model can be made alongside a traditional one, each informing the other, and the card model can act as a safety net for the digital sibling. It is worth considering the collaborative context of the work. Working with a director who is unused to reviewing computer models may lead to miscommunication or false expectations. Likewise a lighting designer may be offended when they see the initial set design that includes lighting states, little realizing that this approach is almost inevitable in the digital model. What is important is that the production team understand the opportunities and limitations of the medium and do not have overly positive or negative preconceptions.

Certain designs lend themselves far more to digital approaches than do others. Projects that are likely to utilize modern materials and forms, for example geometric shapes, projection and kinetics, are more sensibly approached in the digital model, where the modelling and rendering process are likely to produce a more convincing result than traditional techniques. Designs that are likely to draw on chaotic and run-down or organic forms may be better served using card, fimo, balsa and fabric. Although, as a coda to this, look at the work of Roma Patel, currently on the Web site http://www.digitalsetdesign.com/ (particularly the production of 'Amedee'), which illustrates a very textured feel to the world she has created. Certainly, unless the project is very large, requiring many repeated elements, it is likely that ground plans will be produced as quickly and accurately by hand as by a program. Ultimately, there is likely to be some cross-over between methods and a design studio needs to be established that allows for portability between physical and digital domains.

There is no doubt that computer images can be beguiling and engaging. They allow for animated walk-through of the environment, display of lighting effects and even smoke, and a high-quality final image. They indicate high-tech sophistication and high-level production values. The look and the nature of this work can send certain messages to the producer or client and, in the more commercial sector, this might be an important signifier, winning confidence and contracts if used well. For these purposes high-quality rendering and a good use of presentation software is necessary.

When you decide to use digital tools on a project the following management strategies and problems need to be considered.

Filing and storage structures

The effective management of your storage system is vital; without a clear structure you can lose files, overwrite files or accidentally start work on an old version of a project. This may be obvious to many people but it is worth stressing here in order to avoid problems later.

Any single project that you are working on in a program will be saved as a file and files are stored on the computer in locations known as folders, and sometimes directories. These clerical metaphors are useful in providing an appropriate analogy and they serve as graphical icons as well. Folders may contain other folders, known as sub-folders, and all are eventually housed in a storage device such as those mentioned above. Hence you get a structure that looks a little like a tree, with the storage device providing the root and trunk and then the folders and sub-folders branching off. If you were to extend the metaphor the files might be leaves on a branch. A folder that is near the root of this tree is perhaps confusingly referred to as being at a higher level than those further away.

Folders and files must be named and all newer versions of the operating system allow for names of up to 256 letters. A file will also have a three-letter filename extension after the dot in the name. This informs the computer and the users what sort of information is stored in there and how to access it, i.e., what program to use. It is very unwise to enter your own extension, rather allow the computer to allocate the right one. We cannot stress enough how important it is to have a logical directory structure that makes sense, not just at the moment you design it but in three years' time when you have far more files stored. Once a structure is begun it becomes quite difficult to significantly alter it so plan for an increasingly complex environment. It is a good idea to put a word-processed document file directly under the top folder explaining the directory structure, what goes where and any changes that have been made. You should now create your directories making choices about your own working environment and how you would like to set this up.

If you have a thorough and logical folder structure naming should be quite easy, since the folder that a file is in will give the category, the file name can give the detail. This is, of course, fine until you move the file to a different folder. Avoid names that become meaningless as you work on a project: terms such as 'final' should be avoided since inevitably it rarely remains final for long. It is wise to keep older versions of scenes and save the new idea as a new file, thus allowing you to return should the new direction not work out. Naming here becomes particularly crucial. Be aware that it is not only the name that identifies a file content. Your file navigation system, probably Windows Explorer, will allow you to view the last date on which you modified a file and more importantly most programs will allow you to create comments about a file. This is usually called properties or summary information. Use this facility to annotate the content of a file. It will also allow you to view statistics such as creation date, modification dates and so on; all this information helps to identify a particular file and thus manage a project smoothly.

An efficient designer will have a directory structure (set of folders for file storage) that is easy to operate in and simple to maintain. There are likely to be general folders relating to the overall practice of stage design, and specific folders relating to each project. Needless to say any such directory should accommodate other files that you may generate in your work such as correspondence and accounts. Some basic rules should be:

- create a folder at a top level, usually directly under c:\ and use that as the parent directory for all of your work; do not store any work that you have created in any other tree. This is the equivalent of the Windows My Documents folder; it can be re-named. If you start storing files under other folders you run the risk of losing them amongst the program files and potentially in the search for them removing essential files. If, at a later date, you wish to move all your files to a new computer, a common root will assist the process;
- create a directory structure under this top-level folder that reflects your work pattern and includes specific project folders (with sub-folders to cover component parts) and generic library/archive folders;
- always load any program files into the program tree; try to avoid having a range of program files in the My Documents (or equivalent) tree;

- establish a directory tree that recognizes resources that go beyond the life of one project, probably including files for gobos; theatre plans; paintings (arranged by country/date/museum) textures and so on. Naturally each project will have similar directories but once a project is over it is worth centralizing some of the resource as three years down the road you will certainly need some of these again, but will not remember which directory they are in.

A new set of folders should be set up for each project. Remember that not only must this structure allow for the retrieval of files during the life of the project but it must also provide archive material in the future and potentially material for your own digital library. The top-level directory should have the name of the project, e.g., 'Cherry Orchard 2002', underneath which there are likely to be a number of sub-directories. A directory structure might include a 'research' folder, which acts as a repository or scrap book for gathered material; this itself might have sub-directories that might include, 'historical art and architecture', 'textures' and 'costumes'. At the same level as the 'research' folder a 'working model' folder, perhaps sub-divided by 'scene', or by version giving space for different approaches, will contain all model files and ideally a separate folder for working 'texture files'. Textures and maps can cause confusion: on the one hand you need maps specific to each project to be stored in a logical place together with all other project material, on the other hand you may very well wish for maps to be located in a central folder or folders, organized and identified by map type or theme. It is certainly the case that the result of a number of years' research will be very full libraries. Remember also that the location of maps and texture libraries is important since the path to the location may be written into the project model files (by the modelling software), if a map is moved it may not be easy for your software to find. A 'presentation' folder might be used to deposit material that is going to be shown at the next design meeting. This folder might be divided into sub-folders for each meeting, or at least by meeting type. Some kind of 'final design' folder is sensible to separate working models and images from the final ones, although when misused this can easily become the place where files are placed when the designer thinks they have finished, only to be worked on later, thus this becomes a second working directory. A 'schematics' folder housing any theatre plans that have been digitized and the location where you will store ground plans and construction drawings will also prove useful. Finally you should create an 'archive' folder that will be assembled after the project and will contain portfolio material. This may include scanned production photographs as well as digital models.

If time and hard disk space allow it might be worth carrying out an audit after each project, copying useful maps and mesh objects to more general folders organized by theme. It would of course be possible to put shortcuts in these folders, but there may well come a time when a project is relegated to CD storage, and hence the image to which the shortcut refers will be removed. It is certainly a very sensible plan to merge all new mesh objects into separate files, properly identified, so that you may call on them again for a future project. Keep a note of the units used and materials allocated (specific file names). You should be able to store this information in the file's Summary Information or Properties dialog boxes. Name the elements (in a group) something very specific, e.g. avoid calling a chair simply 'chair' as confusions will arise on merging. Of course you could merge these from their original project, but finding them may be hard, and you may not have isolated all necessary information about the mesh.

Establish naming conventions for all files that lead to easy identification and avoid terms such as 'final draft' or 'smaller version', as these rapidly become meaningless. Since a file name can be up to 256 characters long, and most software that did not accept this is now confined to history, it is clearly sensible to use this facility, for although using storage space (very little) it will aid identification.

On the grounds of safety and efficiency it is sensible to make copies of files. For example those in the presentations folder may be duplicates of files in the working folder. However, it has been known for a designer to make different changes to both copies, resulting in extreme confusion. Therefore it is sensible to make presentation material Read Only, which will prevent changes being made to the copy housed there. This has the added advantage that you will be unable to carry out work on a model during a meeting; this is frequently requested by the production team but not often a good idea, although again this will depend on your relationship with the team and, if you are confident with them, you may wish to move basic features around the modelled space as part of the exploration and discussion. However, you will need to set this flexibility up prior to the conference meeting.

Data preservation procedures should be considered before a project is begun. Writable CDs are probably the most sensible means of back-up. They are large enough to hold a single show on one disk and are reasonably robust. Paper copies are also worth keeping. It is certainly worth converting files to the most portable file format that is possible, after the project has ended.

Keeping an index is a sensible approach to organizing the work, perhaps even on a database program, allowing you to search your folders for specific types of image. This is a time-consuming task in the first instance, but there is no doubt that some kind of organizational record will be useful. You should also be prepared to review and amend your directory structures if your working patterns change.

Scheduling and budgeting

Scheduling a project is an important but often overlooked part of design management. The different stages of design development happen at different speeds in a computer than they do in real space but the differential is not linear. A small project with few elements can take longer in the computer than it would in card, whereas a complex multi-element design, particularly one with repeated elements may be substantially quicker to initially model in digital space. Furthermore, re-working a model is generally much quicker in the computer. Therefore you are likely to reach the stage of producing visually compelling models earlier on but spend more time refining details, or even on radical change. The working pattern and design meetings should be planned around this sort of schedule otherwise a bottleneck may occur while the designer is waiting for the normal process of confirmation and consultation. An important point that we have alluded to on a number of occasions before is that, with the nature of digital creativity, it is hard to establish and stick to an end point – it is always possible to 'do a bit more'.

It must be remembered that rendering, particularly of complex animated sequences using lights and atmospheric effects, is time-consuming. It is vital to test-render low-level animation in advance of the final render and to conduct experiments to establish the rendering time of the full sequence.

The final animation should be started with enough time to render it twice before any important conference: once to make the animation and the second time to render it if any unexpected errors occur. An animation of 1 minute will need at least 900 frames for a jerky sequence (at 15 fps) and double that for a smooth version. Since a single frame 320 × 240 pixels may take 2 minutes (or 20, it depends upon complexity) to render if there are a number of shadows and reflections, this might mean 3600 minutes in total, a possible 60 hours, or double that to include correction times. Admittedly, most sequences can be simplified for quicker rendering but this example does give some indication of the problem. During these times, of course, the computer is tied up and so you cannot process any other work for the conference.

Before embarking on a project, or at least at its early stages, it is necessary to undertake a software and hardware audit. Since the point of design is to give an imaginative vision a more concrete form it is important that the tools you have at your disposal are capable of responding to your vision. If a project is likely to require significant projection of moving images, for example falling water, then you must establish whether your software can provide that and whether you know how to achieve it. If not, its purchase and your training must be accounted for in the project schedule and costing. This makes apparent a number of problematic issues. Firstly, of course there is the inevitable desire to make a spectacle. If you find your software can do something clever there is a tendency to attempt to integrate it. In some ways this can be seen as a positive. The program is alerting you to creative possibilities. It is giving you the tools with which to make and test interesting scenic proposals that may have been confined to description in more traditional approaches. The corollary of this is that there is a tendency, particularly for those less familiar with digital technologies, to expect something complex or fancy. While a computer is as capable of representing a lone chair on an empty dusty stage the nature of the medium promotes a feeling that it should offer something more. This undoubtedly has been brought about by the deployment of these technologies in the special effects industry. A good designer will, of course, see these problems and use the tools to serve the needs of the project.

For most theatre designers there is little opportunity to cost the research and development element of a project properly since such activities rarely operate at fixed rates, although some designers working on trade shows, conferences or more complex projects, particularly through production companies, may be in that position. A freelance designer must offset a number of costs generated by the use of computer modelling and while it would be inappropriate to charge many of these to one individual project the designer's annual income must meet these costs.

The capital investment in a computer is likely to depreciate to nearly zero over a 3- to 5-year period, by which time enough of the computer will need upgrading to warrant a completely new purchase. Obsolescence is designed into hardware and software. Since computer prices have traditionally been relatively stable for the past 5 years we can assume that approximately £1000 every 3–5 years, let's say 4 years, will keep the hardware current; that is £250 per year. Adding the occasional new peripheral, if desired, may increase that to an average of £400–£500 per year. However, most people reading this will own a computer anyway, so this is not a new cost, indeed using it for modelling will help it pay for itself. After the initial outlay on software of perhaps £2000 further purchases of extra plug-ins or upgrades are likely to involve far less outlay. A similar figure of £250–£400 per year is ample to keep up-to-date if your ambitions are reasonably realistic. You should also cost personal development time. The initial learning curve is likely to be steep and long.

You will need two dedicated weeks if starting from scratch and this will only be enough to introduce you to the basic use of most software. A month is more realistic in order to develop a deep knowledge of your systems. However, once initial learning is undertaken a week or two a year should be sufficient to learn new procedures and, of course, much is learned on the job. However, ring-fencing some time where learning can follow your agenda rather than the project's is quite useful. Attending courses is extremely helpful but many are commercially run and are very expensive.

Annual costs of keeping a digital design system running are therefore something in the region of £1500 per year, including hardware, software and development time. This may be expensive, depending on your budget, but there are cost benefits, and the hardware cost is likely to be similar to maintaining the standard PC that many individuals now own. A project undertaken solely on a computer costs far less in terms of consumable items than a conventional model does. Materials to make many model boxes may reach a couple of hundred pounds or more. This figure can be cut by a factor of ten for a wholly PC-based project. A number of sheets of high quality printing paper, perhaps an ink cartridge and a CD are the only direct material costs incurred. Naturally, many development costs remain the same and a few, such as Internet connection costs, will be additional. In this respect do be aware that visual image research on the Internet, or downloading software can be a time-consuming and therefore a costly enterprise. It is of course possible that once a designer has become familiar with their software they may well be able to earn some extra income undertaking modelling projects for other types of business such as architectural practices.

The use of the computer to visualize and communicate your ideas for theatre design requires the same sort of process and discipline as if you were using a card model. There are still what we have called four stages to the work. The Conceptual Stage will involve you in assembling research materials that have some resonance or relevance to the work you are undertaking. You will absorb material, written texts, textures and nuances from all areas of your life. These can be collated and placed in a library of files which you may or may not refer to during the course of the process. The Modelling Stage actually involves you using the 3D space of the computer to develop the scenic arrangements of objects, textures and styles within the virtual stage space. This Modelling Stage will also require you to think in terms of the fourth dimension of time. You will use this period to develop ideas of transformation of that space, scene changes and changes of perception for the audience. It is most important that at this stage you are conflating the research and concept of the production with a visualization or number of visualizations that can be shown and discussed. The Schematic Stage allows you to produce the working drawings by which your design might be built. Again, these can be modified as you talk through with makers and the production manager exactly how the modelled environment can be made into a real space–time event. It is most important, then, that the Conference Stage is used throughout this process. The previous stages of Conceptual, Modelling and Schematic are then continually interrupted by the Conference Stage, which enables the sharing of ideas and the changing of the stage space and objects through the assimilation of design ideas. The scenographic team which will include all the designers, possibly makers, and the production manager and director are encouraged through this process to be involved with the event that will occur. We believe this to be an ideal way to make theatre, through collaborative processes that are enhanced by the individuals in the team actively contributing.

Organizing the design for technical purposes

It is likely that the background details and workings of most modelling projects will remain private to the designer; nobody need see the intricacies of the way it has been made. However, at some point in the process it will be extremely useful to be able to pass on specific technical information directly from the files. Indeed there will have to be a way to transfer schematic details from the computer to the stage management team, workshop, lighting team, etc. This may of course be a simple process of 'drawing it' on paper based upon known measurements, or it may be a more sophisticated digital workflow. Whatever the process an effective management of the design process will facilitate or optimize efficiency, accuracy and sharing information.

Setting up units

We have covered units in the basic modelling skills sessions. Using consistent units, ideally across all your projects, but certainly for all elements of one will aid workflow and avoid potentially costly mistakes. However apocryphal it might be, the story that suggests the crash of a probe orbiting Mars was due to the use of both imperial and metric units in its construction is a cautionary tale. The design is eventually going to be built, accurate information about its size must be accessible, and the design team must know that it is going to fit in a specified theatre. We recommend that you follow the standard operating system of your country; in the case of Europe this would be metric, normally using millimetres as the specific unit. Thus a European designer would normally set their system so that one 'unit' in the computer equals one millimetre in real life. Remember there is no need to think in scale in a modelling program, nothing has real dimensions (unlike a card model or drawing) so the designer is always working in the finished dimension.

Throughout the book we have advocated a philosophy based upon 'build what you think looks right' rather than 'build it to a known formula'. In other words experiment with scale, proportion, arrangement rather than assembling a predetermined set of parts (this is the strength of modelling programs). However at some point these experiments must be formalized and eventually built, and exact dimensions will be needed; therefore set your units right at the start of a project and include some kind of dimensional constant (see below).

If you are taking dimensions from your model (to draw onto a paper plan for example) it is tempting to click on a polygon and read off its parameters. This is often unwise since scale transformations may well have changed the apparent size of the object but kept the original creation dimensions intact. Use a ruler tool (in Viz this is accessed via Create > Helpers). If you do not have a ruler tool then create a new simple object in alignment with the object to be measured, reading off the relevant dimensions from the new object. Only take the original (creation) measurements for objects that you know have not been scaled.

It is easy to start 'sketching' an object or design without regard for its size – merely a consideration of its proportion and shape. Indeed you may often import a pre-made object into a design and re-scale it to fit a new project – creating a totally different effect. However, at some point real dimensions will have to be taken.

The dimensional constant

Not only is there no real size in the computer model, but everything can keep changing. It is important to remember the final destination of your design, and build a reminder in to the project. For many designers, using any approach, a human figure is an essential element of a project (see Chapter 9); it reminds us that a performer is an essential and constant presence, and that a design must be scaled around a human (even if that scale is intentionally out of proportion). Even at the end of a project an entire design may be scaled (up or down) in relation to the human figure, but the proportion of the design makes no sense without this presence.

The other constant is of course the stage space for which the design is intended, though for a touring production this may vary somewhat. At the very least a project should set the locations of the stage edges (proscenium if there is one) and extreme seats – this can be done using simple splines and text tools. The computer-provided grid will naturally provide a constant reference, but it can sometimes be hard to use. Think about providing a bolder scale object to assist quick scale calculations. Remember the following:

- the datum point should be 0,0,0. That is to say the intersection of stage floor, centre line and datum/setting line should be at the modelling space's origin;
- do not accidentally scale these references when scaling or otherwise modifying a whole design; they must be constant. It is most sensible to put them on a separate locked layer (see below).

Using ground plans

If you are designing for a specific theatre space you may wish to use the plan (and perhaps section) of the space to assist in setting up your design. There are two basic ways of doing this, with a number of variations; a full appreciation of these may also a require an understanding of layers, covered in the next section.

Importing plans. The theatre may well have digital ground plans available that you can import directly into your modelling program. These are likely to be 2D CAD plans, though some may have 3D versions or even textured models. What the designer really needs are details about dimensions, tab (curtain) lines, entrances, exits, flying locations, etc., so a schematic, thus a symbolic plan is likely to be of more use than a realistic model. Many theatres will make CAD versions available that can be imported directly into a modelling program as shapes, or imported into the designer's CAD program for editing, and then imported into the modeller.

Common file formats for such plans are .dwg, which is a drawing file created in CAD programs and native to Autodesk products, or .dxf, which is a drawing exchange file, and can generally be read by many CAD and vector drawing programs, though some data may be lost. If your modeller is designed to operate in the built environment (architecture, product design, engineering) you are likely to have the facility for importing these drawing files. The results of the importation will very much depend upon how the initial drawing was created, which CAD system was used, what protocols (if any) were followed, etc. A crucial factor to check, perhaps the most important, is what units are used by the imported plan, and that they fit with units that the current design project will use. This information may not import properly and must be checked. Errors are likely to be obvious:

any plan using imperial measurements is likely to have specified an inch as the base unit, so if you are using millimetres then the imported plan will look to be about 4 per cent of its expected size, not difficult to miss. One would hope that plans contain some clear indication of units used but this is not always the case, particularly since they are often set up for printing and may simply have a scale ratio indicated. Ideally at least one item should have a dimension written against it so that this can be used to guide dimensioning. Converting dimensions may be most simply achieved by scaling the entire set of objects imported. A scene where the original units were inches can be converted to the proper size in millimetres by scaling to a factor of 2542 per cent.

When CAD drawings are imported it is likely that new objects will be made of certain organization groups in the drawing, generally the original layers (see below). You should therefore be left with a number of logically constructed objects that may be edited (for their colour, layer, scale) or deleted (or hidden) if they are not relevant to your project.

Upon importing these files the datum point is likely to be properly set since the co-ordinates will remain through the process; if for some reason the datum point of the imported plan does not correspond with your origin the entire set of lines can be moved, so that all elements retain the position relative to both the plan's datum and your origin. If you only move the setting and centre lines to re-set the plan's datum on your origin then all dimensions between datum and fixed architecture will have changed and any dimensioning may be seriously off.

If you have a CAD program available to you then you may wish to import the plan into the CAD program first to carry out editing and checking before importing into the modeller. The advantage to this is that the CAD program is likely to be able to handle the plan information more precisely than the modeller.

Drawing the plan. If you cannot import a plan as a .dwg or .dxf file then you may wish to draw key elements directly into your modelling program. At the very simplest this will include the centre line, datum line, stage edges, sightline and seating extremities, height restrictions/ceiling lines, and perhaps key architectural features. Don't forget these can always be turned off, so the lines do not have to complicate your plan. Generally you are advised to create these using a line tool and by using keyboard entry to ensure accuracy. It should be kept simple and facilitate straightforward use and selection; do not include unnecessary information. If you have the option to use layers all of this should be placed on layer 1.

To aid this drawing process you can import an image of the plan of the theatre (or indeed a plan of your set) as a background to a viewport and draw over it (in Viz Views > Viewport Background > File). These images may be available from the theatre directly, or can be scanned from their technical specification. The problem, of course, is that the origin and datum points may not be properly aligned. Also the constrained resolution may make details a little inaccurate and unclear and the capture method may have distorted the image. However, if these factors are understood, the use of a simple image background while drawing the main features will help the designer get a fuller understanding of the features of the space. The Viewport Background dialog box in Viz offers some control over the manipulation of the background image.

Finally one should bear in mind that in a modelling program (unlike the process of drafting theatre plans) lines can be located in 3D space. It might be very sensible, for example, to use simple lines to represent the edges of the proscenium as seen from the front viewport, or to locate the edge of the fly gallery at the appropriate co-ordinate on the world Z axis (vertical); although this is a symbolic/schematic representation, it might as well be located in 3D space. In the top viewport it will still look like a plan.

Plans serve a function: they give information to the designer to enable the production of a design that can fit in the space, is in proper proportion to the space, and can be seen from the house; plans also then facilitate communication on to stage management and the workshop. Thus clarity is essential. There is no point following conventions if nobody knows what they are!

Using layers

Note: not all modelling programs use layers. This is not essential to the modelling process, but if available is a useful organizational tool. Generally speaking layers are more commonly used in CAD programs.

While technically not an aid to navigating 3D space a layer is an important method of organizing your work in the space. It is useful for anything more than a very simple exploration. Despite the spatial metaphor a layer is a tool of organization and not one based on co-ordinates. Its nearest equivalent is in drafting on a 2D surface where you might use layers of tracing paper or acetate, one laid on top of the other, each representing different components of the drawing. It is an important feature of CAD programs where architectural elements such as foundations, plumbing, steel work, dimension lines, hatching, etc., are assigned to different layers. Layers are a way of grouping associated objects and elements, and are identified as such. For example, the objects may share the same colour or line style. The objects may be switched off so that they do not complicate the workspace. They may be locked so that they cannot be changed or they may share stylistic properties. A complex model may have many hundreds of objects and hundreds of thousands of vertices and lines. Without the ability to identify and isolate these elements a design may soon become too complex to work in effectively.

Some modelling, paint and CAD programs offer layers (Autodesk Viz does) but it is by no means ubiquitous in modelling software. A layer is usually accessed by a Layers dialog box. A new drawing or model will tend to start with one layer only, often called layer 0, and unless new layers are created, all objects and other elements will exist on this one layer. It is worth stressing one more time that a layer is a logical not a spatial tool. Objects on layer 0, for example, may exist at any Z co-ordinate.

Layers are usually easy to set up and are worth becoming familiar with. A dialog box will allow you to specify which layer is current (i.e., which one you are working on), and to set some straightforward properties. Objects will normally be assigned to the layer that is current when they are created, but they may also be assigned to different layers by selecting the object and then selecting the destination layer from the Layers List (in Viz). Layers will tend to offer the following options, though these will vary depending upon the program. The option Create New Layer is self-explanatory. When this button is clicked a new layer will be created; sequentially this will be the last layer in the list. A layer may then be given a name or the default name, which is usually layer X, where X is the sequential number. Naming and numbering conventions are important both for reasons of efficiency but also because a drawing or model may be shared with other members of a design team and they too must know how to navigate through the model or plan. For this very reason standards are being developed that will suggest common stylistic conventions for computer modelling and drawing in theatre. We would urge you to use these conventions.

The next option is layer Colour. Unless changed for individual objects once a colour is set all elements created on that layer will share the same colour. This is for schematic purposes and it will not affect the colour or texture of a rendered 3D object. The Line Style tool is more important for CAD than modelling and is often not available in modelling programs. This tool allows the user to define the line type that will be used, by default, on that layer. Most modelling programs will not offer this option but it is needed for the production of professional plans for circulation to other members of the production team. The Order tool is not present on all programs. This function sets the order in which the layers will be drawn; a higher number here will be drawn after a lower number, hence overlapping it and appearing above others. Multiple layers can be assigned the same order number but again this is a CAD rather than a modelling function.

The Renderable function specifies whether objects on that layer will be rendered. This is useful since a layer can be created that has drawing-aids or other layout functions, but these will not be rendered. Viz also provides a Radiosity On/Off switch, specifying whether radiosity is calculated for objects on that layer. Switching it off saves calculation time.

Lock, On/Off is a very useful feature when you are working in a complex scene where it is all too easy to accidentally select the wrong object. If a layer is locked it cannot be altered by mistake. Display Visible, On/Off enables the layers to have visibility or not. Layers that have their visibility display toggle switched off will not be drawn on the display and will not be printed or rendered. This is extremely useful for complex scenes where you wish to give all your attention to one single object, or to represent different scenes, for example where there are set and lighting arrangements in one model. The Set Current tool will make the selected layer active and thus any new object will be created on that layer. It is quite possible to change an object's layer at a later stage, though this can be time-consuming, so it is better to use this from the start.

Paint programs also operate layers for organizational purposes, though many of the modifiers will be different and oriented to bitmap rather than vector graphics. Lock/Unlock, Visible/Invisible, may remain but they also will include Transparency. This allows a layer to be seen through the one above it. Although any project will tend to suggest what layers should be created we recommend the beneath layers as defined by topic whilst you will need to make sensible choices for your own working environment.

Conventions will shortly be published by the Association of British Theatre Technicians (ABTT) that suggest common naming protocols. These have been identified with CAD users in mind and thus are more focused on technical rather than design needs. However, this should provide a common foundation for your practice. The protocols should shortly be available through the ABTT Web site, http://www.abtt.org.uk. Since these are likely to become industry standard, and a designer may pass their models on to other agencies, it does make sense to follow these conventions where possible.

A basic layer, suggested as layer 1, should include a centre line, the Y axis, the setting line, the X axis, datum line, the Z axis and datum point which should be 0,0,0. This layer might also include extremes of sightlines, stage periphery and other important information needed to set out the project, including building outline. While these are only guidelines and will not be rendered in the final design it is an extremely useful exercise to include simple lines in your model to represent these (even if the layers function is not available in your software these should be included). So use a distinctive colour for this layer instead: the conventions suggest white/black for the main architectural features and yellow for centre, setting and datum lines.

Layer 2 is the stage floor layer and should include the physical properties of the stage, its traps, revolves, pit-edge, etc. This might either be represented by 2D lines that will not render, or by 3D objects that will become part of your model. The conventions suggest colour grey for this layer.

Further layers are sub-floor 3, flying 4, lighting 5, sound 6 and scenic elements 7, services 8, notes 9. For the purposes of this book, therefore, the ABTT conventions suggest layer 7, colour unspecified, should be used for setting. This is important if the file is to be shared elsewhere, but might be restricting during the development of the project where extra layers might be useful to assign to individual scenes, or even different versions of ideas.

The way that you use layers within the project itself (as opposed to their purpose for communication) will depend upon the nature and complexity of the project. 7A might therefore be a permanent set layer indicating any staging that remains fixed for the duration of the play. This may be better located on two layers if you are including both 3D meshes and 2D lines to represent the same information. Layers may be broken down by scene or other logical division for the performance. These layers will contain locations of set at various points in the text. It is quite possible to create an object on one layer and then make a copy placed on a different layer to indicate the same or similar item in different locations. As we have mentioned above each scene might have two layers, one for the meshes and one for the 2D symbolic version. A notes and sketch layer is likely to be discarded as you near completion of the work. This layer may contain miscellaneous information pertinent to the design.

It might also be useful to create layers for the lighting grid and symbols (5), and perhaps a layer for the modeller's lights (5A perhaps).

Each project may suggest a different organization and since it is unlikely that the files will go beyond the project and provided all parties involved use the same conventions, national conventions may not be necessary. If the project is one of visualizing the architecture of a theatre space rather than a set, then commonly recognized conventions may be far more apposite, since this information may be filed in a library that is available to other designers.

In conclusion, use layers to organize your work if your software supports it. If the work is only ever staying on your PC (other than as a rendered model) then the conventions are not necessarily important; clarity and appropriateness are far more so. However, if you want to fit in with the conventions you should finally arrange your project so that layer 1 is for key layout information, layer 2 for stage floor details and layer 7 for set.

Layer 0 is a default layer in some programs but not all, and thus does not feature in the conventions. In other words if you have layer 0 it is a good working layer, the place where objects and shapes are created before being assigned to other layers at a later stage.

Sharing your work

Work is shared with the director or production team for three main reasons, requiring different approaches:

1 to consider creative ideas in an exploratory way considering all aspects from appropriateness to the text to the potential technical problems;
2 to facilitate accurate costing and problem solving prior to final approval;
3 to give precise information to other team members so that elements may be built, bought, etc. In these cases accurate schematic information is required.

The order in which these are considered in the process tends to be the order listed above, though some forward and backward movement may occur.

Exploratory conferences

These may vary from small intimate meetings between one or two members of the team (usually at earlier stages) or a larger presentation to a full department (more often at later stages). The observations below will vary somewhat in importance depending upon the context of the meeting, but by and large they all apply to all conferences. It is always vital that work is presented clearly and in such a way that inspires confidence. Of course digital models facilitate the sharing of material via email and the Web but the face-to-face conference is probably still the most important forum.

The designer will have created their image on screen, so in many ways this is the natural context in which to show it, although there are good reasons to keep print-outs available. As a general rule you should avoid showing work directly from the modelling program but rather you should show pre-rendered animations, still images and possibly VRML models. The reasons for this are that:

- if offered almost unlimited flexibility people will want to see a large number of possible variations; this will be time-consuming and may well get your model into a mess, losing sight of the original formation. At the very least, if you do this, make changes to a copy of the file rather than the original;
- working on complex software while somebody is looking over your shoulder is always a mistake, as the pressure and need for speed and accuracy can easily lead to errors and flustering.

Of course there are always times when the designer and director may work together over a live model, but by and large the work should be done away from conferences. It is always possible to call a half-hour break while the designer does some alterations and re-renders the scene.

A very practical disadvantage of showing the work on computer is the need to have a high-quality computer and display system in the conference space. This should ideally be the one that the image was created on, since variations in display system setting can make significant and unwelcome differences to the image. Furthermore the monitor needs to be large enough to allow several design team members to view it and it must be located away from glare. Always check that the technology works before the conference/meeting. It may be obvious but if the presentation cannot take place or is seriously disrupted by technical failure then not only will valuable consultation time have been wasted, but the team may well (properly) lose faith in your ability. Some common things that can go wrong if you are using a different computer from the one the work was created on are listed below:

- your files are too large to transport on floppy disk and you do not have a CD writer. Consider this in advance and make arrangements, perhaps compressing the files or emailing them to an account that can be accessed from the machine to be used;
- you intended to access the image via the Web, logging on to your home page but (a) the computer that you are using is not Internet-connected, (b) the network is down. Always have a back-up plan, probably having the material on CD;
- the CD drive or the processor on the presentation computer is old and slow, thus animations do not run. Back-up plan: bring a series of stills or lower-resolution animations;
- no software on the computer can read your image files. Solution: bring images in different formats, particularly widely used portable formats such as .jpg (see below). You might also consider bringing an image viewer with you. Use a system that includes its own viewer such as Microsoft's PowerPoint;
- the computer's resolution is set so that your images do not display properly. Familiarize yourself with changing resolutions, checking in advance that you will have proper privileges on the machine.

These are a few common problems, leaving aside the more obvious of having your media formatted for a PC only to find that you are presenting on a Mac. Always check in advance. It is less of a problem if you are presenting on your own machine.

It is of course possible to use a data projector to show your images but these are still too expensive for most projects (starting from about £1000 for one suitable for presentations in a small room). However there is a very real advantage to projecting your proposed design onto a screen in its intended performance space. Check the details of the projector offered, ensuring that they match the space.

For a small conference room where the throw is only 4 or 5 m a brightness of 1000 lumens is fine, particularly if the room can be blacked out completely. However, for a small theatre space where the projector may need to be over 10 m away to produce the required size image you will need at least 2000 lumens to get a good picture. Check the lens on the projector and ensure that it can spread the image sufficiently for the required projection surface.

While these are quite practical issues when conferring over the computer image there are others that are less tangible.

As human beings we learn codes that help us decipher images, allowing us to understand the conventions employed in their creation and therefore enabling us to deal with the material appropriately. A painting is rarely entirely faithful to the way that we perceive the world and certainly the very fact that it is a work of art tells the viewer that it is a mediated interpretation. Both the form and content have been constructed in such a way as to tell us something about the relationship between the artist, subject and viewer. We may see through a pointillist work to the scene beyond, decoding it as a riverside scene, but the pointillist technique mediates the image. It acknowledges artifice and comments on the problem of representation. For the designer the model is also very coded. It is a proposal made of substitute materials on a small scale. It is not the final set but rather a suggestion. However, we do not yet have the same shared conventions for the screen and the conventions that we do have can be problematic.

Firstly we are used to the conventions of another small screen, television, and this medium makes a point of authenticity. The image presented is somehow real both in its reproductive style and in its content. Soap opera, for example, has dominated UK television viewing and it depends upon our belief in the nature of the everyday reality presented. Culturally and scenographically we see real people in real situations, viewing small domestic events on a small screen in our own domestic space. News, sport and consumer programmes such as gardening, cooking and so on all depend on this same authenticity. What the designer is showing, however, is a proposal for a different medium entirely but one which may be decoded as authentic because of the viewing medium. It is certainly true that as we become more used to reading computer-based images we may more easily code and decode these to be separate from television.

Additionally, the conventions or expectations of a computer may come into play. There is a sense in which people, particularly those who are not entirely familiar with computer graphics, expect computer presentations to be interactive and changeable. If a designer presents a still image of a design on screen it is quite likely that the director may assume that the image can be easily manipulated, perhaps viewing it from a different angle or moving a scenic element. Whilst this is possible for the designer to set up in terms of walk-through and camera fly-by, the use of it for discussion and sharing must be clearly considered.

Collaboration

Much emphasis has been placed on the collaborative advantages of working in digital spaces, particularly apparent when considering the relationship of the lighting designer to the project. The rapidity of response coupled with the credibility of the outcome provides a space in which members of the team may share visions with the maximum ease and transparency, in a space that is closely analogous to a theatre space. Braddy et al. have proposed that 'we have created a truly new language with which to communicate theatrical realities. It is a language which does not deal in symbols but in the elements of theatre as they are on stage, before an audience' (Braddy et al., 1993: 20). While the on-screen image may resemble a finished design, the language of the interface surrounding it is generally ill-disposed to transparency. An inexperienced designer or collaborator may well be disempowered by the obtuseness of the programs, resulting in a disenchantment with the process and ill-disposition toward the design. Colin Beardon's and Chris Dyer's work have, separately, sought to address the issue by constructing more theatre-friendly digital environments used by all contributors to the production. There is a potential danger here, for at the furthest extreme one might propose that if an interface is modelled on theatre its user will find it hard to think beyond the confines of contemporary theatre practice and will be unable to challenge and expand it.

Michaeljohn Gold has found slightly different implications in the holistic tendencies of the digital space, arguing that the sharing of creative ideas in a common space might conflate roles:

> The parameters of the exercise, a design for 'The Tempest', required all material and ongoing work to be electronically stored and available to all. There has been thus far only one scheduled meeting between the set and the lighting designer, yet because of the accessibility and ease of adaptation of each other's work, the discussion of the production

concept has developed in purely visual terms. This has resulted in a fascinating and exciting dialogue in which light has become indispensable in the development of set and vice versa. So much so that when the first physical meeting took place, the verbal discussion really only consisted of affirmation and concurrence. The ongoing dialogue engendered by the computer meant that any potential problems had been dealt with not verbally but visually by the shaping and reshaping of each other's ideas. What began as a traditional design relationship has become one where the roles of lighting and set designers are not merely complimentary but inseparable, in some ways almost indistinguishable. (Gold and Fergusson, 1999: 246)

Once the roles are potentially coincident and the ideas of light and object have the same currency, one has to ask whether the theatre needs to place as much emphasis on a creative team collaborating towards its development. Two potential outcomes emerge. Either the contribution of various parties needs to be re-organized or various individual contributions become conflated into the role of one auteur scenographer. This is of course an unlikely scenario. However, the digital space may demystify elements of production, prising private knowledge from the grip of the privileged experts. The technology facilitates sharing images of holistic theatrical moments which may be played in a design conference. The design made by one individual may also be made available via email or Internet to others, each making their contribution or comment and returning it. It was Gold's experience that once such material is transmitted without being mediated by spoken language, the recipient was required to engage simply with the piece itself and once words were done away with, the development was far less prescribed.

Whether the holistic and transparent nature of these technologies encourages the development of an auteur or of a more tightly interwoven team is debatable. While experiments have generally found the latter, we wonder whether those findings emerged out of the collaborative nature of the research projects or the personalities of those present in the team.

Some practicalities for conferring

Presentation formats

One may of course simply show image files in a simple image viewer such as Microsoft's Imaging program, or a paint program. Generally these methods will be best suited to small meetings where informality is not a problem. If, however, you are presenting to a large meeting where a neat and professional presentation is important it might be preferable to organize all material, including notes, research material and final images, into a complete presentation.

PowerPoint is probably one of the best means for showing your work. It allows you to show still visual images in 2D and 3D, providing the perfect format in which to show a storyboard of the production. It allows you to present animations and videos supported by research images, text notes, sounds or music. You can control the order in which images are seen, and it can be used as an anchor to the event; both speakers and audience frequently like a third, distanced element upon which to focus. It also, most importantly for theatre, presents a profile of ideas that are not finished models and will only be finished when the work reaches the stage; this dynamic aspect of

PowerPoint as a presentation tool is very important. PowerPoint operates by asking the author to specify the content of 'slides'. A slide may contain one or a combination of the following:

- still images (single, multiple, collaged);
- text divided into heading, sub-heading, bullet points;
- an animation;
- a .wav (sound) file.

Not only may the user specify the content, but also establish certain stylistic devices such as the way one slide reveals the next, the key strokes needed to advance, the design of the slide and so on. A storyboard is very easily and fluidly shown using PowerPoint and may move from still image to animation. Finally, when the project is complete a portable file is created that contains its own viewer, thereby minimizing the problems of playback.

PowerPoint and other presentation tools can be used to communicate a 'feel' for the project, not simply the design images. The design of the slides can reflect the aesthetic of the production, appropriate music can be played, and a range of inspirational research material collaged in. While this may sum up the gist of the project it may as easily distract from the main business of showing the model and thus needs to be deployed carefully. As a rule the designer of a presentation should concentrate on the clear display of important material. Try to ensure that images are properly centred and are of the same size on the slide, thus as a storyboard is run through the image does not 'jog' around on the slide. Try to avoid over-burdening the slides with text, although bullet points make a useful focus for discussion. These might be key pieces of text from the play itself, identifying major scenographic elements. Do not write reams of text that you will also speak; use the presentation as a focus for discussion and an ordering tool. Equally avoid overly complex graphic design or editing tricks; centred images placed against a plain black background with minimal text will be far more eloquent than a messy jumble of styles and excessive annotation. You should also ensure that the colour and size of the text reads properly over the distance required.

Although not a central concern of this book, PowerPoint can also act as a useful operating facility for digital images projected during production, simply advancing from one slide to the next (including black slides) when the cue is reached.

There are presentation methods other than PowerPoint. A simple set of hypertext pages can be authored in a word processor, and include links from one page to another along with still images, or a more complex Web authoring program might be employed. At the furthest extreme an interactive document might be authored with a program such as Director, resulting in full 'experience' of the project. In terms of cost and development time this is likely to be far beyond the needs and resources of most projects and in fact starts to give rise to a resource and product that is something else entirely – a new form, a new representation of the work.

A note on file types

Naturally an advantage of a digital process is the ability to move images quickly to other members of the team or to receive images from others. In order to ensure an effective sharing of these files it is useful to know a little about file types and emailing processes. There are a number of ways to scan and then to email that scanned image to an email address. You can use the Send To feature of the graphics or scanner program you are using by selecting File > Send and choose Mail Recipient from the menu. To do this you must have a email client on your computer (if you use email from home you will have this). You can send the image direct from your scanner software if this is provided. Usually there is a button option on the software panel and this will open your default email client. The image will be sent via email as an attached file that can be downloaded by the recipient. Or you can open your email and attach your scanned file. Recipients can download it and view it in their own graphics viewer. In this format the image appears as an icon embedded in the file. The recipient must double click the icon to view the image.

When using email to send a graphic for others to open and view you will need to send the image in one of the most common graphics file types. The size of the image can be an issue for the recipient. Therefore it is wise to email an image as a .jpg file; this format is usually a good choice as it allows the user to compress the image and thus keeps the file size small. It is important that you are familiar with the details of common file types and we have covered some of the names elsewhere in this book. However, we include here some definitions of the most common ones. Joint Photographic Experts Group, JPEG files, have the file extension .jpg and their feature is that they can be compressed to a small percentage of the image's original size. JPEG files are universally recognized on the Web and JPEGs, GIFs (Graphics Interchange Format) and PNG (Portable Network Graphics) files are the only files you should use when creating Web pages. Even though JPEG files are small they can still display 16 million colours and are good for saving full-colour photographs. JPEG images are so small because they use a compression scheme. However, if too much compression is used the pictures can become blurred. When you save a JPEG you can choose how much compression to use. You can usually set the compression amount whilst previewing how the picture will look when you save it. This should prevent you from losing too much quality. Multiple editing sessions on a JPEG file may result in loss of quality, so either attempt to reduce the number of editing sessions, or convert the file to a different format. Each time a JPEG is saved with compression, it will result in a reduction in quality from the last iteration; keep compression constant.

Graphics Interchange Format (GIF) images are also very small. GIF images can contain 256 colours. When you save a GIF you are allowed to select one colour in your image that will be replaced by a transparency. GIF files can be combined and sequenced to form an animation. GIFs are best for showing large areas of solid and flat colour. Subtle tones are not so good. Portable Network Graphics (PNG) are an improvement to GIFs. However, older Web browsers may not support PNGs, so they may be difficult for any team member to access if they do not have up-to-date software.

Tagged Image File Format (TIFF) images have a file type with the file extension .tif. A TIFF is used for storage of high quality images. If you have an image that you want to print at a high photographic quality then TIFFs are the best file type for this activity. They can be compressed when they are saved to your hard drive but not to the same degree as JPEG images. However, TIFFs suffer no quality loss when they are compressed.

Encapsulated PostScript (EPS) is actually a language rather than a file type. This can save text and images together. It is most useful for saving bitmap information. EPS files can often have several components such as text, graphics and bitmaps. You can preview EPS files before editing in the correct program for whichever part of the file you wish to alter but remember that the quality of the preview will be relatively poor as really the preview is a representation for placement purposes only.

Adobe Acrobat PDF is a single solution method for creating documents that can be viewed on a PC. Adobe Acrobat can convert any file into a universally readable document. Anyone can download the free PDF viewer from Adobe's site at http://www.adobe.com. However, to create PDF files you will need to purchase the full Adobe Acrobat program. This is unlikely to be a frequent approach for designers.

The schematic stage

For the most part the designer will be interested in objects, materials and lights that will finally represent the design as it will appear on stage. In using a computer the designer's attention is likely to be focused on creating forms that will contribute to the final rendered image. In other words a designer is aiming to produce a digital model that best communicates the look of their idea but this may well be lacking the information needed to build it or set it up on stage. The design team will need accurate ground plans, the workshop will need detailed elevations and sections of pieces. Generally speaking the preparation of these, if done digitally, is the domain of CAD programs and therefore beyond the scope of this book. However, there are a number of approaches that can be undertaken in most modelling programs that will go some way towards the production of necessary schematics. Let us assume that none of the rest of the team use the same modelling program, thus the information will either have to be passed on as fairly generic portable files, or printed out.

It is highly likely that during the modelling process lines and shapes have been created with only haphazard attention to organization (layers, naming, etc.) and it is quite possible that nobody other than the designer will really be able to make full sense of the lines on the screen. The first stage in the process of sharing the technical data is to rationalize names, layers, colour, groups so that the details are clear. This is all covered in previous sections of the book. Once done there are several processes that may be of use; quite probably many projects will need a combination of approaches. Let us work on the assumption that current practice does not generally welcome the use of 3D models as acceptable schematic information, and generally the currency of these details are 2D drawings (whether from computer or not). Of course some designers may have very accepting or IT-savvy stage managers, scenic artists or workshop supervisors who will work from model files.

An important note: so far this book has assumed that the model has been developed from scratch in the digital domain. Obviously in some cases the full ground plan has already been developed on paper and the digital model is being made from that finished plan. In these cases of course these processes are unnecessary, but we also feel that the designer is missing a major creative advantage.

There are four ways to produce usable schematics from a modelling program:

1 reduce the complexity of the 3D model so that one is left with clear, meaningful and properly annotated lines, these can be exported as a .dxf file (or .dwg file) to a CAD program for proper preparation prior to printing. This is usually achieved by a File > Export command;
2 export the whole model to a CAD program and simplify the forms in there;
3 render a simplified wire frame view of the setting or element, however this will generally not have the full range of symbols and notation, and accurate scaling may be very difficult;

4 draw the plans (either on paper or in a CAD program) with reference to the digital model but no direct exportation. Quite frankly, despite the emphasis of this book the authors believe that drawing most ground plans and construction plans directly on paper may be the best solution for many projects.

The ground plan

The overarching aim is to create a clear, simplified and generally conventional set of lines that communicates the layout of the design as seen from above, and in scaled relation to known positions. Ground plans are about clear communication, and also about efficiency: you should find a method of producing the plans that takes as little time as possible, is as accurate as possible but has no unnecessary information.

Either save the work as a new file, or organize the model file so that a layer or a colour can be used to represent the model schematically. Since we will be making some alternative versions of objects, and deleting the mesh of others it is important to keep this separate from your main model.

Maximize the top view and set the viewport to show wire frames (rather than shaded objects). Examine the view. Some geometry may be simple enough that the wire frame clearly represents what it is. Flats are a good example of this, generally being made from assembled boxes or an extruded line. A run of flats seen from the top view contains no extraneous information; although it may not quite fit with conventional notation it is fairly clear what it is. The use of AEC objects (if available to you) such as doors, windows and stairs also present a simple usable plan when seen in wire frame in the top viewport. Similarly rostra are likely to be made of simple boxes that need little further reduction in outline.

However, the majority of objects are likely to contain too much geometry to make sense in a ground plan and there are three ways to provide the simplified image:

1 use splines to draw simplified shapes around existing objects. While this may sound a little inefficient it is probably the quickest method, and leads to easy exportation to a CAD program for further editing and printing. Be sure to select the option that makes the spline renderable. The problem, as with all of these systems, is that you are unlikely to be able to use a line tool that will represent the line styles required for hidden objects, etc.;
2 use a Section tool (if available) (in Viz it is in Create > Shapes > Splines) to create a spline shape based upon the section of an object; this is perhaps more useful for construction drawings than ground plans. Generally ground plans do not use sections, but a section taken from a carefully chosen location may produce a simplified outline of the object;
3 deleting some internal vertices or segments may preserve the outline while removing extraneous structure, however, generally the outline will also collapse. Of course this system also loses the original geometry.

The above processes (including simply leaving the top view of the object as it is) will produce a simplified set of lines that may be used as the basis of a ground plan. You will need to do some editing and tidying up, so consider the following:

- the process so far has not included any conventional symbols such as the diagonal crossed lines inside rostra or the arrows pointing up stairs and rakes; these may be included by the use of splines that will be set to render less thickly than major outlines;
- use splines to put a border around the plan; this clearly indicates where the information stops, is useful as a printing aid, and frames the project neatly;
- use the text tool to annotate the plan (text need not be extruded for this). In the bottom right-hand corner of the drawing area ensure that you have the following information: name of the production, name of the designer, date of the plan (perhaps a version number), units used; if space allows you could also provide a key for layers;
- use text to insert any key information on the plan itself; try to keep text unobtrusive, parallel to the X axis (in top view) and clearly located to the object to which it refers;
- at the very least ensure that the centre line and the setting line are set, and ideally use yellow;
- where possible use proper conventions for line colour and layer. Use names clearly.

Once this is done all original objects can be deleted, hidden or (if layers are available in your program) placed on an inactive and invisible layer. The file may then either be exported as a .dxf file for opening in a CAD program, or rendered as a wire frame, then saved as a .jpg or .gif and printed from a photo-editing program. If exported as a .dxf and opened in a CAD program the operator can then add the more precise elements, including line styles, and then set the printing parameters.

Printing a ground plan to a useful size will require a plotter, which is an expensive piece of equipment rarely owned by individuals or small companies. Plotting agencies will print out large plans for you, although there is a cost to this. Such agencies can be found in the Yellow Pages.

To render wire frames

Your software should allow you to render the wire frame image, thus producing a line drawing schematic; Viz allows this. There may be two ways of achieving this, either by assigning a wire frame material to the object, or by requiring the rendering engine to force a wire frame image when rendering. Splines may or may not be renderable (in Viz they can be made to be, via a check box in the Creation Parameters roll-out). If a spline is not renderable it can be made visible by using it as a path to loft a very small circle.

You may of course set the rendering background to black or white, but will need to adjust wire frame colours accordingly.

Line thickness may be varied by specifying how many units or pixels thick the wire frame will be, thus it is possible to identify some lines as lightweight, some as heavyweight. This is not an ideal tool since there are a number of variables; line colour may be preferable using a range of shades of the main colour.

Of course the final rendered image may be opened in a paint program and printed, or emailed to others, but there is no fixed size or scale that can be applied to it. It is vital that a ruler is included in the image, and given the fact that printers and monitors may distort the aspect ratio of such an image it is preferable to include a ruler in each of the X and Y axes. Also include some key dimension lines.

A ground plan produced by rendering a wire frame image should never be used for final layout purposes, nor for the workshop or lighting team. However, it is sufficient to give an overall impression of a scenic arrangement and will certainly be sufficient for rehearsal room layout, general discussion, blocking diagrams and so on.

Although a modelling program may therefore allow for the generation of plans, there are a number of reasons why a dedicated CAD program may be of use for this task. A modelling program will rarely allow the user to set the drawing for printing, whereas CAD can lay out borders, scales, information boxes, etc., providing properly sized paper copy. Modelling programs are not likely to be equipped with the facilities to offer the different line styles conventionally required in plans. CAD will also allow you to tidy up a plan more easily. It will have many more 2D drafting features than a modelling application. Some modelling programs do include this but, with increasingly effective interfaces between CAD and modelling programs, one is better advised to play to a program's strengths and use each one to complete the specific task.

Always think about what information is required or useful before overcomplicating a project. If you are simply intending to produce the model in the computer and produce plans by hand, which is often an efficient approach in a small project, you may only need to establish basic guidelines. These are the setting line, centre line, datum line and sight-lines.

Construction drawings

Construction drawings may be taken from the model in much the same way as ground plans, and here of course the section tool may be particularly useful. However, in general, items made in a digital model are constructed in a different way than they would be in real life (at whatever scale). Since the computer versions do not have to be self-supporting, they do not need joints and bases, and most importantly are made only from an outer skin, there is rarely an armature or skeleton. Creating spline drawings for the workshop may be time-consuming and in the end not the most helpful approach.

Probably the most effective output from a computer model is a simple rendering of each object, evenly lit, seen from the object's front, side and top. It may also be useful to take a spline section (see above) and render that in addition to or instead of side or top views. Flats should be rendered from a plane aligned to their main face; a section will show architectural details.

An isometric projection may be taken from a user viewport, remembering that isometric is a parallel (orthographic) projection viewing an object so that three planes are seen. Isometric projection should not use perspective diminution.

Using the minimum number of views to describe an object clearly the designer should render the item as simply as possible and then assemble the rendered views on one sheet (a paint program will do) clearly labelling every element. Dimensions are of course vital, and an image file will not keep scale as it is re-sized, printed, etc. Although these are not fully exploded or detailed workshop drawings they will normally provide the information that the workshop needs to build the piece.

The other way around

So far we have examined exporting schematic information from the modelling program, thus assuming most of the work has been done in the computer. However very often you may wish to undertake initial planning on paper and then build a digital model for those plans. A designer's paper and pen sketch of an orthographic view (particularly the top view of course) may be scanned into the computer and assigned as a background to the appropriate viewport. For example a sketched plan would be assigned to the top viewport. Once imported set up the scale of the viewport so that the modelling units correspond to the sketch. Once you have done this the sketch may provide the basis for constructing 3D objects, or for drawing 2D construction lines over the image. A research photograph for example, may be used in much the same way. These background images will not be rendered and they can be switched off, or swapped for another image.

14

Conclusion

The research and practice contained within this book has been specifically designed for students of computer visualizations for theatre. However you may be a professional designer who is endeavouring to engage with this technology for your work and we hope that the book helps you to navigate through the systems and programs that are available. We have set out a context for the use of computer modelling for a variety of processes of visualization for theatre. We hope the exercises have enabled you to grasp that context in an applied manner. They are only the start of the journey.

It is obvious that the personal computer has changed working practices in many working environments. How useful the computer is as a tool for exploration, research and design will depend to a certain extent on the level of engagement the user has with the programs. The use of computer software requires continual research, but more importantly it requires practice, as it is only by practice with their tools that the success of certain programs over others can be ascertained and then disseminated.

Our aim has always been to return to the theatre concepts that form the basis for most explorations into performance. We would like to stress again that you will need to have a competent knowledge of theatre practice in order to align the ideas contained within this book with the use of the computer programs which we have used to illustrate our practice.

The ability to see into the future is not one that we have perfected, however, it is obvious from our investigation here that the majority of changes and developments in software production and application have been caused by users, designers and people with an inquisitive nature investigating, exploring, playing, thinking and dreaming. We feel that, as in other areas of our lives, the computer is a useful exploratory tool. It is also becoming a very powerful means by which to develop visual information for live performance and many companies, artists and individual performers are utilizing the ubiquitous nature of the technology. We would advocate therefore that digital images be experimented with and developed as a part of live performance. Digital modelling and the concomitant images created for performances have no implicit negative effect on productions. They enable different approaches to be explored. Theatre has always embraced new technologies into its craft and the computer is one more technology that can enable new vistas of performance to open up.

This book has only touched the surface. Emerging from 3D modelling there are the related developments of virtual reality on stage, explored particularly by Mark Reaney at the University of Kansas. In a related field immersive experiences have become more like interactive performance;

theorists and practitioners have engaged with a whole new area of cyber performance – Brenda Laurel and team on the Placeholder project, Ivor Benjamin and Mika Tuomola have all (to name but a few) explored these fields in practical experiments. Certainly the emergence of powerful, cheap data projectors has made it relatively easy to show digital images, moving or otherwise, on stage. The facility is not important, anyone can plug in a data projector (or a film projector come to that). It's what you do with these technologies that counts.

This book cannot engage with the art, craft and technology in these areas, but a knowledge of computer modelling not only opens the door on new design processes, but also experimental performance outcomes.

Bibliography

The following texts and other resources were used directly or indirectly in compiling this book. Following the bibliography there is a list of software discussed in the text, with Web addresses of the publishers, and a list of other useful Web sites. None of these lists, particularly the latter, are exhaustive.

Appia, Adolphe, 1989, *Essays, Scenarios and Designs*. Translated by Walther Volbach, edited and with notes and commentary by Richard C. Beacham. Ann Arbor: University of Michigan Research Press.

Barthes, Roland, 1961, 'The Photographic Message'. Translated by Stephen Heath, 1977, in *Image Music Text*. London: Fontana Paperbacks.

Beardon, Colin, 2000 (unpublished), *Creative Practices and the Design of Virtual Environments*. http://www.adr.plym.ac.uk/va/pub.html.

Beardon, Colin and Enright, Terry, 1999a, 'The Visual Assistant: designing software to support creativity'. Conference Proceedings, *Computers in Art & Design Education*. Middlesbrough: University of Teeside, 5–14.

Beardon, Colin and Enright, Terry, 1999b, 'Computers and improvisation: using the Visual Assistant for teaching'. *Digital Creativity* 10 (3), 153–166.

Beardon, Colin, Gollifer, S., Rose, C. and Worden, S. (1997) 'Computer use by artists and designers: some perspectives on two design traditions'. In Kyng, M. and Mathiassen, L. (eds) *Computers and Design in Context*. MIT Press, Camb, Mass, 27–50. Norwood, NJ.

Bijvoet, Marga, 1990, 'How intimate can art and technology really be? – A survey of the art and technology movement of the sixties'. In Hayward, Philip, ed., *Culture Technology and Creativity*. London: John Libby & Company Limited, 15–38.

Birringer, Johannes, 1991, *Theatre Theory, Postmodernism*. Bloomington and Indianapolis: Indiana University Press.

Bolter, David Jay, 1991, *Writing Space, the Computer, Hypertext and the History of Writing*. Hillsdale NJ: Lawrence Erlbaum Associates.

Braddy, Robert E., Cleveland, Annie O. and Cleveland, M. Barrett, 1993, 'The interactive digital design studio'. *Theatre Design & Technology* Fall 1993, 14–20.

Carver, Gavin, 1996, 'Computer aided scenography: some observations on procedures and concepts'. *Studies in Theatre Production* 14, 20–33.

Damisch, Hubert, 1994, *The Origin of Perspective*. Translated by John Goodman. Cambridge MA: MIT Press.

Davis, T., 2001, *Stage Design*. Hove: Rotovision.

DeCuir, L.J., 2000, *Using 3D Studio Max, Painter, and Poser*. Portsmouth NH: Heinemann.

Dorn, Dennis and Shanda, Mark, 1994, *Drafting for the Theatre*. Carbondale and Edwardsville: Southern Illinois University Press.

Dyer, Chris, 1999, 'Virtual_Stages: an interactive model of performance spaces for creative teams, technicians and students'. *Digital Creativity* 10 (3), 143–152.

Giambruno, Mark, 2002, *3D Graphics & Animation*. Second Edition. Indianapolis and London: New Riders.

Gold, Michaeljohn and Fergusson, Cat, 1999, 'Digital Synergy: a humanistic view of modern scenography'. Conference Proceedings, *Computers in Art & Design Education*. Middlesbrough: University of Teeside, 242–248.

Gombrich, Ernst H., 1982, *The Image and the Eye*. Oxford: Phaidon Press.

Harrison, Charles and Wood, Paul, 1993, *Art in Theory 1900–1990: an anthology of changing ideas*. Blackwell Publishers.

Howard, Pamela, 2002, *What is Scenography?* London: Routledge.

Hussey, Michael, 1998, 'Interdisciplinary Instruction by Design'. *Theatre Design & Technology* Fall 1998, 22–29.

King, Mike, 1999, 'The Tyranny and the Liberation of Three Space: a Journey by Ray-Tracer'. *Digital Creativity* 10 (4), 215–227.

Laurel, Brenda, 1991, *Computers as Theatre*. Reading MA: Addison-Wesley.

Laurel, Brenda, Strickland, Rachel and Tow, Rob, 1994, 'Placeholder: landscape and narrative in virtual environments'. *Computer Graphics* 28 (6), 118–126.

Mirzoeff, Nicholas, 1999, *An Introduction to Visual Culture*. London: Routledge.

Morgan, Nigel, 1995, *Stage Lighting for Theatre Designers*. Herbert Press.

Murphie, Andrew, 1990, 'Negotiating presence – performance and new technologies'. In Hayward, Philip, ed., *Culture Technology and Creativity*. London: John Libby & Company Limited, 209–226.

Norton, Peter and Goodman, John, 1999, *Peter Norton's Inside the PC*. Eighth Edition. Indianapolis: Sams Publishing, a division of Macmillan.

Parker, W. Oren and Wolf, R. Craig, 1996, *Scene Design and Stage Lighting*. Holt, Reinhart and Winston.

Payne, Darwin Reid, 1981, *Scenographic Imagination*. Carbondale and Edwardsville: Southern Illinois University Press.

Payne, Darwin Reid, 1985, *Theory and Craft of the Scenographic Model*. Carbondale and Edwardsville: Southern Illinois University Press.

Payne, Darwin Reid, 1994, *Computer Scenographics*. Carbondale and Edwardsville: Southern Illinois University Press.

Reaney, Mark, 1990, 'Three Dimensional Designing'. *Theatre Design & Technology* Fall, 41–46.

Reaney, Mark, 1993, 'The Theatre of Virtual Reality'. *Theatre Design & Technology* Spring, 29–32.

Reaney, Mark, 1996, 'Virtual Scenography: the actor audience computer interface'. *Theatre Design & Technology* Winter, 36–43.

Reid, Francis, 1996, *Designing for the Theatre*. London: Routledge.

Rush, Michael, 1999, *New Media in Late 20th Century Art*. London: Thames and Hudson.

Salmon, Virginia L., 1993, 'Computing trends in theatre production'. *Theatre Design & Technology* Fall, 21–24.

Street, Rita, 1998, *Computer Animation: A Whole New World*. Massachusetts: Rockport Publishers Inc.

Strindberg, A.,1888, *Preface to Miss Julie*. Translated by Michael Meyer 1964. London: Secker and Warburg.

Svoboda, Josef, 1993, *The Secret of Theatrical Space*. Translated and edited by J.M. Burian. New York: Applause.

Unruh, Delbert, 1996, 'Virtual Reality in the Theatre: new questions about time and space'. *Theatre Design & Technology* Winter, 44–47.

Volbach, Walther R., 1968, *Adolphe Appia, Prophet of the Modern Theatre: a profile*. Middletown CT: Wesleyan University Press.

Walton, J. Michael, 1983, *Craig on Theatre*. London: Methuen.

Weishar, Peter, 1998, *Digital Space: designing virtual environments*. New York: McGraw Hill.

Welsh, Jeremy, 1990, 'Power access and ingenuity – electronic imaging technologies and contemporary visual art'. In Hayward, Philip, ed., *Culture Technology and Creativity*. London: John Libby & Company Limited, 149–162.

Wentk, Richard, 2001. *The Which? Guide to Computers* (revised edn). London: Which Books.

White, Christine, 2001, *Technical Theatre*. London: Arnold.

Web sites

Web sites concerning computer modelling and the theatre. These sites contain many links themselves, and since they are able to be updated more frequently than this book, we have kept this list short.

Mark Reaney, and the Institute for the Exploration of Virtual Realities (i.e.,VR).
http://www.ukans.edu/~mreaney/index.html

Roma Patel, Digital Set Design. Theatre designers using computer modelling.
http://www.digitalsetdesign.com/

Darwin Reid Payne. Computer scenographics studio.
http://www.wfu.edu/~drp/frontdr.htm

L.J.DeCuire. An introduction to computer assisted design for the theatre.
http://web.utk.edu/~ldecuir/compbook.htm

Cad4Theatre. Mostly CAD related, hosts the standards for CAD in theatre developed with the Association of British Theatre Technicians.
http://www.cad4theatre.org.uk/

ModelBox. A CAD for theatre agency.
http://www.modelbox.co.uk/index2.html

General Web sites

Association of British Theatre Technicians (ABTT)
http://www.abtt.org.uk

David Hersey Associates (DHA), manufacturer of Gobos. From this site you will be able to download
   image files of gobos for use when lighting the digital model.
http://www.dhalighting.co.uk/gobos-t.htm

Filename Extensions. A site that will help you to identify unknown file types.
http://www.webdesk.com/filename-extensions/

3D Café. A very useful general site for computer modelling, including free models and images.
http://www.3dcafe.com/asp/default.asp

Software

The following listings are not intended to be exhaustive, nor are they recommendations. The lists
and addresses identify software that is mentioned in this book. Autodesk Viz is the main software
referred to in the text.

Openstages. Theatre-specific visualization program. Trial download available.
http://www.openstages.com/

Visual Assistant. Simple software, particularly useful in the creation of storyboards.
http://www.adr.plym.ac.uk/va/index.html

Autodesk Viz (previously 3D Studio Viz), produced by Autodesk. 15 day free demo available. This
   is also the site for other Autodesk products including AutoCAD, AutoSketch and AutoCAD LT.
www.autodesk.co.uk

AutoCAD, AutoCAD LT and AutoSketch.
www.autodesk.co.uk

3ds Max. Distributed by Discreet.
http://www.discreet.com/index-nf.html

Poser. Figure generating software, produced by Curiouslabs (previously Metacreations).
http://www.curiouslabs.com/

TurboCAD. Produced by IMSI.
http://www.turbocad.com

LightWave 3D. Modelling software by New Tek.
http://www.newtek.com/

Softimage|3D. High-end modelling by Softimage.
http://www.softimage.com/home/

Maya. High-end modelling program by Alias Wavefront.
http://www.aliaswavefront.com/

Carrara. Modelling program by Eovia.
http://www.eovia.com/home.jsp

True Space. Modelling program produced by Caligari.
http://www.caligari.com/

Strata 3D. Modelling software produced by Strata.
http://www.strata.com/

Paintshop Pro. Produced by JASC.
http://www.jasc.com/

People for People. Premade human models for use in design projects.
www.peopleforpeople.com

Meshpaint 3D. For applying surface colour directly to 3D meshes, produced by Texture Tools.
http://www.texturetools.com/meshpaint.shtml

Photoshop. A paint and photo-editing program, produced by Adobe.
http://www.adobe.com/products/photoshop/main.html

PhotoPlus. Simple image editing software by Serif.
http://www.serif.com/

WYSIWIG. Dedicated theatre lighting software produced by Cast Lighting.
http://www.castlighting.com

RPC (Rich Photorealistic Content). Photorealistic people for inclusion in models, by ArchVision.
http://www.rpcnet.com/

Powerpoint. Presentation software by Microsoft.
http://www.microsoft.com

Piranesi. A 3D painting system, by Informatix Software International.
http://www.informatix.co.uk/index.shtml

Premier. Video editing software by Adobe.
http://www.adobe.com/products/premiere/main.html

Glossary

Ambient colour   A value of a material that suggests the colour (hue) it displays when not directly illuminated, it suggests the effect of bounced, indirect, light in a scene.

Ambient light   A general level of non-directional illumination suggesting (but not exactly calculating) the effect of bounced light in a scene. The level for ambient light can be set in the rendering module/engine. The notable effect is normally detected in the shadows in a scene.

Array   A number of copies of a single, original object, generated to form a pattern or specified arrangement.

Aspect ratio   The ratio of the height of an image (or any rectangular form) to its width (height/width). The normal aspect ratio for computer images is 1.33, hence, for example, images of 640 × 480 pixels.

Attenuation   The decay or fall-off of light over distance.

Axis   (pl. axes) One of the three imaginary/notional lines, all perpendicular to each other, that reference direction and location in a 3D space – up/down, left/right, front/back (though these terms have little meaning in 3D space). The axis is also the line (or pivot) around which an object or camera rotates, bends, twists or otherwise moves. See also co-ordinates. Axes are normally named X, Y and Z – the orientation of these (i.e., which is front to back) will depend upon your software and the mode that the co-ordinates are set to, orientating themselves around the world, an object, the screen or other user-defined orientation. Generally in world mode X is front to back of the scene/stage, Y is left to right, X is up and down. With reference to the screen X is left to right, Y is up and down.

Axonometric view   A view in which the scene is viewed without the effect of perspective; specifically this term is applied to those views that are not aligned with the co-ordinate systems in use in the scene. This view is useful for accurate construction of scenes.

Boolean operation   A process whereby the geometry of one object is subtracted from or added to another; this process is normally used to cut holes for doors or windows.

Bump map   A bit map (image file) or procedural map that creates the illusion of a 3D textured surface (such as the relief of bricks and mortar) on an object when applied as part of a material. A bump map uses the greyscale values of the image to suggest relief.

Centre line   A notional line that bisects the stage, running from the centre of the front of the stage (often the centre of the proscenium opening) to the centre of the back wall. It is an important line for locating setting on stage. The centre line will normally correspond to the front to back axis of the 3D model.

Clone   A method of duplicating an existing object. There are a number of variations in Viz including copy, instance and reference.

Colour temperature   A value that describes the colour of a light source in relation to the colour of dull metal when heated. Thus a light of colour temperature 3200 Kelvin (will look slightly amber – the normal colour of theatre lights) has the same colour as a dull metal when heated to that temperature.

Co-ordinates   The three digits that describe the location of a point in space with regard to the axis/ co-ordinate system in use.

Copy   A unique duplicate of the original object which behaves autonomously once created.

Datum point   In theatre this is the point on the level of the stage floor where the centre line and the setting line cross. This should be coincident with the origin point (i.e., co-ordinates 0,0,0 in the 3D world).

Diffuse colour   The colour of an object under normal direct illumination.

Diffuse map   A bit map or procedural map applied to a material as a pattern or texture.

Directional light   Light coming from a single source where all the rays are parallel, in essence this simulates the effect of sunlight – it should not be used to replicate theatre spotlights.

Dolly   The movement of the camera forward or away from the scene.

Edge   A line acting as a boundary to a polygon, thus a line connecting two vertices.

Environment parameters   A set of variables that define rendering parameters in Viz, most notably the level of ambient light, the background colour and any atmospheric effects such as fog.

Extrusion   A process by which a 2D shape is turned into a 3D object by extending it in the third (missing) axis.

Face   The smallest element of a mesh; the smallest face is the triangular surface defined by three vertexes.

FOV, Field of View   The angle, measured from the camera's position, that sets how much the camera sees.

Gel   A term used for coloured or frosted filters placed in front of theatre lights.

Gizmo   A non-rendered object in a Viz scene used to control a function, thus a gizmo might represent the scale and orientation of the mapping co-ordinates.

Grid   The non-rendered lines in a 3D scene (like graph paper) that aid in the positioning and sizing of objects.

Gobo   In theatre a cut-out piece of metal placed between the bulb and the lens of a theatre light, thus shaping the beam and creating a projected silhouette. In digital 3D this effect can be achieved with a projector.

HSV; Hue, Saturation, Value   A set of three variables (usually on a scale of 0–255) that define 'colour'. Hue is the pigment or chroma, saturation is the intensity of the pigment, and value is the brightness or amount of black and white in the colour. See also RGB.

Import/export   Importing is the process whereby a file that is not native to the software is brought into a program, exporting is similarly the process where a file is saved in a non-native or cross-platform format.

Instance   A duplicate of an original that may affect all other duplicates and the original if it is modified.

Keyframe   In animation a frame that defines a significant event in the sequence; the computer calculates all frames between keyframes – which the user defines.

Keystoning   The distortion effect created when the beam of a projector is not perpendicular to the projection surface.

Lantern   The term used for all theatre lights, sometimes Luminaire.

Lathe   The process of spinning a shape around an axis to create a 3D object, usually with a circular section and profile defined by the original shape.

Layers   A system for organizing digital plans (normally found in CAD programs but present in some modelling programs) in which elements of the design are assigned to notional 'layers' or organizational groups. Each layer may have its own colour, line type, name, etc.

Local axes/co-ordinates   A co-ordinate system that is constant to the object (rather than the screen or the world).

Lofting/loft   Similiar to extrusion, a 2D shape is extended in the third (missing) dimension along a pre-defined path.

Map/texture map   Generally the term applied to a bit map or graphic-generating procedure that is assigned to a material to create a pattern on an image on the surface of an object.

Mapping co-ordinates   see also UVW axes. The co-ordinates that specify the orientation of a material on an object's surface.

Material/texture   A material is a combination of parameters (and sometimes maps) which define the surface properties of an object; these properties may include its colour, shininess, transparency and any pattern or texture.

Mesh   The representation of the series of vertices and connecting lines that make up a 3D object; the term 'mesh' may apply to an object or a whole scene.

NURBS, Non-Uniform Rational B-Splines   A type of spline (a line) that has control points or handles away from the line itself, creating smooth lines.

Omni-light   A digital light source that radiates in all directions (omni-directional), also called a point light.

Opacity map   An image file or procedural map that defines areas of transparency and opacity in a material. Generally black is transparent, white opaque and grey represents degrees of semi-transparency. This process can create the effect of a cut-out or a painted gauze.

Origin, or origin point   The intersection of X,Y,Z axes, co-ordinates 0,0,0.

Orthographic view   A parallel view usually aligned to one of the defined world planes; such a view does not represent perspective.

Pel   A term used to describe the picture element of a monitor display.

Perspective view   A view of a scene (often seen from any position) which calculates the effect of perspective. Using certain parameters this may become a camera view.

Pixel   The smallest component part of an image, a picture element.

Plane   A surface (imaginary or real) or view of a scene, normally defined by two axes, thus the XY axes will normally define a plane parallel with the 'ground'.

Polygon   A closed shape with three or more sides, defined by lines and vertices at each angle/intersection. Polygons form the basis of normal 3D modelling, known as polygonal modelling.

Primitive   A pre-made, basic, geometric form.

Radiosity   The effect produced by light bouncing off one object and thereby illuminating another object, colouring or otherwise affecting the light as it does so. A radiosity renderer calculates the effect of bounced (indirect) light.

RAM, Random Access Memory   Used for temporary storage while operations are performed.

Raytracing   A sophisticated rendering calculation in which each pixel of the image is calculated by tracing the ray of light backwards into the scene, calculating each intersection with a surface.

Reference   A duplicate of an object that is affected by transforms applied to the original.

Render   The process by which the computer calculates and displays the combined effect of geometry, material, light and effects. There are different qualities of rendered output defined by rendering algorithms. The result may be a still image or an animation. A rendered image cannot be manipulated in the way a mesh scene can.

Resolution   The clarity and complexity of an image; in computing terms this is determined by the number of pixels it contains, expressed as horizontal pixels by vertical pixels.

RGB   Red, Green, Blue; an expression of colour based upon the amount of the three primary colours present, each measured on a scale of 0–255. RGB is also a term used to set monitor colour.

Screen axes/co-ordinates   A set of co-ordinates relative to the viewport (rather than the world). Whichever the view of the scene the co-ordinates relate to the screen itself, X is left to right, Y is up and down and Z forward and back (into the screen).

Segment   A subdivision of a mesh object.

Setting line   In theatre the term used to describe the notional/imaginary line usually at the downstage extremity of the set. The setting line is frequently located immediately upstage of the proscenium arch. The setting line should normally correspond to the Y axis.

Shape   A 2D form constructed of lines and vertices. A shape is not normally rendered itself but used to construct a 3D object using extrude or lath functions. A closed shape is one where the defining line is connected to itself at each end, thus defining an inside and an outside to the shape. Some functions require a closed shape.

Snap   A tool that forces the cursor to jump to the nearest pre-defined point, a grid line, the intersection of meshes, etc.

Specular highlight   The intense area of brightness seen on shiny objects, caused by the reflection of a light source.

Spline   A line constructed with and modified by control points, facilitating smooth curves. Bezier, B-spline and NURBS are all different types of spline.

Spotlight   A digital light source that replicates the effect of a theatre spot (or lantern). A spotlight has a defined but variable beam angle and may usually be set to project an image file.

Truck   In theatre the term (used as a noun and verb) for elements of scenery that move (or truck) on- and off-stage.

UVW axes   The set of co-ordinates that refer to the geometry of an object however it is rotated in the world co-ordinates. UVW co-ordinates are most commonly used to describe the placement of a material on an object.

Vertex   A point in 2D or 3D space, located by co-ordinates, that forms the key points of a mesh. The plural may be either vertexes or vertices, the latter being more common.

Volume light   A light source that has had an effect assigned to suggest the presence of fog/smoke/mist in the beam.

World axes/co-ordinates   The main co-ordinates around which a 3D scene is orientated. These co-ordinates do not change with a change of view, nor when an object is moved.

Wire frame   A display mode (or rendered output) that shows the object as a mesh form rather than fully textured.

Index

Note: this index includes references to processes in the computer only where the text introduces or explains the process; it does not include every reference in specific exercises. For example 'colour' is only indexed where the page explains the use of colour, not where an exercise asks the user to set an object's colour. Similarly program names are listed when the text introduces their functionality rather than when they are referred to in exercises.

3D Studio Max, *see* Max
3D Studio Viz, *see* Viz
3D World, 22
3dsmax, *see* Max

Aardman Animations, 177
Adding Machine, The, 2
Adobe:
   Acrobat, 205
   Photoshop, 17, 18, 27
   Portable Document Format, *see* PDF
   Premier, 181
Alias Wavefront Maya, 21
Ambient light, 122
AMD Athlon, 29–30
Amedee, or how to get rid of it, 187
Amiga, 21
Animation, 173–4, 176–85
Appia, Adolphe, 138
Apple, 27, 200
Architectural elements, 15, 70, 76, 206
   making a cornice, 167
Array, 168–9
Association of British Theatre Technicians (ABTT), 197
   CAD standards, 197
Attenuation, of light, *see* Lighting, attenuation
AutoCAD, 16

Autodesk, ix, 15, 16, 19, 21, 27
Autodesk Viz, *see* Viz
Axis, 43–5, 195
Axonometric, 43
   views, 46

Barthes, Roland, 158
Bauhaus, 158
Bauprobe, 66, 71
Beam angle, 124
Beardon, Colin, 3, 11, 56, 142, 157, 201
Benjamin, Ivor, 211
Bevel, 166
Bezier, 160–1
Bitmap, 16
Bits, 31
Blinn shading, 95
Bolter, David, 141
Book, making a model, 162–5
Boolean, 68–9, 165
Box sets, 76–7
Braddy, Bob, 10, 201
Bump map, in materials, 96, 103–5
Bytes, 31

CAD programs, 4, 6–8, 10, 38, 195–6, 205–8
   general overview, 13–16

Camera, in a computer model, 151–2
  focal length of lens, 153
Camera Obscura, 2
Carrera Studio, 22
Cartesian co-ordinates, *see* Co-ordinates
Cathode Ray Tube (CRT) Monitor, *see* Monitor
CD, 32, 192, 200
Centre Line, 47, 197, 208
Chandelier, making, 167–80
Cherry Orchard, The, 189
Chiaroscuro, 116
Cinematography, 173
Clone 63, *see also* Array
Colorado State University, 10
Colour, 88–9,
  colour temperature, 126
  HSV setting, 89
  in light, 114, 123, 133–4
  RGB setting, 89
Computer Aided Scenography, 7
Computer Arts, 22
Computer Scenographics, 7
Computers in theatre design, xii
  advantages and disadvantages, 8–9, 158,
    186–7
  as a tool, 3,
  choice of platform, 26–7
  history, 9–12
  modes of use, 4–7
  to facilitate experimentation, 12, 139–42
  use in design team meetings, 199–201,
Construction drawings, 6, 151, 208–9
Construction plane, 50, 60
Co-ordinates, 43–4, 47
  world co-ordinates, 45
Costume Design, 4, 147
CPU (Central Processor Unit), 29–30
Craig on Theatre, 174
Craig, Edward Gordon, 107, 173–4

Da Vinci, Leonardo, 1
Damisch, Hubert, 42
Datum point, 47, 194–5, 208
David Hersey Associates (DHA), 129–30
Descartes, Rene, 43

Design:
  2D exploration, 4, 18
  3D exploration, 5–6, 71–6, *see also* Modelling
    for theatre design
  box sets, 76–8
  bricolage, 5, 18
  by error, 140
  change over time, 141–2, 173–4
  collaboration, 10, 192, 201–2
  composition of images, 153
  conferences, 199–201, 202–3
  reading the model, 157–9, 200–1,
  stages in the design process, 4–7, 140, 192
  strategies for problem solving, 3–4,
  the effect of light on form, 114–15
  the importance of human figures, 143–4, 153
  using colour and texture, 87–8,
Diffuse Colour map, in materials, 95–6
Digipeople, 149
Digit, 22
Digital camera, 18, 38–40, 103, 110
Digital technologies, and the arts, 2, 9
Dudley, William, 12
Durer, Albrecht, 1, 42
DVD (Digital Versatile Disk), 32
Dye Sublimation printers, 37
Dyer, Chris, 10, 178, 201

Email, to exchange images, 200, 204
EIDE (Enhanced Integrated Drive Electronics), 32
EPS (Encapsulated postscript), 204
Euclid, 43
Evans, David, 13
Export, 209
Extrude, 163, 164, 166–7,

Fergusson, Cat, 202
Files:
  file types for images, 203–5,
  filename extensions, 188, 203–5
  naming and organizing, 187–90,
Flats, 76
Floppy disk, 32
Fly-bys, 184, 201

Folders, *see* Files
Frame, 177
Fresnel Lantern, 137

General Electric Company, 19
General Motors, 13
GIF (Graphics Interchange format), 204
Gobo, 129–30,
Gold, Michaeljohn, 201–2
Gombrich, Ernst, 3
Gouraud shading, 54
Graphics cards, 35–6
Graphics programs, *see* Paint/photo programs
Grids, as drawing aids, 50–1, 79
Ground plans, 6, 15–16, 194–5, 206–7
  exporting plans to a CAD program, 20, 205–6
  importing plans from a CAD program, 20,
    194–5
  library of theatre plans, 7
Grouping, 63–4, 83

Hard disk, 32
Human maquette, 143

IBM, 26–7, 29
Importing plans, 194
Improvisation, 142
IMSI TurboCAD, 16
Intel, 27
Internet searching, for maps, 109, 129
Inverse Kinematics, 147, *see also* Animation
Inverse Square Law, 125

JPEG (Joint Photographics Expert Group), 204

Kelvin, *see* Colour, colour temperature
Keyframes, 177
KIDDS (Kent Interactive Digital Design Studio),
  11–12, 37, 107

Laserjet printers, 37
Lathe, 170–1
Laurel, Brenda, 211
Layers, 196–8
LCD monitors, *see* Monitor
Lighting, *see also:* Omnidrectional light, Ambient
    light, Spotlight, Colour
  angle of incidence, 121
  attenuation, 125
  control of intensity, 123–4
  creative approaches, 114–15
  faking bounced light, 132, *see also* Radiosity
  in the computer, 52–3
  theatre lantern types, 137
Lightscape, 53, 118
Lines, making models from, 160–1, 162
  extruding, *see* Extrude
Lofting, 167
Lowry, L.S., 143
Lucas, George, 9
Lumens, 124, 126

Macintosh comnputer, *see* Apple
Maps, 52, 95–105, 109
Martin Centre for Architectural and Urban Studies
    at Cambridge University, 23
Materials, 51–2, 87–8, 89- 94
  collecting maps for, 109–12,
  creative deployment of, 103–7
  editing and creating, 94–101, 103
  mapping/applying materials to objects, 89–90.
    92–3
  on a human maquette, 146–7,
Max, ix, x, 21, 26
Merging files, 165
Mesh object, 48, 85–6
Mesh Paint, 147
Microsoft, 28
  DOS, 28
  Explorer, 188
  Imaging, 202
  Powerpoint, 175–6, 200, 202–3
  Windows, 26–8, 30, 188
Model Box Bureau, 7

Modelling for theatre design, 56, *see also* Design
　basic approaches in a computer, 48, 56
　effective use of materials, 102–7
　producing schematics, *see* Ground drawings,
　　Construction plans
　the use of model people, 143–4,
　use of a card model, 3, 158
　using lines and shapes, 160–1, *see also* Lines,
　　Shapes
　using primitives, 64–6, 71–8
Modelling programs, 4, 6–9, 208
　general overview, 19–23
　useful features, 22–3
Modifier, *see* Transformations and modifications
Modifier list, 85, 163
Monitor, 33–5
　dot pitch, 34

New Media in the 20ᵗʰ Century, 2
Nine Evenings: theatre and engineering, 2
NSTC, 177
NURBS (Non-Uniform Rational B-Splines), 49,
　147, 160, 171–2

Occlusion, 41
Omnidirectional light, 53, 120–1
Opacity map, in materials, 97–102, 106–7, 149,
　　see also Transparency
　to create a human figure, 149, 150
　using a photo/paint program to create, 98
OpenStages, 10–11, 12, 178
Operating system, 28
Opposite click (with mouse), x
Orthographic, 43–6, 151, 208

Paint/photo programs, 4, 8, 104, 111, 197
　general overview of, 16–19
PAL, 177
Parcan, 137
Patel, Roma, 187
Path:
　for animation, 184
　for lofting objects, 167
PDF (Portable Document Format), 205
Pebble convex lantern (PC), 137

Perspective:
　to represent 3D space, 41–2,
　viewports in a computer, 43, 46
Phoenix Theatre, 11
Phong shading, 54
Photo editing programs, *see* Paint/photo programs
Photometric lights, 118, 120, 126
Picture plane, 42, *see also* Perspective
Pivot point, 60,
　in an array, 168–9,
Pixel, 16, 33–4, 55, 156, 207
Placeholder project, 211
Planes (in 3D space), 44–5, 46
Plano convex lantern, *see* Pebble convex lantern
Poser, 23, 148
Primitive objects, 64–7, 78–83, 144
　definition of and creating, 57–9
　making model people with, 144–7
　transforming and modifying, *see* Transformations
　　and modifications
Printers, 36–8
Printing images, 157
Projector:
　creating in a digital scene, 126, 129
　data projector for showing images, 200, 211
Profile lantern, 122, 136–7,

Radiosity, 54
RAM (Random Access Memory), 30–3
　on graphics cards, 36
Raytracing, 11, 125
　Renaissance use of, 1
Reaney, Mark 2, 10, 210
Reflection map, in materials, 96–7
Reid Payne, Darwin, 5, 10, 140
Rendering, 41, 53–5, 64, 151,
　animations, 183–4
　composition for, 153–5
　effects, 155–6
Resolution, 33–4, 156–7
　for printing, 37, 157
Romeo and Juliet, 176
Rotation, 62
RPC modeling, 150
Rush, Michael, 2

Scale, 62, 139, 143, 158
Scanline rendering, 54
Scanner, 18, 39, 103
    for creating material maps, 110–11
Scenographic team, 192
SCSI (Small Computer Systems Interface), 32, 38
Serif Photostudio, 18
Serlio, 99, 106
Setting line, 47, 208
Shakers, 78
Shapes, modeling with, 160, 167–8, *see also*
    Extrude
Shininess, in materials, 94
Sightlines, 208
Silicon Graphics, 21, 27
Smoke, duplicating the effect of, *see* Volumetric
    lights
Snap drawing aid, 50–1, 79
Softimage, 21
Spline, 49, 160
Spotlight, 53, 122–3
Storyboards, 4, 11, 153–4, 174–6, 183, 202
Strata Studio Base, 22
Strindberg, August, 77
Sutherland, Ivan, 13, 19
Svoboda, Josef, 134, 139, 141

Table, making in the computer, 76–86
Technical drawings, *see* Ground plans,
    Construction drawings
Tempest, The, 201
Terry, Ellen, 107
Text, creating in a model, 164
Theatre Design and Technology, 10
TIFF (Tagged Image Format), 204
Time configuration, 179
Transformations and modifications, of objects,
    61–4, 66–9, 85
Transparency, in materials, 94, 103
Truespace, 22
Tuomola, Mika, 211

Units of measurement, 78, 193
University of Kansas, 210
Unix, 21, 27

USB, 38
UVW, map, 90, 105, 146, 165
UVW modifier, 92

Vanishing point, 42
Vase, making a, 170–2
VCR, 38
Vector graphics, 17
Vectors, 14, 16–17
Vertex (Vertices), 43, 48, 160
    modification of, 84–6
Viewport, 44–6, 47, 127
    composition in, 151
    for focusing lights, 127, 130
    importing an image to, 195
    user defined, 46
Virtual dub, 181
Virtual reality, 210
virtual_Stages, *see* OpenStages
Visual Assistant, 11–12, 24–5, 56, 157, 175
Visualization programs, *see* Modelling programs
Viz, ix, x, 16, 20–1, 26, 44–5,
Volumetric lights, 134–6, 155–6
VRML (Virtual Reality Modelling Language),
    10–11, 199

Walton, Michael, 174
Walk-through, 184, 201
Weishar, Peter, 186
Weta Digital Ltd, 9
White card model, 3
Windows, *see* Microsoft
Wire frames, 160, 207–8, *see also* Mesh object
    rendering, 207
World co-ordinates, 45
World wide web:
    for collecting images, 109, 129
    for sharing images, 200
    image files for web browsers, 204
Word-processor, compared to computer modeling,
    141
WYSIWYG, 24

Zip drive, 32

Focal Press

www.focalpress.com
Join Focal Press on-line
As a member you will enjoy the following benefits:

- an email bulletin with **information on new books**

- a regular **Focal Press Newsletter**:

  - featuring a selection of new titles

  - keeps you informed of **special offers, discounts and freebies**

  - alerts you to **Focal Press news and events** such as author signings and seminars

- complete access to **free content** and reference material on the focalpress site, such as the focalXtra articles and commentary from our authors

- a **Sneak Preview** of selected titles (sample chapters) *before* they publish

- a chance to have your say on our **discussion boards** and **review books** for other Focal readers

Focal Club Members are invited to give us feedback on our products and services.
Email: worldmarketing@focalpress.com – we want to hear your views!

Membership is **FREE**. To join, visit our website and register. If you require any further information regarding the on-line club please contact:

Lucy Lomas-Walker
Email: l.lomas@elsevier.com
Tel: +44 (0) 1865 314438
Fax: +44 (0)1865 314572
Address: Focal Press, Linacre House,
Jordan Hill, Oxford, UK, OX2 8DP

Catalogue
For information on all Focal Press titles, our full catalogue is available online at www.focalpress.com and all titles can be purchased here via secure online ordering, or contact us for a free printed version:

USA
Email: christine.degon@bhusa.com
Tel: +1 781 904 2607 T

Europe and rest of world
Email: j.blackford@elsevier.com
Tel: +44 (0)1865 314220

Potential authors
If you have an idea for a book, please get in touch:

USA
editors@focalpress.com

Europe and rest of world
focal.press@elsevier.com